WOMEN'S RIGHTS AND LAW CODES IN EARLY INDIA, 600 BCE–570 ACE

This book looks at the first eight Sanskrit law codes written in India, between 600 BCE and 570 ACE. It focuses on the legal, religious, and ethical customs that were codified in this period and their impact on the social and political life of women.

The volume analyzes texts such as the *Dharma Sūtras*, the *Arthaśāstra*, the *Manu Smṛiti*, the *Yājñyavalkya Smṛiti*, and the *Nārada Smṛiti*, among others. It studies discourses on justice, conduct, virtues, and duties, and how early laws were used to systematize patriarchy and the *varna* caste system in South Asia. It examines how patrimonial laws and male property rights highlighted social anxieties about female chastity and *varna* lineage, which led to the subordination of women and the lower *varnas*. These anxieties are most evident in codes from the late Vedic-early classical eras when diverse new settlers arrived upon the subcontinent. At this time, kings decentralized governance and allowed local groups to practice communal laws, while they meted out court justice with a specific law code. As the state became prosperous from trade conducted by merchants of diverse castes, sects, and classes, and social peace was ensured by officials from disparate backgrounds, kings began to rely upon a law code that aspired for equity above intolerance. These chapters examine heterodox Therāvada Buddhism and Jainism, their origins in the oligarchic state, their impact on the royal Sanskritic state, as seen in canonical literature. They especially focus on women's roles in heterodox sects, and the emergence of new spaces for women, as such changes were adopted in disparate ways and degrees by other South Asian communities.

The volume will be a useful resource for students and researchers of history, women and gender studies, social anthropology, sociology, and law. It will also serve as an information guide for readers who are interested in the political and social life of women in early India.

Sita Anantha Raman is Emerita Associate Professor, Santa Clara University, where she taught South Asian history and SE Asian history. She is the author of the books *Women in India: A Social and Cultural History* (Vols.1& 2; 2009); *A. Madhaviah: A Biography and a Novella* ('Muthumeenakshi', trans. by Vasantha Surya; 2004); and *Getting Girls to School: Social Reform in the Tamil Districts, 1870–1930* (1996); and of various journal articles.

WOMEN'S RIGHTS AND LAW CODES IN EARLY INDIA, 600 BCE–570 ACE

Sita Anantha Raman

Routledge
Taylor & Francis Group
LONDON AND NEW YORK

First published 2020
by Routledge
2 Park Square, Milton Park, Abingdon, Oxon OX14 4RN

and by Routledge
52 Vanderbilt Avenue, New York, NY 10017

Routledge is an imprint of the Taylor & Francis Group, an informa business

British Library Cataloguing-in-Publication Data
A catalogue record for this book is available from the British Library

Library of Congress Cataloging-in-Publication Data
A catalog record for this book has been requested

ISBN: 978-0-367-19869-5 (hbk)
ISBN: 978-0-367-49692-0 (pbk)
ISBN: 978-0-429-26006-3 (ebk)

Typeset in Sabon
by Apex CoVantage, LLC

Dedicated with gratitude to
Professor Stanley Wolpert (1927–2019)
&
Professor Damodar R. SarDesai (1931–2016),
who inculcated respect for humane laws

CONTENTS

INTRODUCTION

Sanskrit law codes and the royal state

This is a study of the first eight Sanskrit law codes used by kings in early India during a millennium (600 BCE–570 ACE) of notable political, social, religious, and cultural innovations. We analyze each code's guidelines for kings, women, and occupational classes (*varnas*) through the lens of historical events in the era of its composition. The *varnas* were priestly *brāhmans*, *kşatŗiya* kings and soldiers, *vaiśya* folk, and *śudra* workers. Our study has four chronological sections. Part I is a historical prelude (Chapters 1–2); Part II is on the later Vedic era (Chapters 3–5) kingdoms, society, and the first codes, the *Dharma Sūtras* (ca. 600–300 BCE). Part III covers the heterodox Mauryan Empire (320–184 BCE) and early classical era (ca. 184 BCE–200 ACE) of dynamic political-social changes, the royal code *Arthaśāstra* (320 BCE–150 ACE), and the *Manu Smŗiti* (100 BCE–100 ACE). Part IV is on the later classical era of stable pre-Guptan and Guptan empires, when monarchs meted out justice with two fairly liberal codes, the *Yājñyavalkya Smŗiti* (200 ACE) and *Nārada Smŗiti* (400 ACE).

In the later Vedic era (1000–300 BCE), Sanskritic territorial expansion resulted in the formation of large political states (*janapada*) across the northern regions. These states included kingdoms and oligarchies (ca. 800 BCE), whose leaders were elite men of the martial class/caste (*varna*) of *kşatŗiyas*. When kingdoms began to dominate oligarchic states, scholarly *brāhmans* composed the *Dharma Sūtras* (600–300 BCE) to guide kings on statecraft and court justice. The royal state reached its apex in the heterodox Mauryan Empire (320–184 BCE), for which Kauţilya composed the initial sections of the *Arthaśāstra*. Mauryan collapse triggered political disarray, succeeded by new empires in the early classical era (ca. 200 BCE–200 ACE). Kauţilya's eponyms now expanded the *Arthaśāstra*, which Vişnugupta completed ca. 150 ACE. There also now appeared the first *Dharma Śāstra*, that is, the orthodox *Mānava Dharma Śāstra/Manu Smŗiti* (100 BCE–100 ACE). In the later classical era (200–570 ACE) of more stable, prosperous political states, less orthodox *brāhmans* composed two new *Dharma Śāstras*, the *Yājñyavalkya Smŗiti* (ca. 200 ACE) and *Nārada Smŗiti* (ca. 400 ACE). Pre-Guptan kings relied on the *Yājñyavalkya Smŗiti*, which Guptan emperors (320–570 ACE)[1] used in conjunction with the *Nārada Smṛiti*. The *Yājñyavalkya* and *Nārada Smṛitis* highlighted the king's righteous duty (*dharma*) to govern and dispense unbiased justice (*nyāya*) to all subjects based on norms in their era. As code writers were all *brāhman* men, their codes often began by describing the *dharmas* of the four *varnas*. Yet the writers' chief purpose was temporal, as they wished to define the king's *dharma* to govern and mete out justice to all subjects in a righteous manner.

The theoretical basis of this study is that Sanskritic clans followed amorphous patriarchal customs until political states (*janapada*) emerged in the later Vedic era. When kingdoms began to dominate oligarchies, the authors of the *Dharma Sūtras* legally validated patriarchal customs on marriage and patrilineal inheritance. These laws had serious social implications, as they subordinated women in the state and in society. This study examines each code through the lens of political and social events in that historical era, a method that clarifies the author's motivations, the main political-economic factors of that era, and the code's impact. The codes were often adopted as customary laws by the four Sanskritic *varnas* of *brāhmans, kṣatṛiyas, vaiśyas,* and *śudras,* and these laws filtered into the practices of non-Sanskritic and heterodox subjects. Meanwhile, many autonomous tribal and Dravidian groups retained diverse forms of ancient matriliny. The codes present a range of male perspectives, such as benign paternalism, stern orthodoxy, misogyny, unorthodox patriarchy, and simple humanity. Interestingly, in a millennium of epochal intellectual ferment by seers of the *Upaniṣads* and by heterodox sages like Gautama Buddha and Mahāvīra, even heterodox and unorthodox monarchs chose a code written by *brāhmans*. This was probably because in early India, most sects and cultural groups shared a common value for *dharma* (Sanskrit)/*dhamma* (Pāli) as the underlying social principle/foundation (Skt. root '*dhr*') of ethical conduct by individuals, and righteous governance by kings.

South Asia's rich layers of ethno-cultural diversity indicate that countless humans have settled in, and merged in this region from the dawn of antiquity to the present day. The first layers were prehistoric groups who spoke Austric, Tibeto-Burman, and Dravidian languages, followed by Indo-Āryan clans speaking Sanskrit (ca. 2200–2000 BCE) and later arrivals from Asia, Europe, Arabia, and Africa. This study's four chronological sections are synopsized below.

Part I – Historical prelude

In Chapter 1, 'Antecedents and Preview', the author analyzes artifacts that shed light on early beliefs, women, and society in South Asia. These include prehistorical sculptures depicting women and archaeological remains from the urban Indus/Harappan Civilization (2700–1700 BCE). The chapter has a short discussion of recent scholarship on the linguistic/ethnic origin of the inhabitants of the Indus cities and their interaction with patriarchal clans of Indo-Āryan settlers (ca. 2200–2000 BCE).

Chapter 2, 'Early Vedic Era', examines historical events on the subcontinent ca. 2000–1000 BCE. Indo-Āryan Sanskrit language speakers arrived on the subcontinent in the last few centuries of the Indus civilization. As Sanskritic clans then consisted predominantly of males, genetic interactions with earlier Dravidian, Austric, and Tibeto-Burman language speakers were numerous and ongoing. The clans moved across vast swathes of territory, eventually reaching the Gangetic plains (ca. 1000 BCE). Each territorial expansion and settlement created an early South Asian population of mixed ancestry, followed by genetic amalgams with later immigrants in the classical, medieval, and modern centuries.[2] Creative bards drew upon early Indo-Āryan myths to compose the sacred *Rig Veda* (ca. 1900–1000 BCE). The *Rig Veda*'s ten volumes inform us of the territorial expansion of Sanskritic clans led by martial *kṣatṛiya* leaders (*rājans*); of the first occupational *varnas* of *brāhmans*, *kṣatṛiyas*, and *vaiśya* folk; and the creation of the fourth *varna* of *śudra* workers inducted from local communities. The elite three *varnas* were now called the 'twice born' (*dvīja*). While *dvīja* women initially had the right to study the *Vedas*, perform rituals, own property, and remarry, when society and state grew increasingly diverse (ca. 1000 BCE), restrictions increased. *Dvīja* women were forbidden to have sexual contact outside their *varna*, especially with men who were *śudras*, or of mixed caste, or foreigners without caste (*mlecchas*). In contrast, *dvīja* men were allowed polygamous marriages across *varna* lines, and their sons of such mixed ancestry sometimes claimed their paternal lineage, but others were ranked as mixed castes with fewer rights.

Part II – Later Vedic era and *Dharma Sūtras*

Chapter 3, 'Vedic Scriptures, *Janapadas*, and Women', provides an overview of the later Vedic era. This era witnessed the first Sanskritic territorial states (*janapadas/mahājanapadas*), which included kingdoms (*rājyas*) on fertile Gangetic plains and oligarchies (*gana sanghas*) on surrounding hillsides.[3] By 800 BCE, there were sixteen major *rājyas* and *gana sanghas*, whose leaders were often elite *kṣatṛiyas*. Social, political, and intellectual ferment appear in orthodox and heterodox literature from this period. The Vedic corpus was expanded with the addition of the *Sāma*, *Yajur*, and *Atharva Vedas*, each having a hymnal (*Samhita*), liturgy (*Brāhmana*, ca. 1000–500 BCE), meditative forest book (*Āraṇyakā*), and spiritual philosophical book (*Upaniṣad*, 800–300 BCE). The *Brāhmanas* comprised chants for sacrificial rites, which were grandiose for kings upon their ascensions and victories.

The Sanskritic clans rapidly expanded over the Gangetic plains, but they expanded more slowly into hilly regions of eastern Uttar Pradesh and northern Bihar. These became the domains of oligarchic political states (*gana sanghas*), whose indigenous hill tribes and non-Sanskritic groups did not rapidly absorb Sanskritic mores of patriarchy and social classes/caste (*varna*). As *gana sangha* leaders did not often perform *brāhmanical* rituals, some orthodox Sanskritic texts expressed dislike for these oligarchs. Although the *Upaniṣad* seers dissented against the rituals in the *Brāhmana* texts within the *Vedas*, their scriptures were absorbed into the *Vedas*, as the seers respected the *Rig, Sāma, Yajur Vedas*, and the gods. This is evident in the early *Chāndogya Upaniṣad* (1.4.1–5).[4] The *Upaniṣads* also sent a powerful message of the unity of the individual soul (Ātman) and the universal spirit (Brahman). Other Vedic-era Sanskrit scriptures were the epics *Rāmāyana* and *Mahābhārata* (800–300 BCE), with myths about heroic kings, queens, and ethical conduct as *dharma;* demoniac rivals; and the *Mahābhārata*'s addendum, the *Bhagavad Gīta* (ca. 300 BCE). The *Bhagavad Gīta* is a discourse between divine Ķrişnā and Arjuna in which Ķrişnā declares that human actions (*karma*) cause a cycle of birth and death but that freedom (*mokśa*) is possible through three paths, which became the undercurrent of Hindu belief and practice. These are the way of knowledge (*jñāna*) taken by renunciants, the way of *karma* in which an individual performs ethical acts of *dharma* without egoism, and the way of devotion (*bhakti*) to the Supreme.

In contrast, heterodox thinkers vigorously opposed Vedic celebratory rituals for royal accessions and victories, and they broke off from the orthodox mainstream. These beliefs ranged widely from agnosticism embraced by Siddharta Gautama, a.k.a the Buddha ('Enlightened One'; 563–484 BCE), founder of Theravāda Buddhism; Jaina denial of a supreme Deity yet belief in a soul (*jīva*) for all living things, as taught by Vardhamāna Mahāvīra, a.k.a. Jina ('Conqueror, or 'Great Hero'; 540–468 BCE), founder of Jainism; the atheism of the Ājīvikas; and radical materialism of the Chārvākas. The two most significant sects were Buddhism and Jainism, which strongly appealed to the lower *varnas* and pre-Āryan groups. Our study examines the two most notable innovators, the Buddha and Mahāvīra whose divergent philosophies reflect not only religious issues but also the struggle between royal and oligarchic states. Both thinkers were *kşatŗiyas* from *gana sanghas* that were inhabited by indigenous linguistic-cultural groups. While both orthodox and heterodox dissenters objected to *Brāhmana* rituals, they shared a common belief that ethical *dharma* (Skt.)/*dhamma* (Pāli) was the foundation (Skt. root '*dhr*') of civil society.

Chapter 4, 'Jaina and Buddhist Canon, States, and Women', expands the discussion on Therāvada Buddhism and Jainism and their key principles as introduced in Chapter 3. This chapter focuses specifically on the links between their founders and the *gana sanghas*, women's innovative roles in both sects, and the spread of their beliefs across the subcontinent in the next centuries.[5] Siddharta Gautama was an aristocratic *kşatŗiya* of the Śākya *gana sangha* in Nepal who left his patrimony and family to meditate upon sorrow. His benign solutions earned him the honorific of the Buddha. Early Therāvada canon includes the *Tripitaka* (Three Baskets) and *Jātaka* (Birth Tales) in Pāli. Jainism's founder Vardhamāna Mahāvīra was the last of twenty-four preceptors (*tīrthankaras)* was also known as 'Jina' (Conqueror). The son of a *kṣatṛiya* from the Jṇātṛikā *gana sangha* in Vaiśāli (n. Bihar), Mahavīrā became revered as the last *tīrthankara*. Jaina canon includes the *Āchārānga Sūtra, Kalpa* Sūtra, and other scriptures written in Prākrit folk dialects like Ardha Magadhi derived from Sanskrit and local languages.[6] The common thread uniting the orthodox followers of *Vedic* texts, and heterodox Buddhists, and Jainas was the belief in ethical conduct (*dharma*). This is seen in the Jaina and Buddhist canon exalting nonviolence (*ahimsa*) and its political implications. This chapter also examines women ascetics in Buddhism and Jainism and some representations in art, the *Āchārānga Sūtra* and *Kalpa Sūtra* in Prakrits, derived from Sanskrit and local languages. Buddhist canon includes the *Tripitaka* (Three Baskets), which includes the *Digha Nikaya* and the *Jātaka* (Birth Tales) in the Pāli language. Āśoka Maurya's royal edicts were in Pāli, often in the Brahmi script, the script in which the first Tamil edicts were written. Āśoka introduced Theravāda Buddhism to Srī Lanka, from where it spread across Southeast Asia, and in the classical era, the new sect of Mahāyana Buddhism reached Central Asia, China, Korea, and Japan.

When kingdoms dominated the oligarchies (ca. 600 BCE), male *brāhmans* composed the first temporal law codes. The first codes were the *Dharma Sūtras*,[7] which were composed as guidelines for *kṣatṛiya* kings on their righteous duties (*dharma*). These codes also defined the *dharmas* of the three upper *varnas* ranks (*dvījas*), that is, *brāhman* priests, *kṣatṛiya* soldiers, and *vaiśya* merchants and farmers, and the rights and roles of women.[8] The *Dharma Sūtras* validated male polygamy and patrilineal inheritance for kings and *dvījas*, rulings that profoundly affected women's rights. While some sacred texts describe women as scholars, others idealize rites to goddesses of wealth in the climate of rivalry among *mahājanapada* kingdoms like Kosala, Magadha, and the Vṛjjī confederacy. Oligarchs often adopted Buddhist or Jaina tenets, while lower-caste Nandas and Mauryas established dynasties. As economic clout increased with territorial acquisition through matrimonial alliances, women became pawns in royal rivalries. A queen's dower (*strīdhana*) of valuable domains was often seized by her polygamous husband. At the same time, important Hindu, Buddhist, and Jaina ideals of *dharma* shaped the conduct of rulers and subjects in this era. These discussions provide the context for the next chapter on the *Dharma Sūtras* (600–300 BCE) and its ideals on kingly governance, *varna*, and women.

Chapter 5, '*Dharma Sūtras*', examines the *Dharma Sūtras* of four male *brāhmans*, Āpastamba, Gautama, Baudhāyana, and Vasiṣṭha, whose views ranged from paternalism to stern orthodoxy. Although grounded in *dvīja* culture of Vedic study in order to perform rites, the codes had two powerful temporal aims. The first was to uphold ethical laws (*dharma*) for a society based on *varna*, and the second was to define a *kṣatṛiya* ruler's duties to defend, tax, and mete out justice. Yet they also legally endorsed patrilineal/ patrimonial inheritance to garner wealth for males of the higher *varnas* or the 'twice born' (*dvījas*) over *śudra* and non-Sanskritic subjects. Their rulings left an indelible imprint on women's rights in marriage and access to landed property. The *Dharma Sūtra* authors mandated celibacy for male students, but they did not mention female students, a fact that indicates that girls no longer studied the *Vedas* alongside boys. The codes lauded women's premarital celibacy and marital chastity to ensure 'pure' paternal Sanskritic lineage, but they validated polygamy for male *dvījas,* who could marry *śudra* wives. They established patrilineal inheritance so that kings and other men could garner wealth. While protecting female dower (*strīdhana*), only the southerner Āpastamba familiar with matriliny gave a widow the right to inherit her husband's property. Vasiṣṭha's (ca. 300 BCE) list of numerous mixed castes reflects a genetically diverse society, but his male *dvīja* anxiety appears in his ruling on childhood marriage for girls and eternal chastity for wives. Later elite male *dvīja* code writers followed their lead in promulgating Sanskritic patriarchy and *varna* hierarchy, which defined women and *śudras* as subsidiaries under their jurisdiction. These norms effectively penetrated surrounding Dravidian and tribal communities, even those with primal matriarchal rights. While some pre-Āryan groups accepted Sanskritic ideas, others retained their matrilineal patterns of inheritance partially or completely.

Part III: Mauryan–classical era: *Arthaśāstra* and *Manu Smṛiti*

Chapter 6, 'Mauryan Empire and *Arthaśāstra*', discusses the patrilineal royal state that exalted kingship, which attained new glamour and authority in the heterodox Mauryan Empire (321–184 BCE), and Kauṭilya's seminal work on statecraft, the *Arthaśāstra*, which was later expanded by his eponyms and completed by Viṣnugupta (ca. 150 ACE).[9] While these first heterodox rulers were probably inspired by Jaina and Buddhist doctrines on ethical conduct, they only governed the Mauryan Empire with the *Arthaśāstra* written in Sanskrit by the *brāhman* Kauṭilya. Yet the Mauryan Empire changed the ideal of governance, once predicated on orthodox *brāhmanical* norms, in surrounding states and eras, as the *Arthaśāstra* vividly describes the ideal king's duties (*dharma*).

Sources include Megasthenes's *Indika* in Greek, Buddhist and Jaina canon, Hindu *Purānas*, emperor Aśoka's pillar and rock edicts, and historical records. The founder was the gifted non-*dvīja* general Chandragupta,[10] whose *brāhman* mentor Kauṭilya wrote the *Arthaśāstra* code.[11] Chandragupta later became a Jaina monk under the tutelage of seer Bhadrabāhu

(367–298 BCE), the accredited author of two Jaina canonical texts, the *Kalpa Sūtra* and *Bhadrabāhu Samhita*. The central Jaina tenet is ethical conduct (*dharma*), with the most supreme being nonviolence (*ahimsa*),[12] which has had a profound political and social impact on South Asia. The Jaina text *Āchārānga Sūtra* emphasizes nonviolence, a tenet later adopted by the Mauryan emperor Chandragupta, who retired as a Digambara Jaina monk in Karnataka where he died. Jainas believe the canons were orally transmitted until formally inscribed in the next centuries.

The term *dharma* also reverberates in the Buddhist ideal of the 'wheel of law' (*dhamma chakka:* Pāli), through symbolic, doctrinal comparison of the royal chariot wheel and the cycle of ethical morality. The emperor Aśoka (272–232 BCE) promoted this ideal by carving it on pillars and walls of funerary memorials (*stūpas*). Hindu, Buddhist, and Jaina practices had a mutual influence, as sects, ethnic groups, and cultures had to coexist in a region that was increasingly diverse. The Mauryan Empire reached its peak under his grandson Aśoka, who spread Theravāda Buddhism to Srī Lanka. Theravādā Buddhists now composed their canon of *dhamma* rules, the *Tripitaka* (Three Baskets) with three sections, namely *Vinaya Pitaka* (Conduct), *Sutta Pitaka* (Discourses), and *Abhidhamma Pitaka* (Supplementary Doctrines). *Vinaya* and *Sutta Pitakas* describe moral rules of conduct, which no doubt influenced Mauryan ideas on *dhamma*.

This chapter has a detailed examination of the *Arthaśāstra*'s laws on kingly governance, diplomatic relations with the Graeco-Bactrian Empire in the northwest, and Aśoka's Buddhist *dhamma*. The chapter also compares Kauṭilya's earlier sections of the *Arthaśāstra* describing queens, workers, courtesans, women's sexual rights, and humane punishments with sections written by eponyms in the classical era who suspected women of treachery. In the post-Mauryan, early classical centuries of invasions, migrations, and new kingdoms (ca. 200 BCE–200 ACE), eponyms expanded the *Arthaśāstra* for heterodox and unorthodox monarchs. Less tolerant to women than Kauṭilya, their verses suspect women, yet these are not as misogynist as verses in the contemporary early classical code, the *Manu Smṛiti* (100 BCE–150 ACE).

Chapter 7, 'Early Classical Era', tries to decode the post-Mauryan, early classical era (200 BCE–200 ACE), where there were political upheavals and invasions that introduced new immigrants. Despite social turmoil, the newcomers added to the region's ethnic, sectarian, and cultural diversity. Kauṭilya's eponyms now expanded the *Arthaśāstra*, which was completed by Viṣnugupta (ca. 150 ACE). The authors were probably upper-caste men, but they shared the vision of nonsectarian royal justice endorsed by Kauṭilya and Aśoka Maurya. The expanded *Arthaśāstra* now appealed to both heterodox and tolerant Hindu kings whose trading economies thrived with communal harmony and whose policy of decentralized governance sanctioned local autonomy. In an era of dramatic political and sociocultural changes, subjects were united by a common belief in righteous conduct and laws as *dharma*. Yet such changes also stirred xenophobic, misogynist anxiety in the orthodox, as seen in the first *Dharma Śāstra*, namely the *Mānava Dharma Śāstra/Manu Smṛiti* (100 BCE–105 ACE).

As new religious sects burgeoned, kings and emperors promoted a particular sectarian vision, which was expressed in art. There now appeared an array of sacred Buddhist, Jaina, and devotional (*bhakti*) Hindu texts in Sanskrit, Pāli, local Praķrits, and Tamil. Decentralized governance was the new royal policy that promoted local authority and communal peace among diverse communal groups. Monarchs also did not interfere unduly into the subjects' customary laws until a crime necessitated royal intervention or when disagreements led individuals to appeal to the king, who then used a particular Sanskritic code to dispense justice. This study focuses only on the specified eight Sanskrit codes, and it does not examine the laws of diverse communities in early India.

Chapter 8, '*Arthaśāstra* and *Manu Smṛiti*', is a discussion of the early classical era's kingdoms, societies, and women (180 BCE–200 ACE), and it introduces the *Arthaśāstra*'s later sections and the *Manu Smṛiti*. Elite male anxiety appears in misogynist and/or xenophobic verses in the *Arthaśāstra*'s later verses and the *Mānava Dharma Śāstra/Manu Smṛiti* (100 BCE–150 ACE). The focus is on social changes, royal governance, and women's rights in these dynamic centuries of invasions, as well as of genetic mergers and religio-cultural syncretisms. This chapter contains an analysis of political events, kingship, kingdoms, and society after the fall of the Mauryan Empire. There now occurred invasions by Persians, Greco-Bactrians, and Central Asian Śakas and Kuṣānas, which resulted in migrations by local tribes like the Ābhīras. While newcomers brought in Persian notions of kingship, they also adopted *kṣatṛiya* identities and Sanskritic titles like *rājā* and *mahārājā*. Trade expanded over land and sea with Rome, Asia, Africa, and southeast Asia, making local kings, like the Dravidian Pāndyas, Cheras, and the Śātavāhanas, tolerant to merchants of all sects and tribes. As kings battled over territories and won and lost in quick succession, royal governance grew more decentralized. As society grew ethnically diverse and culturally layered, kings recognized the importance of tolerance. Sources include Sanskrit inscriptions by the Śaka king Rudradāman and Tamil Sangam-era texts exalting heroic women. Meanwhile, the *Manu Smṛiti* depicted women and lower castes as intellectually inferior. This chapter examines the two codes, *Arthaśāstra* and *Manu Smṛiti*, in detail. The *Arthaśāstra* was used by heterodox and tolerant Hindu rulers, while orthodox rulers used the *Manu Smṛiti* to govern and mete out justice. Eponyms and Viṣnugupta (2nd century ACE) expanded and completed the *Arthaśāstra*. In this era, indigenous Hindu kings may have been drawn to the orthodox *Manu Smṛiti*, which exalted *kṣatṛiya* kings. The chapter analyzes attitudes toward women, whose chastity became central to notions of paternal Sanskritic *varna* lineages, and Manu's rulings on *kṣatṛiya* kings, *varna*, and women's marital and property rights.

Part IV: Later classical era: *Yājñyavalkya Smṛiti* and *Nārada Smṛiti*

Chapter 9, 'Pre-Guptan and Guptan Monarchs', describes powerful, dynastic kingdoms (200–570 ACE), their socioeconomic moorings, and the spread of Sanskritic norms but also syncretic interactions with Dravidian and tribal groups. As Śaka, Kuṣāna, and Śātavahana emperors had granted regional authority to governors and feudatories (*satraps*), their mighty kingdoms began to weaken (ca. 100 ACE). Their *satraps* and tribal confederacies (*gana sanghas*) now seized power, and these changes affected land routes in the north upon southern kingdoms. Kings began to highlight justice as their most important duty, and they relied on the ethical *Yāĵñavalkya Smṛiti*. Guptan emperors (320–570 ACE) relied on the *Yājñyavalkya Smṛiti* and the *Nārada Smṛiti*. This chapter describes these kingdoms and some powerful queens like Prabhāvati Gupta, who married a Deccan king, as well as their focus on prosperity and culture.

While Manu followed Kauṭilya's guidelines on the importance of precise laws (*vivādā*) and legal procedures (*vyavahāra*), these were fine-tuned by Yājñyavalkya and Nārada, who focused on ethical justice. Our study proposes that in the classical and medieval centuries, many Hindu kings did not solely depend on the *Manu Smṛiti* but relied instead on two more liberal *Dharma Śāstras* that promoted communal harmony and emphasized equitable royal justice (*nyāya*). The pre-Guptan *Yājñyavalkya Smṛiti* and Guptan *Nārada Smṛiti* were cited in two major medieval commentaries (*prabandhas*), which were regional laws till the colonial era.

Chapter 10, '*Yāĵñyavalkya* and *Nārada Smṛitis*', examines laws in these codes on royal justice, women, and *varna*, and their great impact on medieval laws. The *Yāĵñyavalkya Smṛiti* (ca. 250 ACE) and *Nārada Smṛiti* (ca. 400 CE) reveal that elite male fears over female chastity and *varna* lineage became less overt in stable, prosperous dynastic kingdoms. As the king's chief duty was now juridical, rulers relied on the *Yājñyavalkya Smṛiti* and the *Nārada Smṛiti*, both of which had more humane laws on women and emphasized ethical justice (*nyāya*) in court. The chapter has a comparative analysis of the codes on kingship and *varna*; describes female education, marriage, and property rights; and examines each code's laws on women. The *Yājñyavalkya* and *Nārada Smṛitis* were cited in medieval *prabandha*, such as Vijñāneśvara's *Mītākṣarā* (ca.11th century ACE) and Jīmutavāhanā's *Dāyabhāga* (ca. 13th century ACE), which became regional laws in the north, Bengal, and Deccan. Yet later *brāhmans* directed British colonial jurists to the *Manu Smṛiti* as the most earliest and most definitive Hindu code, setting aside the still more ancient *Āpastamba Dharma Sūtra* that favored women and the *Arthaśāstra* whose fewer caste biases appealed to heterodox and unorthodox kings. The *Manu Smṛiti* thus became the basis of colonial Hindu law, whose residual effects appear in legislative and juridical debates even today, despite free India's equitable constitution. It is important that we now view the *Manu Smṛiti* as an archaic document reflecting the society of a bygone era.

Notes

1 This study is entitled *Women's Rights and Law Codes in Early India, 600 BCE–570 ACE*. The ending date (570 ACE) is derived from the theory that although the Guptan Empire disintegrated after Skanda Gupta (d. 467 ACE) and Bengal was lost (ca. 544 ACE), their administrative efficiency and patterns of justice with the *Yājñavalkya Smṛiti* and *Nārada Smṛiti* led subsequent dynasties to emulate their governance. After Skanda Gupta, north India was invaded violently by Central Asian Hunas, who wrested Punjab away (ca. 500 ACE), a blow that triggered internal revolts in Kathiawar, Mālwa, Kashmir, Rājputana, Nepāl, Orissa, Assām, and Bengal by 544 ACE. Inscriptions indicate that a Budha Gupta (d. 495) from a minor, rival Guptan line continued in Magadha in the Gangetic region. Guptan unification no doubt inspired Harsha Vardhana, who ascended the throne of Thānesar near Delhi and once again united northern India (606–647). For historical surveys of the post-Gupta period, see Romila Thapar, *Early India: From the Origins to AD 1300*, Berkeley: University of California Press, 2002, 250–289; Ramashankar Tripathi, *History of Ancient India*, New Delhi: Motilal Banarsidass, 1999 (9th ed.; 1st ed. 1942), 249–277; Stanley Wolpert, *A New History of India*, New York: Oxford University Press, 2000 (7th ed.; 1st ed. 1977), 92–94. For information on *Jīmutavāhanā's Dāyabhāga*, which gave widows inheritance rights in Bengal and was influenced by *Yājñavalkya Smṛiti*, see Ashutosh Dayal Mathur, *Medieval Hindu Law: Historical Evolution and Enlightened Rebellion*, New Delhi: Oxford University Press, 2012, 71; Ludo Rocher, trans., ed., *Jīmutavāhanā's Dāyabhāga: The Hindu Law of Inheritance in Bengal*, New York and Oxford: Oxford University Press, 2002, 1–32, 177–186. Also see Justice Markandey Katju, "The Importance of Mitakshara in the 21st Century", in *Practical Lawyer*, Lucknow: Eastern Book House, 2005 at this website: http://www.ebc-india.com/lawyer/articles/200573.htm, 1–6; and N.N. Bhattacharya, "Property Rights of Women in Ancient India", in L.K. Tripathi, ed., *Position and Status of Women in Ancient India*, Vol. I, Varanasi: Benares Hindu University, 1988, 62–71, *vide.*, 69–71 on Vijñāneśvara's *Mītākṣarā*, and Jīmutavāhanā's *Dāyabhāga*.

2 Mitochondrial DNA studies of many South Asians, notably those who speak Austric/Munda languages indicate that the first humans migrated out of Africa in the Paleolithic era (ca. 65,000–50,000 years ago), some travelling via the Red Sea to the coasts of South Asia, to islands like Sri Lanka, and thence to Southeast Asia. A second overland wave reached the Middle East where agriculture developed at Elam, and some migrants left Elam for the Indus region (ca. 10,000 BCE). The Indus/Harappan civilization (7000–2000 BCE), whose population spoke a Dravidian-Elamite language, now traded along the western coast, so that its speakers reached south India. In the Bronze Age, Tibeto-Burmese speakers occupied the north-northeastern regions of the subcontinent, while Indo-Āryan clans speaking Sanskrit arrived in the northwest (ca. 2200–2000 BCE). South

Asia's numerous language groups include 1) Austric/Munda, related to SE Asian languages; 2) Tibeto-Burmese of northeastern tribes like the Khasis; 3) Dravidian in south India (e.g., Tamil, Telegu, Malayalam, Kannada) and vestigial Brahui Dravidian in the Indus region; 4) Sanskritic languages (e.g., Hindi, Urdu, Sindhi, Punjabi, Rajasthani, Bengali, Assamese, Oriya, Pali, Prakrits, Gujarati, Marathi, Konkani, Sinhalese, and Dardic admixtures like Kashmiri, to name a few), as well as Persian, Arabic, English, and French, which have shaped modern society.

South Asia's ethno-cultural underpinnings have intrigued scholars for centuries, but recent genetic research has begun to shed light on such issues. Despite cultural diversity, South Asians reveal varying patterns of genetic interaction with other groups. Some tribes are virtually untouched, like the Andamanese; the Brahui speak a proto-Dravidian language but live in the Indus region among other language speakers with whom they share genetic markers; some Sanskritic speakers have more Indo-Āryan genetic markers than others; some Dravidian speakers have more Indo-Āryan genes than others, depending on caste. A few publications that encapsulate the main scientific conclusions for ordinary readers include: Tony Joseph, *Early Indians: The Story of Our Ancestors and Where We Came From*, New Delhi: Juggernaut Books, 2018; Partha C. Majumder, "The Human Genetic History of South Asia", in *Current Biology*, Vol. 20, February 23, 2010, 184–187; Mait Metspalu, Mayukh Mondal, and Gyaneshwer Chaubey, "The Genetic Makings of South Asia", in *Science Direct*, Vol. 53, December 2018, 125–133, Elsevier Ltd.; G. David Poznik, Yali Xue, Fernando L. Mendez, Peter Underhill, et al., "Punctuated Bursts in Human Male Demography Inferred from 1,244 Worldwide Y-Chromosome Sequences", in *Nature Genetics*, Vol. 48, 2016, 593–599.

3 For the most insightful exposition of the *gana sanghas,* see R. Thapar, *Early India: From the Origins to AD 1300, op. cit.*, 146–150.

4 Ainslee T. Embree, ed., *Sources of Indian Tradition, Volume 1: From the Beginning to 1800,* New York: Columbia University Press, 1988 (2nd ed.), 43–45, (1st ed. 1958 by Wm. Theodore deBary, A.L. Basham, et al.)

5 Embree, *ibid.*, 43–199.

6 Padmanabh S. Jaini, *Collected Papers on Jaina Studies*, Delhi: Motilal Banarsidass, 2000, 3–11, 11–27; and Padmanabha S. Jaini, *Gender and Salvation, op. cit.,* xvi–xx, 1–35, 52–59, 72–73, 82–92.

7 The *Dharma Sūtras* in Sanskrit are available as PDF files at: www.hinduonline.co/DigitalLibrary.html. See apastamba_dharma_sutra.pdf; baudhayana_dharma_sutra.pdf.; gautama_dharma_sutra.pdf.; vasishta_dharma_sutra.pdf.

8 See also Patrick Olivelle's notable critical translation, *Dharmasūtras: The Law Codes of Āpastamba, Gautama, Baudhāyana, and Vasiṣṭha*, Oxford: Oxford University Press, 1999. Also see his historical analyses: P. Olivelle, ed., *Between the Empires: Society in India 300 BCE to 400 CE*, Oxford: Oxford University Press, 2006; P. Olivelle, *Language, Texts and Society: Explorations in Ancient Indian Culture and Religion*, New Delhi: Firenze University Press and Munshiram Manoharlal, 2005.

9 Patrick Olivelle's notable studies of the *Arthaśāstra* and *Manu Smṛiti* include: P. Olivelle, trans., ed., *King, Governance and Law in Ancient India: Kautilya's Arthaśāstra: A New Annotated Translation*, New York: Oxford University Press, 2013; P. Olivelle, "Manu and the 'Arthaśāstra': A Study in Sastric Intertexuality", in *Journal of Indian Philosophy*, Vol. 34, No. 2–3, June 2004, 281–291; P. Olivelle, *The Law Code of Manu: A New Translation Based on the Critical Edition*, Oxford: Oxford University Press (Oxford Classics), 2004; P. Olivelle, trans., ed., *Manu's Code of Law: A Critical Edition and Translation of the*

Mānava-Dharmáśāstra with the Editorial Assistance of Suman Olivelle, Oxford and New York: Oxford University Press, 2005; P. Olivelle, *The Law Code of Manu: A New Translation Based on the Critical Edition, op. cit.*

10 Romila Thapar, *Aśoka and the Decline of the Mauryas*, Oxford and Delhi: Oxford University Press, 1961 (3rd ed.). Thapar describes Kauṭilya as 'the theorist of the politico-economic Mauryan state' (p. 56) who composed the first sections, including Vol. II of the *Arthaśāstra.* Thapar makes a persuasive argument that the *Arthaśāstra*'s references to silk, which was brought into India ca. 130 BCE from China, indicate that the code was revised in the classical era and that it was completed by Viṣnugupta (200 ACE), *vide.,* Appendix I, 217–225. See also Romila Thapar, *A History of India,* Vol. 1 (Pelican: 1966), New Delhi: Penguin Books, 2000 (12th ed.); R. Thapar, *Early India: From the Origins to AD 1300, op. cit.*, 184–185. Patrick Olivelle and Mark McClish recently proposed a date for the *Arthaśāstra* between the Mauryan and Kuṣāna Empires, *vide.,* P. Olivelle and M. McClish, trans., *Arthaśāstra: Selections from the Classic Indian Work on Statecraft*, Indianapolis: Hackett Publishing Co., 2012, xx.

11 The first translation was by R. Shamasastry, *Kautilya's Arthaśāstra (1915)*, Mysore: Mysore Printing and Publishing Works, 1967 (8th ed.). Shamasastry attributed a Mauryan date, endorsed by scholar S. Radhakrishnan. For the Sanskrit text, see Sanjeev Sabhlok, ed., *Chanakya (Kautilya)'s Arthashastra in Sanskrit,* with R. Shamasastry's trans., Melbourne, Australia, at this website: www.sabhlokcity.com/2012/09/chanakya-Kautalya-arthashastra-chanakya-niti-chanakya-sutras-full-text-sanskrit-and-translations/. Kauṭilya declared his authorship of Vol. I (*AŚ* I.1.19): 'So that happiness and victory may arise from these verses, Kauṭilya has composed this work of enlightenment' ('*sukha grihana vijayam artha pada niśchitam, kauṭilyena kṛtam śāstram vimukta granth vistāram*'). Early historians like K.A. Nilkanta Sastri endorsed Shamasastry's view that the *Arthaśāstra* was composed for the Mauryan Empire, *vide.,* K.A.N. Sastri, "Mauryan Polity", in K.A.N. Sastri, ed., *Age of the Nandas and Mauryas*, New Delhi: Motitlal Banarsidass, 1967 (rpt. 1996), 171–191.

12 *Āchārānga Sūtra* (1.4.1; 1.1) translated by A.L. Basham, in Ainslie T. Embree, ed., *Sources of Indian Tradition, Volume 1: From the Beginning to 1800, op. cit.*, 58, 64–66.

Part I

HISTORICAL PRELUDE

1

ANTECEDENTS AND PREVIEW

Early South Asian civilization was notable for its unique creative endeavors, as well as sociocultural mergers of diverse linguistic and ethnic groups.[1] This feature of immersion and borrowing, yet distinction, remains a feature of the region even today, with women playing a crucial part in the transfer of heritage. Paleolithic sites reveal that hunter-gatherers attributed nature's fertility to female sexual power, as seen in the discovery of an animistic icon of the vulva-womb (*yoni*; ca. 6000 BCE) in a cave shrine in Baghor, Madhya Pradesh, a symbol of divine female energy that is still venerated today.[2] Women were respected as economic producers, as well as for being the reproducers of clans, a trait still evident among some tribes in south India.[3] This is evident in Mesolithic caves in Bhimbetka, Madhya Pradesh, and Kurnool, Andhra (30,000–10,000 BCE), whose paintings reveal women working alongside men.

Harappan-Indus civilization

Such religio-cultural beliefs were reaffirmed with the spread of agriculture in the Neolithic and Chalcolithic (Bronze) ages (5000–2800 BCE), as women helped to plant and reap crops for the clan. As the home was regarded as the sacred site of births, women probably also conducted rites to the goddess of fecundity, a practice that remains common even today. Archaeology also provides clues on gender relations in the first urban experiment of the Indus-Harappan civilization (ca. 7000–2700–1700 BCE).[4] Numerous terracotta and bone icons of goddesses, some of nursing mothers, were strewn across Harappan sites such as Mehrgarh (7000 BCE), Kulli, Zhob, Nal, Harappa, and Mohenjo-dāro (2700–1900 BCE).[5] Their profusion and the clay lamps unearthed outside street homes indicate the prevalence of matriarchal customs, including domestic rites by women. Yet the small but imposing limestone statue of a contemplative priest-king ('*śramana*') also suggests that the overarching religio-political authority lay in male hands. This civilization was notable for its extensive town planning, granaries, docks, and smaller artifacts such as a bronze dancing woman; beads; and terracotta seals, one engraved with an image of a plant emerging from a woman and another of a male god who resembles Śivā as Mahāyogi.[6] The prosperity of this large civilization depended on an agricultural, industrial, and mercantile workforce, which must have included women.

Scholars who have tried to decipher the Harappan seals have offered various theories on the language and script. As the earliest Indus sites predate the arrival of Indo-Āryans who spoke Sanskrit (ca. 2200 BCE), some notable epigraphists have proposed that the Indus inhabitants spoke proto-Dravidian, the matrix of later south Indian languages. Finnish scholar Asko Parpola used computers and scientific methods to unravel the Indus script, which he concluded was in a proto-Dravidian language. Epigraphist Iravatham Mahadevan, a scholar of Tamil-Brahmi rock inscriptions (200–400 BCE), concurred that the Indus script was proto-Dravidian.[7] Recent studies strongly indicate that Harappans were descendents of Middle Eastern groups from Elam, where agriculture developed.

The mature phase of the Harappan civilization (ca. 2200–1900 BCE) marked the arrival of pastoral, patriarchal Indo-Āryan clans who spoke Sanskrit (ca. 2200 BCE).[8] Archaeologists have unearthed settlements of Indo-Āryans near the Caspian and Black Sea region, which was probably the initial Indo/Iranian/European homeland. Linguists favor Eastern Europe as the homeland, as it has numerous Indo-Āryan languages, unlike South Asia and early Iran, each having a single language like Sanskrit and early Persian. Similarities between early Persian and Sanskrit suggest that these two groups initially travelled together into Central Asia before one went to Iran and the other entered South Asia. What is truly significant is that fairly soon after their arrival, considerable genetic interaction between Sanskrit speakers and indigenous proto-Dravidian/tribal ethnic groups forged new communities with shared linguistic heritages.

Teams of international geneticists have done studies on the Y-chromosomes of male subjects from Asia.[9] These scientific studies confirm that there occurred a significant dispersal of Indo-Āryan male chromosomes from the Caspian and Black Sea region (ca. 5000 BCE) into Central Asia and thence into South Asia (ca. 2200 BCE). As the patriarchal Indo-Āryan clans were predominantly male, they had relations with or married local women, who bore progeny with both sets of genes. Earlier genome studies were inconclusive on Indo-Āryan genetic heritage, as the studies were chiefly of matrilineal DNA that connected subjects to maternal ancestors in South Asia. The arrival of early tribal and disparate caste groups is also being studied by geneticists (see Introduction, fn. 2). These scientific discoveries negate theories that South Asia was the original Indo-Āryan homeland.[10]

Although Indo-Āryan arrival coincided with the later stages of the Harappan civilization, it is unlikely that pastoralist warriors, who arrived in trickles, could have destroyed the fortified walls of complex cities. They may have been encouraged by the availability of grain and other wealth, and minor skirmishes were more likely than a military 'invasion'. The Indus cities also do not appear to have buildings for military battalions or for weapons, but, as they depended on trade of agricultural and manufactured products, they probably encouraged visitors. Moreover, despite Indo-Āryan pride in martial prowess, the small clans would have been unlikely to collide with a vast, urban civilization of great wealth and power. Instead, cooperation and integration would have mutually benefited immigrants and the Indus elite. What is known is sometime after settling in South Asia, Sanskrit-language priests composed the scriptural *Rig Veda*'s first volume (ca. 1900 BCE), completing its final, tenth volume (ca. 1000 BCE) after the Sanskritic clans reached the Yamuna region. The *Rig Veda* does not refer to battles between spear-wielding pastoralists and massive armies emanating from Indus fortifications.

In the waning Harappan era, it is likely that Sanskritic *brāhman* priests shared their religious ideas with the Indus priestly elite, to whom they were now related. This is suggested in the excavation at Kālibangān (ca. 2000 BCE) of large fire mounds, often termed 'fire altars', near a large building possibly used for priestly rituals.[11] Given the paucity of women in the early Sanskrit clans, it is entirely probable that Indo-Āryan clansmen won access to Harappan women and that mixed offspring expanded the Sanskritic clans. In return, clansmen acquired knowledge on managing an urban empire, with access to vast territories with an agricultural and industrial labor force. The strategic creed to 'live and let live, and to skirmish with Others only if unavoidable' now became the established pattern of Indic civilization. Over the next millennium, Sanskrit texts reveal dynamic genetic-cultural medleys in the spate of socioreligious interfaces between Sanskritic and Dravidian/tribal groups, who adopted each other's languages, beliefs, and practices.

Preview: Vedic era (ca. 2000–300 BCE)

During the early and later Vedic periods (ca. 2000–800–300 BCE), Indo-Āryan clans extended sway over the northern Gangetic regions. Sanskrit became the language of the elite, who publicized their ideals on royal authority, women's roles, and the functions of the *varnas,* that is, *brāhman* priests, *kṣatṛiya* kings/soldiers, *vaiśya* folk/merchants, and *śudra* workers. Indo-Āryan territorial and social expansion appears in the scriptural *Rig Veda*, whose first book was composed (ca. 1800 BCE) after their arrival on the subcontinent and whose tenth and final book (ca. 1000 BCE) shows their initial slow advance to the Yamuna-Gangetic Doab near Delhi. Over the next centuries, Sanskritic groups acquired large territories in the north, west, and east into the Ganges plains, soon dominating earlier inhabitants, including diverse communities who spoke their own languages. Territorial expansion led to the creation of the political state (800 BCE) as kingdoms and oligarchies, whose leaders were *kṣatṛiyas*, some having *brāhman* advisors. As patriarchal customs allowed polygamy for elite *varna* men, they took multiple wives from local communities, thus effectively bequeathing Sanskritic paternal lineage, cultural heritage, and norms to their mixed offspring. This was an ongoing process in the Vedic eras, and it continued during the millennia of further occupation across the peninsula. This process explains the subtle local transformations of Sanskritic norms across the peninsula. The connotation of the term 'Sanskritic' is thus linguistic/cultural/ethnic, rather than racial, as all humans belong to the race of *Homo sapiens sapiens*. This study proposes that the formation of the Sanskritic state facilitated the adoption of Sanskritic cultural norms across the peninsula.

Between 1000 and 300 BCE, Sanskritic political and social dominance reshaped local beliefs, languages, cultures, and indigenous practices, which in turn infused Sanskritic society. By 1000 BCE, the Sanskrit *Vedic* corpus was expanded to comprise four major scriptures, that is, the *Rig Veda, Sāma Veda, Yajur Veda,* and *Atharva Veda*, and by 800 BCE, each had four sections, a hymnal (*Saṁhitā*), liturgy (*Brāhmanā*), forest texts (*Āraṇyaka*), and philosophical works (*Upaniṣads*). The growing power of kingdoms over oligarchies led *brāhman* priests to the liturgical *Brāhmanās*, which catered to *kṣatṛiya* kings who wished for large fire rituals upon ascension and victory. Yet these rites burned large forests and destroyed their denizens, including indigenous tribal groups. Two dissident streams of thought then challenged orthodox *Brāhmanā* ritualism. The less radical appear in the early *Upaniṣads*, such as the *Iśāvāsyo U., Aitareyo U., Chāndogya,* and *Taittarīya U.* Sage-composers now advocated meditation on the inner Breath (*Prāna*) and detachment, which give insights into the Truth, that is, the spiritual unity of the individual (*Ātman*) and the cosmic Being (*Brahman*).

Devotional movements were inspired by myths of *Vedic* gods seen through the lens of Vedic-classical society. These deities appear in secondary, or 'remembered' texts (*smṛitīs*) such as the Sanskrit epics *Rāmāyana* (ca. 800–500 BCE) and *Mahābhārata* (ca. 900–200 BCE) and the *Mahābhārata*'s devotional addendum, the *Bhagavad Gīta* (ca. 300 BCE), which highlights the path of dedicated, selfless acts (*karma*) and devotion (*bhakti*) to the Supreme in a deified form. The formation of the royal kingdom is celebrated in the *Rāmāyana* and *Mahābhārata.* The *Rāmāyana* may have originally been an ancient Indo-Āryan myth about a heroic king who rescues his wife, but it was now set in the kingdom of Ayodhya (in Uttar Pradesh), whose heroic king Rāmā rescues his abducted wife Sīta, daughter of the king of Mithila (in Bihar), from the demon king Rāvanā (in Srī Lankā). The core of the *Mahābhārata* set in the Yamuna-Ganges confluence near Hastināpurā (Delhi) may be older than the *Rāmāyana*, but it was completed later. The *Mahābhārata* revolves around a struggle for the throne between two factions, namely the virtuous Pāṇdavā brothers led by Arjunā and their ruthless Kauravā cousins. The Pāṇdavās are assisted by Kṛṣṇa, king of Dwārakā (in Gujarat), whose divine intervention saves queen Draupadi from Duryodanā's clutches. The *Mahābhārata*'s poetic addendum, *Bhagavad Gīta* (ca. 300 BCE), is set on the battlefield as a metaphor for life and its struggles. In this highly sacred work, Kṛṣṇa urges Arjuna to fight bravely, as selfless endeavors in a righteous cause and devotion (*bhakti*) bear their just rewards. In the early and later classical centuries, the *Bhagavad Gīta* gave rise to the *Purānas* (200 BCE–400 ACE), epic tales which celebrate the pantheon of Hindu goddesses and gods. This era also produced numerous notable, temporal texts on logic, law, poetic drama, medicine, yoga, mathematics, and art.

The later Vedic centuries also gave rise to streams of heterodox seers dissenting from orthodox *brāhmanical* rituals. While some questioned ritualism but still respected Vedic deities, others were agnostics or atheistic materialists. The most significant agnostics were Siddhartha Gautama, the Buddha or Enlightened One (563–486 BCE), prince of the Śākya clan in modern Nepal, who established Theravāda Buddhism, and Vardhamāna Mahāvira (540–468 BCE) from the Jñātrika *gana sangha* in Vaiśāli (Bihar), who founded Jainism and is revered as the last of twenty-four preceptors (*tīsrthankara*).[12] Jainism questions the existence of a supreme being but reiterates belief in a soul (*jīva*) in every form of life. This central tenet led to Jaina emphasis on nonviolence (*ahimsa*) as the pre-eminent *dharma*. Seers of the *Upaniṣads* and of the Jaina and Buddhist sects emphasized the principle of righteous conduct (*dharma:* Skt.; *dhamma:* Pāli) as the foundation (Skt. root '*dhr*') of all civil society. Later Buddhist and Jaina thinkers produced a rich array of heterodox canons, such as the Buddhist *Tripitaka* and *Digha Nikaya*, and the Jaina *Āchārānga Sūtra* and *Kalpa Sūtra*. Buddhist scriptures were composed in Pāli, and Jaina canon were in Prakrits, languages derived from Sanskrit and local dialects.

In the Mauryan Empire, founder Chandragupta Maurya (b. 324 BCE) abdicated his throne (ca. 301 BCE) to become a Digambara Jaina monk in the south (Karnataka). His grandson Āśoka became devout Buddhist who spread these beliefs across his empire, into Srī Lanka. His royal edicts in Pāli used several scripts, the most notable being the Brahmi script in which Dravidan Tamil edicts first appear in south India.

The fundamental principle of ethical *dharma* united the orthodox, unorthodox, and heterodox in early India. This principle was adopted by temporal rulers based on temporal codes in kingdoms. The importance of righteous royal governance is evident in the titles that orthodox *brāhmans* gave to their royal codes, such as the *Dharma Sūtras* and classical *Dharma Śāstras*. In the classical era (300 BCE–600 ACE), new immigrants arrived from across Asia, Europe, and Africa, and Sanskrit was the language of many royal courts, as seen in the edicts of the Śaka king Rudradāman and of the imperial Guptas (320–550 ACE). At the same time, Dravidian kings hosted Tamil literary conferences (Sangam) exhibiting works of aphorisms, poetry, and epics that highlighted righteous conduct among kings and ordinary men and women (200 BCE–500 ACE). Sanskrit and Dravidian languages borrowed from each other, and linguistic-cultural threads were woven into a multiethnic fabric, a pattern replicated over the next millennia.

The next chapters examine scriptural references to *dharma*, kings, and women in the *Brāhmanas, Upaniṣads, Rāmāyana, Mahābhārata,* and *Bhagavad Gītā* and in important heterodox scriptures, like the Jaina *Āchārānga Sūtra* and the Buddhist *Tripitaka*.

Notes

1 As stated previously in the Introduction (*vide.*, endnote 2), mitochondrial DNA studies reveal that when humans migrated from Africa in the Paleolithic era (ca. 65,000–50,000 years ago), some groups travelled via the Red Sea to South Asian coasts, and to islands like Sri Lanka. Their descendents include South Asian tribes who speak Austri/Munda languages. Another wave left overland for the Middle East where agriculture developed in Elam, and subsequently, some migrants from Elam settled near the Indus River (ca. 10,000 BCE). Inhabitants of the Indus-Harappan civilization (7000–1800 BCE) thus probably spoke a Dravidian language akin to Elamite, and as they traded peacefully along the western and southern coasts of South Asia, they reached south India, thus leading to the spread of Dravidian languages in southern India. In the Bronze Age (ca. 2500 BCE), Tibeto-Burmese speakers reached the northeast. On this subject, see Tony Joseph, *Early Indians: The Story of Our Ancestors and Where We Came From*, *op. cit.*; Partha C. Majumder, "The Human Genetic History of South Asia", in *Current Biology, op. cit.*; Mait Metspalu, Mayukh Mondal, and Gyaneshwer Chaubey, "The Genetic Makings of South Asia", in *Science Direct*, *op. cit.*; G. David Poznik, Yali Xue, Fernando L. Mendez, Peter Underhill, et al., "Punctuated Bursts in Human Male Demography Inferred from 1,244 Worldwide Y-Chromosome Sequences", in *Nature Genetics*, *op. cit.*

2 J.M. Kenoyer, et al., "An Upper Paleolithic Shrine in India?", in *Antiquity*, Vol. 57, 1983, 88–94. Excavations at a cave in Baghor, Madhya Pradesh, unearthed a shrine (ca. 6550 BCE) with an icon of the female principle (*yoni*) associated with the Hindu mother goddess Shakti. See Mark Kenoyer, et al., "Preliminary Report on Excavation at the Late Paleolithic Occupation Site at Baghor", in G.R. Sharma and J.D. Clark, eds., *Palaeoenvironment and Prehistory in the Middle Son Valley (Madhya Pradesh, North India)*, Allahabad: Abinash Prakashan, 1983, 117–142; Mark Kenoyer, "Socio-Ritual Artifacts of Upper Paleolithic Hunter-Gatherers in South Asia," in Gregory Possehl, ed., *South Asian Archaeological Studies*, New Delhi: Oxford IBH, 1992, 233–251; Mark Kenoyer, *Ancient Cities of the Indus Valley Civilization*, Karachi: Oxford University Press, 1998; Gregory Possehl, *The Indus Civilization: A Contemporary Perspective*, Walnut Creek: Altamira, 1998.

3 For example, some Kerala tribes, like the Malampantaram, Ullatar, Mannan, and Narikkurava tribes, worshipped menstruation as fertility even in the late 20th century, *vide.,* Rajan Gurukkal, "Sabarimala Through the Ages," Opinion

section, *The Hindu*, January 10, 2019, website: www.thehindu.com/opinion/op-ed/sabarimala-through-the-ages/article25952897.ece?homepage=true

4 Sita Anantha Raman, *Women in India: A Social and Cultural History,* Santa Barbara: Praegar, ABC-CLIO, 2009, 4–6. Two interesting studies of ancient Indian art are: Vidhya Dehejia, *Indian Art*, London: Phaidon, 1997, 25–34; Roy C. Craven, *Indian Art: A Concise History,* London and New York: Thames and Hudson, 1997 (revised ed.), 7–23.

5 Mehrgarh goddess images can be seen at: www.pinterest.com/pin/549228117034746113/

6 Dilip K. Chakrabarti, *India: An Archaeological History: Paleolithic Beginnings to Early Historic Foundations*, New Delhi: Oxford University Press, 2003 (1st ed. 1999), 82–86, 99, 151–204. Asko Parpola, renowned Finnish scholar on the Indus script, believes that the Indus cities were founded by Dravidian speakers: Asko Parpola, *Deciphering the Indus Script*, Cambridge: Cambridge University Press, 1994; "The Coming of the Aryans to Iran and the Cultural and Ethnic Identity of the Dāsas," in *Studia Orientalia*, Vol. 64, 1988, 195–302, The Finnish Oriental Society.

7 See Iravatham Mahadevan, *Indus Script–Texts, Concordance and Tables*, New Delhi: Director General, Archaeological Survey of India, 1977; Iravatham Mahadevan, *Early Tamil Epigraphy from the Earliest Times to the Sixth Century*, Chennai: Central Institute of Classical Tamil, 1977 (revised ed. 2014). In addition, Mahadevan wrote short articles for *The Hindu,* which the journal republished as a memoriam in November 2018, *vide.,* Iravatham Mahadevan, "The Earliest Inscription in Malayalam," June 7, 2012; I. Mahadevan, "An Epigraphic Perspective on the Antiquity of Tamil," January 24, 2010; Iravatham Mahadevan, "Parpola and the Indus Script," June 17, 2010; M.V. Bhaskar and Iravatham Mahadevan, "Unearthing Stories from Stone," January 5, 2013.

8 See Tony Joseph's article on recent genome breakthroughs: "How Genetics Is Settling the Aryan Migration Debate", in *The Hindu*, June 17, 2017, at this website: www.thehindu.com/sci-tech/how-genetics-is-settling-the-aryan-migration-debate/article19090301.ece. Joseph cites lead geneticists who co-authored two scientific journal articles validating archaeological discoveries and historical theories. The first study is by Martin Richards (Huddersfield, U.K.), Silva, M., Oliveira, M., Vieira, D., et al. "A Genetic Chronology for the Indian Subcontinent Points to Heavily Sex-Biased Dispersals", in *BMC Evolutionary Biology*, Vol. 17, No. 1, 2017. ISSN 1471-2148. The other is by G. David Poznik, Yali Xue (both from Stanford University), Fernando L. Mendez, Peter Underhill, et al., "Punctuated Bursts in Human Male Demography Inferred from 1,244 Worldwide Y-Chromosome Sequences", in *Nature Genetics*, *op. cit.*

9 For linguistic paleontology, archaeology, and the original homelands of the Indo-Europeans/Āryans in the Pontic-Caspian region of modern Ukraine, see J.P. Mallory, *In Search of the Indo-Europeans: Language, Archaeology and Myth*, London: Thames and Hudson, 2001, 35–42, 151–157, 182–188, 222–231. Mallory cites the British linguist Robert Gordon Latham, who first proposed that linguistic science pointed to this region, rather than to Asia, as the original homeland of those who spoke the Indo-European languages. Also see Maria Gimbutas, "Primary and Secondary Homeland of the Indo-Europeans," in *Journal of Indo-European Studies*, Vol. 13, 1985, 185–202. Maria Gimbutas is well known for her work, *The Goddesses and Gods of Old Europe, 6500–3500: Myths and Cult Images,* Berkeley: University of California Press, 1982 (1st ed. 1974). British scholar Colin Renfrew believes that the Indo-Āryans originated in

Anatolia. See: A.C. Renfrew, *Archaeology and Language: The Puzzle of Indo-European Origins*, London: Pimlico, 1987.

10 Some theorists still favor South Asia as the Indo-Āryan homeland, *vide.,* Michael Danino, "Aryans and the Indus Civilization: Archaeological, Skeletal, and Molecular Evidence", in Gwen Robbins Schug and Subash R. Walimbe, eds., *A Companion to South Asia in the Past,* John Wiley & Sons, 2016, 205–224.

11 Dilip K. Chakrabarti, *India: An Archaeological History, op. cit.,* 200.

12 For Buddhism and Jainism, see Ainslee T. Embree, ed., *Sources of Indian Tradition, Volume 1: From the Beginning to 1800*, *op. cit.*, 43–199.

2

EARLY VEDIC ERA

I. *Rājans* and *varna*

Sometime after settling near the Indus,[1] Indo-Āryan bards drew upon ancient oral myths to compose the first hymns of the Sanskrit *Rig Veda*, whose ten volumes were composed over a period of nearly one thousand years (2000–1000 BCE). Not only does this oldest Indo-Āryan text have religious and literary significance, it is a valuable document on the social history of the peninsula. The clans highly valued their patrimonial heritage as the 'noble ones' (*āryas*), but they allowed sons born to their indigenous wives to continue their scriptural and social legacy. In the early Vedic era, society consisted of three occupational classes: priests (*brāhmans*), warrior-leaders (*kṣatṛiyas*), and folk (*vaiśyas*). As they spread toward the Yamuna, the clans conquered valuable domains so that they assimilated other locals into Sanskritic society. The *varna* order became more hierarchical, comprising three elite 'twice-born' (*dvījas*), *brāhmans, kṣatṛiyas,* and *vaiśyas* allowed to learn the *Vedas*, and *śudra* workers, who were denied this right. The *Puruṣa Śukta* hymn in the *Rig Veda*'s final volume (*RV* 10.90) describes the emergence of the four *varna* classes from a sacrifice of a Primal Male.[2] The term '*varna*' stems from the root 'to cover' (Skt.: *var*), possibly referring to a color identification of each rank to be worn on clothing, such as red for *kṣatṛiya* warriors. This meaning eluded colonial scholars preoccupied with European racial theories, who erroneously concluded that *varna* referred to skin color and that *śudras* were dark-skinned pre-Āryans. Suffice it say there were dark *brahmans* as well as dark *śudras*, since sexual interaction was an ongoing feature of Indo-Āryan settlement. From prehistory to the post-colonial era, the subcontinent has been genetically reinvented with each migrant influx. Sanskritic cultural norms, deities, and practices were adopted selectively by local communities who spoke Dravidian, Tibeto-Burman, and Austroasiatic (Munda) languages, while those speaking Sanskrit married into local groups, adopted their tools and clothes, and honored patrilineal and/or matrilineal customs. Progeny bore Sanskrit names and carried on Vedic traditions, but they also carried the mitochondrial DNA of local matriarchs.

At late Harappan sites (ca. 1400 BCE) near the fertile Yamuna-Ganges Doab, archaeologists have unearthed the iron hoes, sickles, and plows of pre-Āryan inhabitants. The tenth and final book of the *Rig Veda* (ca. 1000 BCE) indicates that the Indo-Āryan clans had now reached the Doab, where they lived in agricultural villages. Adopting the iron instruments of earlier indigenous inhabitants, they farmed extensively and produced a variety of grains.[3]

II. Women in the *Rig Veda*

Class and gender distinctions were less pronounced in the early Vedic period (2000–1000 BCE). *Rig Vedic* hymns refer to an oligarchic assembly (*sabhā*) and a later folk assembly (*samītī*) attended by women. Exalting the martial skills of powerful men with weapons (*kşatra*), the *samītī* chose a *rājan* as protector, although kingship was not hereditary.[4] Hymns laud valiant male *kşatṛiya* 'warriors' on 'spotted steeds'. Others describe a '*rājan* who scattered one-and-twenty people of both Vaikarna tribes through lust of glory' (*RV* 7. 18. 10–11) and a heroic 'Battle of Ten Kings' (*RV* 7. 33).[5] Other hymns invoke the gods Agni and Indra (*RV* 1.141.10–11, 6.1–2) and goddess Dawn for war's 'bounty rich in chariots, kine, and horses' (*RV* 7.76.5). Men of the clan owned the wealth collectively, but the *samītī* distributed it as shares (*bhāga*).

Daughters enjoyed some indirect rights to paternal wealth, and daughters had a marriage dower (*dyaur*) inherited by their girls. An early hymn thus instructs a man without sons to bequeath his property to his daughter's son rather than to his own brothers (*RV* 3.31.1–2), as wealth must be transferred from one generation to the next.[6] The 'Wedding Hymn' for the goddess Surya in the *Rig Veda*'s final book (*RV* 10.85.7, 25) describes the bride's *dyaur* as heaven and earth, and it blesses her with 'fine sons'/offspring (*suputra:* sons/progeny), and 'her share of good fortune' (*subhāgati*).[7] Clearly, a wife was entitled to a 'good share' of her husband's fortune. The next verse states that she had the right to speak in the public arena: 'Go the house to be the household's mistress and speak as lady to thy gathered people' (*RV* 10.85.26).[8] Initially, both males and females of the higher 'twice born' (*dvīja*) castes were initiated into Vedic study through the sacred thread ritual (*upanāyana*). The early hymns thus refer to women sages (*brāmavādinīs*), teachers (*āchāryas*), and preceptors (*upādhyāyinīs*).[9] Although the clans valued premarital and marital chastity, couples married after maturity amid prayers for progeny, who were essential for clan survival. A late hymn (*RV* 10.18) instructs a widow to remarry after a mourning period. Other customs were levirate remarriage for a widow (*niyoga*) and male polygamy across *varna* lines.

Notes

1 Despite some primary genetic markers, South Asians also display patterns of genetic and cultural interaction with other groups. Some groups are virtually untouched, like the Andamanese; the Brahui speak a proto-Dravidian language but live in the Indus region among other language speakers with whom they share genetic markers; some Sanskritic speakers have more Indo-Āryan genetic markers than others; some Dravidian speakers have more Indo-Āryan genes, sometimes depending on caste. South Asian ethno-cultural diversity has led to genetic studies, as stated earlier in the Introduction (endnote 2); and in Chapter 1 (endnotes 1, 8). Some recent texts that encapsulate scientific findings for the general public are: Tony Joseph, *Early Indians: The Story of Our Ancestors and Where We Came From, op. cit.*; Partha C. Majumder, "The Human Genetic History of South Asia", in *Current Biology, op. cit.*; Mait Metspalu, Mayukh Mondal, and Gyaneshwer Chaubey, "The Genetic Makings of South Asia", in *Science Direct, op. cit.*; G. David Poznik, Yali Xue, Fernando L. Mendez, Peter Underhill, et al., "Punctuated Bursts in Human Male Demography Inferred from 1, 244 Worldwide Y-Chromosome Sequences", in *Nature Genetics, op. cit.*

2 *Rig Veda*, translated by R.T.H. Griffith, *op. cit.,* in Sanskrit with English translations. *Rig Veda,* 10.90.11): 'When they divided Puruṣa how many portions did they make? What do they call his mouth, his arms? What do they call his thighs and feet? 12): The Brahman was his mouth, of both his arms was the Rājanya made; His thighs became the Vaiśya, from his feet the Śudra was produced'. The Sanskrit verse reads thus: (11: *yat puruṣaṃ vyadadhuḥ katidhā vyakalpayan* | *mukhaṃ kimasya kau bāhū kā ūrū pādā ucyete* || 12: *brāhmaṇo asya mukhamāsīd bāhū rājanyaḥ kṛtaḥ* | *ūrūtadasya yad vaiśyaḥ padbhyāṃ śūdro ajāyata* ||)

3 On ochre colored pottery (OCP), painted grey ware (PGW), northern black polished ware (NBPW), wooden wheels, and iron farming implements at late Harappan sites at Hulas, Atranjikhera, and Kurukshetra on the Yamuna-Ganges Doab, see Dilip K. Chakrabarti, *India: An Archaeological History, op. cit.,* 247–254, 256–264.

4 On the *sabha* and *samīti,* see Ram Sharan Sharma, *Aspects of Political Ideas and Institutions in Ancient India,* Delhi: Motilal Banarsidass, 1991, 105–117 (3rd revised ed.), *vide,* 114.

5 *Rig Veda*, translated by R.T.H. Griffith, *op. cit.* These verses are *RV* 7. 18. 2, 10–11:

RV 7.18. 2: 'For like a King among his wives thou dwellest: with glories, as a Sage, surround and help us. Make us, thy servants, strong for wealth, and honour our songs wirth kine and steeds and decoration' ('*rājeva hi janibhiḥ kṣeṣyevāva dyubhirabhi viduṣ kaviḥ san, piśā ghiro maghavan ghobhiraśvaistvāyataḥ śiśīhirāye asmān*');

RV 7.18.10: 'They went like kine unherded from the pasture, each clinging to a friend as chance directed. They who drive spotted steeds, sent down by Pṛśni, gave ear, the Warriors and the harnessed horses' ('*īyurghāvo na yavasādaghopā yathākṛtamabhi mitraṃ citāsaḥ, pṛśnighāvaḥ pṛśninipreṣitāsaḥ śruṣṭiṃ cakrurniyuto rantayaśca*');

RV 7.18.11: 'The King who scattered one-and-twenty people of both Vaikarna tribes through lust of glory – As the skilled priest clips grass within the chamber, so hath the Hero Indra, wrought their downfall' *('ekaṃ ca yo viṃśatiṃ ca śravasyā vaikarṇayorjanān rājā nyastaḥ, dasmo na sadman ni śiśāti barhiḥ śūraḥ sarghamakṛṇodindra eṣām*').

R.T.H. Griffith, *op. cit.,* also translated these verses, *Rig Veda* 7.33.5–6:

RV 33.5: 'Like thirsty men they looked to heaven, in battle with the Ten Kings, surrounded and imploring'. *('ud dyāmivet tṛṣṇajo nāthitāso adīdhayurdāśarājñe vṛtāsaḥ, vasiṣṭhasya stuvata indro aśrodurum tṛtsubhyo akṛṇodu lokam'*;

RV 33. 6: 'Like sticks and staves wherewith they drive the cattle, stripped bare, the Bharatas were found defenceless: Vasiṣṭha then became their chief and leader: then widely were the Trtsus' clans extended' ('*daṇḍā ived ghoajanāsa āsan parichinnā bharatā arbhakāsaḥ* I *abhavacca puraetā vasiṣṭha ādit tṛtsūnāṃ viśo aprathanta*').

6 *Rig Veda* 3.31.1–2 states that a man's wealth can be inherited by his daughter's son generationally, rather than between siblings. R.T.H. Griffith, trans., *Rig Veda, op. cit.,* 3.31.1: 'WISE, teaching, following the thought of Order, the sonless gained a grandson from his daughter. Fain, as a sire, to see his child prolific, he sped to meet her with an eager spirit' ('*sāsad vihvar duhiturnaptyaṃ ghād vidvān ṛtasya dīdhitāsparyanā; pitā yatra duhituḥ sekaṃ ṛañjan saṃ śaghmyena manasā dadhanve*');

(3.31.2) 'The Son left not his portion to the brother, he made a home to hold him who should gain, it. What time his Parents gave the Priest his being, of the good pair one acted, one promoted' ('*na jāmaye tānvo rikthamauraka cakāra garbhaṃ saniturnidhānam; yadī mātaro janayanta vahnimanyaḥ kartā sukṛtoranya ṛandhan*').

7 *Rig Veda* 10.85. 7, 25 ("The Marriage of Surya"), R.T.H. Griffith, *op. cit.* His translation reads: 10.85.7: 'Thought was the pillow of her couch, sight was the unguent for her eyes: Her treasury was earth and heaven when Sūrya went unto here' *('cittirā upabarhaṇaṃ cakṣurā abhyañjanam, dyaurbhūmiḥkośa āsīd yadayāt sūryā patim'*);

10.85. 25 reads: 'Hence, and not thence, I send these free. I make thee softly fettered there. That, Bounteous Indra, she may live blest in her fortune and her sons' *('preto muñcāmi nāmutaḥ subaddhāmamutas karam, yatheyamindra mīḍhvaḥ suputrā subhaghāsati'*).

Also see Wendy Doniger O'Flaherty, trans., *The Rig Veda,* 267–271 of these verses: 10.85.7: 'Intelligence was the pillow; sight was the balm. Heaven and Earth were the hope-chest when Surya went to her husband';

10.85. 25: 'I free her from here, but not from there. I have bound her firmly there, so that through the grace of Indra she will have fine sons and be fortunate in her fortunate in her husband's love'. Doniger's translations are poetic and modern, but her interpretation of '*subhagati*' (v.25) is problematic. The word simply means 'she who is fortunate/or has her share of good fortune' and not 'she who is fortunate in her husband's love'.

8 *Rig Veda* 10.85.26–27, as translated by R.T.H. Griffith, *op. cit.*

10.85.26: 'Let Pūṣan take thy hand and hence conduct thee; may the two Aśvins on their car transport thee. Go to the house to be the household's mistress and speak as lady to thy gathered people' ('*pūṣā tveto nayatu hastaghṛhyāśvinā tvā pra vahatāṃrathena; ghṛhān ghacha ghṛhapatnī yathāso vaśinī tvaṃvidathamā vadāsi*');

10.85.27: 'Happy be thou and prosper with thy children here; be vigilant to rule thy household in this home. Closely unite thy body with this man, thy lord. So shall ye, full of years, address your company' ('*iha priyaṃ prajayā te saṃ ṛdhyatāmasmin ghṛhe ghārhapatyāyajāghṛhi; enā patyā tanvaṃ saṃ sṛjasvādhā jivrī vidathamā vadāthaḥ*').

9 Sita Anantha Raman, *Women in India: A Social and Cultural History, op. cit.,* 31–32.

Part II

LATER VEDIC ERA AND *DHARMA SŪTRAS*

3

VEDIC SCRIPTURES, *JANAPADAS*, AND WOMEN

I. Later Vedic era

A. Vedas, *epics, and* Bhagavad Gīta

Territorial expansion by Sanskritic clans into the Gangetic Valley set into motion dynamic social, political, and economic changes. Between 1000 and 300 BCE, seers expanded the *Vedas*, which now comprised the *Rig, Sāma, Yajur,* and *Atharva Vedas*, each with four sections: hymnals (*Samhītas*); liturgies for sacrificial rites (*Brāhmanas*; 1000–500 BCE), often conducted for kings; meditative forest texts (*Āraṇyakās*); and spiritual philosophical texts (*Upaniṣads:* 800–300 BCE).

Social and political changes are reflected in the *Brāhmanas* and the *Upaniṣads* (800–300 BCE), the Sanskrit epics *Mahābhārata* and *Rāmāyana* (800–300 BCE), and the heterodox Buddhist canon in Pāli and Jaina scriptures in Prākrit (500–300 BCE). The discovery of iron near modern Delhi improved *ksatṛiya* weapons with which they battled local enemies and rival Āryan clans over arable land. The *Rig Veda*'s liturgical *Aitareya Brāhmana* (1.3.13–14, 23) describes battles lost by the gods (*devās*) to demons (*aśurās*) with superior iron fortifications (*durga*). A clear analogy was thus drawn between local enemies and *aśuras*. The *Śatapatha Brāhmana* (*SB* 1.3,2:14–15) in the *Yajur Veda* also describes a battle between clans, after which victorious *kṣatṛiyas* exacted tribute (*bali*) from rival village leaders (*vaiśya*).[1] While *kṣatṛiya* leaders (*rājans*) often claimed an extra share,[2] the *samītī* had to approve land allotments (*SB* 7.1.4).[3] Iron tools also facilitated the clearing of dense forests during migrations east along the Ganges and southwest into Mālwa-Gujarāt. In their search for high-revenue lands, the clans forged alliances that were the nucleus of the first *janapada* states, which included kingdoms (*rājyas*) and oligarchies (*gana sanghas*). In the eastern Gangetic plains and foothills, there emerged two rival kingdoms of particular historical significance. These were the Kosala (Uttar Pradesh) and Magadha (north Bihar) kingdoms and the Licchaavi *gana sangha* confederacy.

Brāhmana liturgies reflect that *kşatŗiya* kings and *brāhman* priests now controlled large forests, and their ritual sacrifices for kings often destroyed woods, animals, and human denizens. Early bards (*rişīs*) retreated into the forests, sometimes initially accompanied by their wives, to meditate upon life. Such *rişīs* composed the esoteric early *Upanişads* and concluded that sacrificial rites to the god Fire (Agnī) had symbolic meanings, while the Truth is the unity of the inner essence of all beings (Ātman) and the cosmic spirit (Brahman).[4] The *Brihadaranyaka Upanişad* has such discourses between *rişī* Yājňavalkya, who teaches his wife Maitreyī and the brilliant woman ascetic (*rişīkā*) Gārgī. The sage states that only through 'hearing, reflecting and meditation' can one spiritually realize the Truth that is Ātman (*BU:* 2.4.5).[5]

The first verse of the *Chāndogya Upanişad* (1.4.1–5) declares that one can know Ātman by meditating upon the god Udgīta as 'OM', or the Breath of life (Prāna).[6] The text later states that the melodious sound of 'Om' was Sāman, as by chanting it, the singer devotee could reach the divine Sun and the cosmos (*CU* 1.7.7), as Sāman encapsulated all virtue, while all that unworthy was termed Asāman (*CU* 2.1.1).[7]

While these innovative sages disagreed with orthodox ritualism, their *Upanişads* were soon inducted into the *Vedas*, partly because the sages accepted Vedic deism as the lesser truth underlying the monistic principle of the unity of Ātman and Brahman.[8] The *Īsa Upanişad* (*Īsa Up.* 1.1) begins by urging one to renounce greed, to perform righteous acts, and to know that a single divine Spirit (Īśa) permeates the universe:

> Om; *Īsa* (the Lord) envelops all that changes in this universe of worlds;
> Embrace what is given, renounce all else, do not covet the wealth of others.[9]

Some enlightened sage-composers were men of lower or mixed-caste ancestry, as described in early *Upanişads*. Aitareya, author of the *Aitareya Upanişad, Samhīta*, and *Brāhmana*, had a pre-Āryan *śudra* mother and a *brāhman* father. His *Aitareya Up.* (*A. Up.*1.1) begins with this vision of primal creation:

> Truly, in the beginning, all this was Ātman; no rival ever existed;
> It then thought: Let me create the worlds.[10]

The *Chāndogya Up.* (*Ch. Up.* 4.4.1–5) also describes how castes merged in this period. A young man, Satyakāma Jābalā, was born to a *śudra* maid, Jābalā, but he was eager to learn the *Vedas*. Satyakāma first asked his mother Jābālā who his father was, but she replied that she did not know, as she had conceived him as a maid working in a large household. Satyakāma still approached the high-caste sage Haridrumata Gautama to teach him the *Vedas*. When this sage asked him about his paternal lineage, the boy repeated his mother's words, and offered his name and matronymic as Satyakāma Jābalā. Impressed with Satyakāma's honesty and intelligence, the sage replied that as Satyakāma wished to tell the truth (*satya*), he was a true *brāhman*, and he called for wood for a Vedic sacrificial fire ritual to consecrate Satyakāma as a *brāhman*.[11]

Changes are also recorded in the Sanskrit epics *Mahābhārata* and *Rāmāyana* (800–300 BCE), the heterodox Buddhist canon in Pāli, and the Jaina canons in Prākrits, based on local variations and local languages (500–300 BCE). The 'remembered' texts (*smṛiti*), that is, the epics *Rāmāyana* (800–500 BCE) and *Mahābhārata* (900–200 BCE), relate myths about heroic kings, queens, *dharma*, and demoniac rivals, all of which powerfully shaped social and political norms in early India. The *smṛiti* texts describe the expansion of kingdoms, exalt righteous kings, and condemn unjust *kşaṭriyā* rivals. These Sanskrit epics and the heterodox Buddhist and Jaina canon describe the first *janapadas*, whose *rājans* contested over regions with fertile lands and natural products. The *janapadas* included kingdoms, oligarchies, and oligarchic *gana sanghas*, all of whose *rājans* belonged to elite *kşatṛiya* families (*rāja kula*). The chief difference lay in the role of the assembly, which governed the oligarchy but was largely an advisory body in the monarchy.[12] The emergence of kingdoms is celebrated in the *Rāmāyanā* and *Mahābhārata*. The *Rāmāyanā* may have been based on an even earlier Indo-Āryan myth about a heroic king who rescues his wife, but it was now set in the kingdom of Ayodhya (modern Uttar Pradesh). In it, the heroic king Rāmā rescues his abducted wife Sīta from the demon king Rāvanā in Srī Lanka.

The *Mahābhārata* is set in the Yamuna-Ganges confluence, or Doab, in the kingdom of Hastināpurā (modern Delhi). This epic also revolves around the struggle for a throne between virtuous Pandavā princes and their rival Kauravās led by ruthless Duryodanā. When Duryodanā humiliates the Pandavā queen Draupadi, a major war results, but the Pandavā ally is divine Kṛişṇa, king of Dwārakā (Gujarat). The epics thus set certain normative standards for royal ethical conduct.

The *Mahābharata*'s (900–200 BCE) spiritual addendum, the *Bhagavad Gītā* (300 BCE), reflects the transition from ritualism to personal devotion or *bhakti*. The *Bhagavad Gītā* (ca. 300 BCE) is set on the battlefield, as a metaphor for life's struggles between the good and worse impulses among human beings. Divine Kṛişṇa urges his friend Arjuna to do his duty as a *kşatṛiya* and to fight bravely for a cause based on righteousness (*dharma*), as our unselfish endeavors and devotion (*bhakti*) bear their own rewards. The *Bhagavad Gītā* reaffirms the *Upanişads*' message of the unity of Ātman-Brahman through deistic faith in Kṛişṇa, who declares three paths (*mārga*) of righteous conduct (*dharma*), namely the paths of knowledge (*jñāna*), work (*karma*), and devotion (*bhakti*). He declares that *bhakti* offers spiritual comfort to all who seek it, as everyone is equal in the eyes of the Lord. Kṛiṣṇa urges Arjuna that the ideal *dharma* for ordinary individuals was to take the middle path of *karma*, performing acts without egoism (B.G.7.17–18) but strengthened by *bhakti* (*BG* 7.8–10; 9.26–29). The scripture also contains a poignant reminder that all devotees are equal in the eyes of the Lord. These verses explain the *Bhagavad Gītā*'s appeal to the ordinary person and show why this scripture became the undercurrent of Hindu beliefs:[13]

> (*BG* 9.26): Whoever offers Me a leaf, flower, fruit, or water with devotion,
> I will accept these as the gift of a pure minded devotee.
>
> (*BG* 9.29): I am the same to all beings, none is hateful or more beloved;
> Those who worship Me with devotion are in Me, and I am in them.[14]

In the classical eras, the *Bhagavad Gītā*'s devotional message inspired others to compose the *Purānas* (200 BCE–400 ACE), which celebrate the mythical pantheon of Hindu gods and goddesses envisaged through the social lens of classical India. While Sanskritic dominance reshaped local beliefs, languages, and practices, indigenous cultures in turn infused Sanskritic society. Hindu religious ideas appear in the scriptures, which were infused in the later Vedic era by the beliefs of non-Sanskritic communities. Such scriptures were followed in the classical era by temporal texts on logic, law, poetic drama, medicine, yoga, mathematics, and art.

B. Janapadas*: kings and oligarchs*

The later Vedic era witnessed the first Sanskritic territorial states (*janapadas/mahājanapadas*), which included kingdoms (*rājyas*) on fertile Gangetic plains and oligarchies (*gana sanghas*) on surrounding hillsides.[15] By 800 BCE, there were sixteen major *rājyas* and *gana sanghas*, whose leaders were often elite *kṣatṛiyas*. Social, political, and intellectual ferment appear in orthodox and heterodox literature from this period. The Vedic corpus was expanded with the addition of the *Sāma, Yajur,* and *Atharva Vedas*, each having a hymnal (*Samhita*), liturgy (*Brāhmana*, ca. 1000–500 BCE), meditative forest books (*Āraṇyakā*), and spiritual philosophies (*Upaniṣad*, 800–300 BCE). The *Brāhmanas* comprised chants for sacrificial rites, which were grandiose for kings upon their ascensions and victories.

The Sanskritic clans rapidly expanded over the Gangetic plains, but they expanded more slowly into the hilly regions of eastern Uttar Pradesh and northern Bihar. These became the domains of oligarchic *gana sanghas*, whose indigenous hill tribes and non-Sanskritic groups did not rapidly absorb Sanskritic mores of patriarchy and social classes/caste (*varna*). As *gana sangha* leaders did not often perform *brāhmanical* rituals, some orthodox Sanskritic texts expressed dislike for these oligarchs. Although the seers of the *Upaniṣads* also questioned the value of ritualism, their scriptures were included into the *Vedas*, as the seers respected the *Rig, Sama,* and *Yajur Vedas* and gods, for example, as seen in the early *Chāndogya Upaniṣad* (1.4.1–5).[16] The *Upaniṣads* also sent a powerful message of the unity of the individual soul (Ātman) and the universal spirit (Brahman). Other Sanskrit scriptures were the epics *Rāmāyana* and *Mahābhārata* (800–300 BCE), with myths about heroic kings, queens, ethical conduct as *dharma*, and demoniac rivals. The *Mahābhārata*'s addendum, the *Bhagavad Gīta* (ca. 300 BCE), is a discourse between divine Ķrişnā and Arjuna. Ķrişnā declares that human actions (*karma*) cause a cycle of birth and death but that freedom (*mokśa*) is possible through three paths, which became the undercurrent of Hindu belief and practice. These were the paths of: 1) knowledge (*jňāna*) taken by renunciants; 2) *karma*, in which individuals perform ethical acts of *dharma* without egoism; and 3) devotion (*bhakti*) to the Supreme.

There were also heterodox movements, of which the two most significant were Buddhism and Jainism, which appealed to non-*dvīja* and pre-Āryan groups. Siddhartha Gautama (563–483 BCE) was an aristocratic *kşatŗiya* of the Śākya *gana sangha* in Nepal, who left his patrimony and family to meditate upon sorrow. His benign solutions earned him the honorific of the Buddha ('Enlightened One'), and he founded Therāvada Buddhism. Early Therāvada canon includes the *Tripitaka* (Three Baskets) and *Jātaka* (Birth Tales) in Pāli. The other major heterodox dissident was Mahavīrā, or 'Jina' (Conqueror; d. 468 BCE), who founded Jainism. The son of a *kşatŗiya* from the Jņātŗikā *gana sangha* in Vaiśāli (n. Bihar), Mahavīrā became revered as the last of twenty-four Jaina preceptors (*tīrthankaras*). Jaina canon includes the *Āchāranga Sūtra* and other works in Prākrit folk dialects like Ardha Magadhi. These heterodox sects spread across the subcontinent in the next centuries.[17] Our study examines the key principles of Therāvada Buddhism and Jainism, their founders' origins in *gana sanghas*, and women's roles in these sects.

When kingdoms dominated the oligarchies (ca. 600 BCE), male *brāhmans* composed the first temporal law codes. The first codes were the *Dharma Sūtras*,[18] composed as guidelines for *kşatŗiya* kings on their righteous duties (*dharma*). These codes also defined the *dharmas* of the three upper *varnas* ranks (*dvījās*), that is, *brāhman* priests, *kşatŗiya* soldiers, and *vaiśya* merchants and farmers, and the rights and roles of women. The *Dharma Sūtras* validated male polygamy and patrilineal inheritance for kings and *dvījās*, rulings that profoundly affected women's rights. While some sacred texts describe women as scholars, other idealize rites to goddesses of wealth in the climate of rivalry among *mahājanapada* kingdoms like Kosala, Magadha, and the Vṛjjī confederacy. Oligarchs often adopted Buddhist or Jaina tenets, while lower-caste Nandas and Mauryas established dynasties. As economic clout increased with territorial acquisition through matrimonial alliances, women became pawns in royal rivalries. A queen's dower (*strīdhana*) of valuable domains was often seized by her polygamous husband. At the same time, important Hindu, Buddhist, and Jaina ideals of *dharma* shaped the conduct of rulers and subjects in this era. These discussions provide the context for the next chapter on the *Dharma Sūtras* (600–300 BCE) and its ideals on kingly governance, *varna*, and women.

Orthodox *Brāhmana* liturgies and early Buddhist canon (ca. 300 BCE) offer different theories on the origin of the *janapadas*. As the early *Brāhmanas* indicate that *brāhmans* were initially dismayed by the growing temporal power of *kṣatṛiyas*, some scholars have inferred that these complex, orally transmitted liturgies were intended to deter *kṣatṛiyas*, *vaiśyas*, and women from initiating Vedic rites. It is more probable, however, that the *brāhman* authors wished to exclude powerful local leaders, whom they regarded as *śudras*, from performing the rites. A watershed reconciliation soon redefined the roles of *brāhmans* and *kṣatṛiyas* in the *janapadas*.

The *Aitareya Brāhmana* (1.14,23) thus contains a myth in which the gods elected Varuna, the god of justice, as their king to lead battles against the demons.[19] The *Taittirīya Brāhmana* (1.5.9) in the *Yajur Veda* describes another legend in which Prajāpati, the father of the gods, chose Indra, his eldest son (*jyeṣṭha putra*) and the god of war, as *rājan*. After Indra defeated the demons, the gods crowned him in an elaborate ritual (*rājasūya*).[20] A corollary myth states that the gods then appointed *kṣatṛiyas* earthly kings, as they resembled mighty Indra and benevolent Varuna. Now reassured of their political relevance, *brāhmans* vigorously undertook *kṣatṛiya* coronations, while kings appointed priests as advisors who upheld morality (*dharma*).

A *rājan* and his male kin enjoyed considerable advantages, such as a larger share of tax from villagers (*viś*). At first, the *rājan* was succeeded by a male relative, but patrimonial kingship became hereditary when rulers reaffirmed their authority in flamboyant annual rites. *Samhīta* chants (*TS* 1.8.1–3) and various *Brāhmana* liturgies describe the coronations of *rājans*, whose search for new dominions *brāhmans* lauded in the prestigious horse sacrifice (*aśvamedha*). The *Taittirīya Samhīta* (*TS* 4.4.2) and *Śatapatha Brāhmana* (*SB* 13.1–5) describe the *aśvamedha*. In this elaborate ritual, the king's stallion was let free to roam over adjacent lands, which the king would then claim. Those local leaders who did not contest him lost their autonomy, while the challengers encountered his superior *kṣatṛiya* might. This earthly ambition deeply troubled the ascetics of the Upaniṣads, as seen in the *Bṛhadāranyaka Upaniṣad*, which ironically occurs at the end of the *Śatapatha Brāhmana*. The *Bṛhadāranyaka Upaniṣad* (1.1) begins with a meditative verse on the divine symbolism of *aśvamedha* as superior to the mundane ritual act.[21] Yet, as in the later Vedic era, almost no ruler had a large standing army or police force; kings exacted periodic taxes, as stated in the *Dharma Sūtra* law codes, but refrained from interfering in local rites or customary laws on marriage or property. This probably remained a feature of governance in the centralized Mauryan Empire with diverse communal groups, while in the classical era, decentralized governance was a hallmark of most empires.

A contrasting view on the primal state is offered in the Buddhist text *Digha Nikaya* (ca. 300 BCE). Theravāda Buddhist tenets were established by Siddhartha Gautama, known as the Buddha or 'Enlightened One' (563–484 BCE). A set of Buddha's sermons is found in the canonical *Tripitaka* ('Three Baskets'), that is, *Vinaya Pitaka* (Discipline Basket), *Sūtta Pitaka* (Sermon Basket), and *Abhidamma Pitaka* (Metaphysical Basket). *Sūtta Pitaka*'s first book has a sermon on the Buddha's death ('Mahāparinirvāna Sūtta', 5–6). It also describes the prosperous cities Rājagriha, Sāvatthi, Campā, Kōsambī, and Kāsī, inhabited by wealthy *kşatŗiyas, vaiśyas,* and *brāhmans*, and the city of Kūśinārā, whose Malla oligarchy witnessed Buddha's death. The sermon on creation has a secondary myth on the first state.[22] This postulates that in the beginning, there existed neither wealth, social classes, nor the ownership of women in marriage. As injustices increased over time, leaders and the folk met in an assembly, and their pact formed the first state. The leader had three titles: the chosen leader of all the folk (*mahāsammata*), the lord of the fields (*khattiya*), and the *rājan* who upheld *dharma*. However, this pristine state dwindled into a monarchy due to the greed of *rājans/khattiyas* who owned fields.[23] The most significant heterodox thinkers who disagreed with Vedic *brāhmanical* texts and rituals were the Buddhists and the Jaina followers of Vardhamāna Mahāvīra (540–468 BCE), who is revered as the last of twenty-four Jaina preceptors (*tīthankaras*). Buddhists and Jainas did not dismiss land ownership, as it was the foundation of all territorial states. Yet these sects originated in oligarchic states (*gana sanghas*) that opposed rigid *brāhmanical* laws, and they also later thrived as semi-autonomous communities in kingdoms, such as in Gujarāt, whose rulers valued Jaina merchants and bankers who enriched the economy.

In large *rājyas* of the later Vedic era, *kşatŗiya* kings/chieftans (*rājans*) recognized their need for a temporal law code with which to govern and to validate patrimonial succession. This led scholarly *brāhmans* to now frame the first law codes, the *Dharma Sūtras*. The authors endorsed new ideals of kingship, which reshaped women's roles in Sanskritic states. Female legal subordination was further affirmed when hereditary kingdoms dominated *gana sanghas*.[24] Amid wars, economic expansion, and sectarian and ethnic challenges, male succession thus became the lynchpin of the royal state. The *Dharma Sūtra* authors also endorsed the occupational (*varna*) hierarchy of *brāhman* priests and advisors, *kşatŗiya* soldiers and kings, *vaiśya* farmers and merchants, and *śudra* artisans and laborers. The three elite castes, or 'twice born' (*dvījas*), learned the *Vedas* to perform its rites, but in large states with complex economies, as landowners, they also wielded considerable mundane authority.

The emergent state and the dominance of kingdoms over oligarchies coincides with new meanings for two terms. '*Dharma*', which originally signified righteous or sacred duties of individuals, now also meant the righteous laws of a temporal state in the *Dharma Sūtras*. In the Mauryan Empire, the term *kşatŗiya*, which originally specified the elite *varna* of kings and soldiers, was now used to describe the gifted non-*dvīja* military Chandragupta emperor based in Pātaliputra, Magadha (Patna, Bihar). His mentor and *brāhman* Kauţilya composed the *Arthaśāstra*, basing his kingly ideal on Chandragupta, while reaffirming patrimonial succession and *varna* occupations.[25] Buddhist, Jaina, and Roman sources indicate that Chandragupta Maurya was not a *kşatŗiya* or *dvīja* but the plebian son of the chief of the Moriya tribe of peacock trainers in Pipphalivana (Pātaliputra; modern Patna, Bihar). Several historians attest that he later became a Jaina monk who died in Saravanabelagola, Karnataka.[26] Mauryan imperial expansion was facilitated by this founder's pragmatic acceptance of Vedic norms, balanced by respect for local cultural proclivities. It is interesting that his mentor Kauţilya began his *Arthaśāstra* by lauding the *Vedas* and four *varnas*.[27]

II. Women, *varna*, state: changing norms

Despite attempts by *brāhmans* and *kşatŗiyas* to guard *varna* distinctions, the rules on marriage, exogamy, endogamy, and female inheritance remained fluid in the early centuries. The clans imbibed matrilineal customs from local groups, while pervasive sexual interactions resulted in diverse sub-castes. Local matriarchies provided wives for higher-ranking patriarchal clans, although both lineages were deemed important. This is seen in *Mahābhāratā* legends of the Kurū-Pānchala kingdom (Yamuna-Ganges Doab) and the Vŗşnī oligarchy (Punjab-Mālwa), some of which concern powerful, heroic women.[28] The marriage of princess Draupadi (Pānchāli) to the five Pāndavā brothers of the Kurū kingdom indicates an alliance with sub-Himālayan polyandrous tribes. An early tale concerns high-ranking Sāvitrī, who chose the tribal hero Satyavān as her husband. When he died suddenly in their forest home, Sāvitrī relentlessly pursued Yamā, the god of Death, whom she outwitted to reclaim her lover's life. Important myths also grew around the dark-hued hero Kŗişna, son of Vāsudevā of the Vŗişni-Yādavā oligarchy. Yet Kŗişna is first described as the son of Dēvakī (Dēvakī *putra*) in the *Chāndōgya Upanişad* (3.17.6) of the *Sāma Veda* (ca. 750 BCE).[29] In the *Mahābhārata*, Kŗişna defeats his demoniacal maternal uncle's bid for the throne and then rules Dwāraka in the west. The legend suggests the dominance of a patrimonial kingdom over a matriarchal oligarchy.[30]

After settlement, land ownership reinforced patrilineal inheritance, and it also reshaped the *varna* hierarchy dominated by *dvīja* men. The iron plow brought prosperity for those with land, but as R.S. Sharma suggests, this heavy instrument also deterred women from tilling the fields.[31] Women hoed, harvested, threshed grains, and tended dairy cattle, but their agricultural labor was now regarded as an extension of domestic work. No longer tillers of the soil, they were not viewed as the owners of land, so that women's voices became muted in the public assembly (*samiti*). Ironically, the fertile, furrowed field (*sītā*) was originally associated with earth goddess Āditi, in whose furrow her infant daughter Sītā was discovered by king Janaka in the *Rāmāyana*. The term for agriculture was *sītādhyaksha*, but farmed acreage became the domain of kings and elite men.[32] As kingdoms and oligarchies acquired territories and the economy grew complex, there were other repercussions for women and the lower castes. Conquered indigenous groups were reduced to agricultural and menial slaves/serfs (*dāsās*). The *varna* order metamorphosed into a less flexible economic system in which *dāsas* formed the lowest laboring class. Some *dāsās* were inducted into the hierarchy as lowly *śudras*, while others served as outcaste (*chandāla*) drudges for elite Sanskritic groups.[33] This large workforce benefitted the state, and it reduced the need for *dvīja* female labor, whose chaste domesticity became highly valued.

When kingdoms dominated oligarchic states (ca. 600 BCE), male *brāhmans* composed the first temporal law codes as guidelines on governance based on righteousness as *dharma* for *kşatŗiya* kings. The *Dharma Sūtras*[34] also defined the *dharmas* of the three upper *varnas* ranks (*dvījas*), that is, *brāhman* priests, *kşatŗiya* soldiers, and *vaiśya* merchants and farmers, and the rights and roles of women. The *Dharma Sūtras* validated male polygamy and patrilineal inheritance for kings and *dvījas*, rulings that profoundly affected women's rights. While some sacred texts describe women as scholars, other idealize rites to goddesses of wealth in the climate of rivalry among *mahājanapada* kingdoms like Kosala, Magadha, and the Vŗjjī confederacy. Oligarchs often adopted Buddhist or Jaina tenets, while lower-caste Nandas and Mauryas established dynasties. As economic clout increased with territorial acquisition through matrimonial alliances, women became pawns in royal rivalries. A queen's dower (*strīdhana*) of valuable domains was often seized by her polygamous husband. At the same time, important Hindu, Buddhist, and Jaina ideals of *dharma* shaped the conduct of rulers and subjects in this era. These discussions provide the context for a further discussion (Chapter 5) of the *Dharma Sūtras* (600–300 BCE), and their ideals on kingly governance, *varna*, and women.

A. Ritual rights and wrongs: adhikāra

Brāhmana liturgies attest to priestly preference for kings whom they anointed and advised over oligarchs, who were often independent and sometimes heterodox. In return for priestly exaltation of royal authority (*kşatra*), kings endorsed Vedic rites supervised by male *brāhmans* and the *varna* hierarchy. These political alignments helped to push *dvīja* women into domestic shade and *śudras* into drudgery. As shown by feminist scholars, women's ritual authority (*adhikāra*) now declined. Although in previous centuries, *dvīja* boys and girls had undertaken the sacred thread initiation (*upanāyana*) before studying the *Vedas*, this important rite was restricted increasingly to males. McGee's study of the *Taittirīya Brāhmana* confirms that as fewer girls now enrolled in Vedic schools, there were fewer female sages (*brahmachārinīs*) or priests with the *adhikāra* to conduct rites on their own. The marriage rite had replaced the *upanāyana* as the pre-eminent rite for women. As the worthy half of a 'married pair', a wife was allowed to kindle the sacrificial fire for household rites, but this *adhikāra* was now denied to single women.[35]

Some Vedic texts emphasized women's inferiority and the need to chastise them into submission. As I have shown elsewhere, they reflect male sexual anxieties rather than religious insights.[36] The *Taittirīya Samhīta* (*TS* 6.5.8.1–2) stated that the root of such tensions lay in women's ability to bear offspring yet give us glimpses of heaven. The poet compared the womb to a cup of Soma, but as the god Soma did not wish to be drunk by women, the other deities fashioned a lightning bolt from melted butter (*ghee*) to chastise women. He compared women's distressed cries to the sacred flame's sizzle caused by libations of *ghee:*

> Soma could not bear being drawn for women; making the ghee a bolt they beat it, they drew it when it had lost its power; therefore, women are powerless, have no inheritance, and speak more humbly than even a bad man.[37]

This analogy also appears in the *Śatapatha Brāhmana* (*ŚB* 4.2.13), but its description of chastised women is more vivid and violent:

> and by that thunderbolt, the ghee, the gods smote the wives and unmanned them, and thus smitten and unmanned they neither owned any self nor did they own any heritage. And in like manner does he now, by that thunderbolt, the ghee, smite the wives and unman them; and thus smitten and unmanned, they neither own any self nor do they own any heritage.[38]

In another verse, the *Śatapatha Brāhmana* (*ŚB* 14.1.1.31) instructed the sacrificer to be abstinent in his diet and to avoid contact with women and *śudras:*

> And whilst not coming into contact with Śudras and remains of food; for this Dharma is he that shines yonder, and he is excellence, truth, and light; but woman, the Śudra, the dog, and the black bird (the crow), are untruth: he should not look at these, lest he should mingle excellence and sin, light and darkness, truth and untruth.[39]

In her perceptive study of the *Jaiminiya Brāhmana* in the *Sāma Veda*, O'Flaherty points out that solemn rituals allayed the fear of death in an era when life was often precarious. At the same time, fearing female sexuality as a power that 'devoured' men, male *brāhmans* frequently portrayed women as 'demonaic' seducers who could wantonly destroy the sacrificial fire (*JB* 1. 125–26). Male *angst* also appears in their creation myth (*JB* 1.154–55), which excluded females from the primal struggle between *devas* and *aśuras*.[40]

Although O'Flaherty does not explain why misogyny increased in the later Vedic era, the Sanskrit epics dramatize diverse sociosexual tensions within the clans and with local groups. Complex confrontations probably led many elite *dvija* patriarchs to clamp down on their women who defied commands or who openly voiced their dissent in the public arena. In the *Rāmāyana*, the hero Rāma allied himself with the virtuous pre-Āryan prince Vibhīśana, who helped him to wreak revenge on his brother, the demonaic (*rākśāsa*) Rāvana, who had abducted Rāma's chaste wife Sīta. The *Mahābhārata* war emanated from a dynastic struggle between the arrogant Kuru princes led by Duryōdhana and the righteous Pāndavas led by Yudhiştara, son of Dharma. Its immediate cause, however, was Duryōdhana's public humiliation of proud Draupadi, polyandrous wife of the five Pāndava brothers.

Legal scholar Chawla shows that the early codes had a residual effect on modern women's right to property. Āpastamba, a southerner familiar with Dravidian matrilineal laws, granted wives and daughters some inheritance rights in his *Dharma Sūtra*. These were later rejected by Baudhāyana, another southern *brāhman*, who declared: 'Women are considered to be devoid of strength and not to inherit property, says a Vedic text' (*BDS* 2.3.46). Baudhāyana quoted the *Taittirīya Samhīta*'s verse on female weaknesses, which made them unfit to manage property. Medieval and colonial rulings (1878, 1889) cited Baudhāyana to prevent women from owning property, but some scholars challenge these interpretations.[41]

Jamis on argues that *brāhmans* conceded women's mental 'agency' to act independently, but, as they suspected their motives, they tried to 'rein' in female talent. Men thus granted women some authority, but only if they chastely fulfilled their domestic functions. Her otherwise valid theory is weakened by her reliance on a few of his terms instead of the substance of his code. She describes Āpastamba as a misogynist because he used the 'pregnant masculine dual' (*svāminau*; *ĀDS* 2.4.10–13) for the male-female 'married pair'.[42] Historically, the languages of most patriarchal societies employed a male compound noun for mixed-gender groups, for example, as in the English term 'mankind' for all humanity and the Sanskrit term *suputra* (good sons) for male and female progeny. While this rightly offends us today, two thousand years ago, Āpastamba tried to grant women some legal rights in his stratified society. Was he a misogynist because he didn't go far enough, or was he simply a patriarch defined by the culture of his era?

Despite the hierarchies of gender and *varna*, other texts reveal that *dvīja* women and *śudra* men challenged impediments to their study of the *Vedas*, and victorious non-*dīvjas* assumed the mantle of *kṣatṛiya* kings for several more centuries.[43] The *Vedas* were composed largely by men, but there are significant differences within the corpus. The *Brāhmanas* presented a dominant male perspective, but the seers (*ṛṣīs*) of the *Upaniṣads* proclaimed that a single neuter spirit united all beings, a truth that transcended illusory, physical differences. The discourses of some female sages (*brahmavādinīs*) with male teachers are recorded in the *Bṛhadāraṇyaka Upaniṣad*. This influential scripture can be partly dated from its reference to Magadha's king Ajātaśatru (491–460 BCE) (*BU* 2.1.1–20). In the *Bṛhadāraṇyaka Upaniṣad*, venerable sage Yāĵñyavalkya enlightened his wife Maitreyi (*BU* 2.4.1–14; 4.5.1–15) on esoteric subjects, and his answers to the probing questions of his brilliant female student Gārgi appear in two discourses (*BU* 3.6.1; and 3.8.1–12).[44] Also in this era, the enlightened *śudra* sage Mahidāsa Aitareya's *Brāhmana, Āranyaka*, and *Upaniṣad* were incorporated into the *Rig Veda*. The *Chāndōgya Upaniṣad* (*CU* 4.4–1–5) relates a similar tale of a prescient *śudra* who was taught the *Vedas*. Satyakāma Jābala was born as the illegitimate son of a *śudra* maid yet wished to learn the *Vedas* from the *dvīja* sage Haridhrumath Gautama. When Satyakāma Jābala asked his mother Jabāla about his father, she replied that as a maid in a large household, she did not know which master had impregnated her and hence gave Satyakāma his matronymic name of Jābala. When the sage questioned Satyakāma Jābala about his lineage, the boy honestly related his mother's words and that he was simply Satyakāma Jābala. Impressed by the boy's intelligence and honesty, the sage agreed to teach him.[45]

Heterodox Buddhist and Jaina canons and Roman accounts also shed light on early political states in which some non-*dvījas* became rulers. Three states in the northeast that were especially powerful were the kingdom of Kośala on the Sarāyu river, the kingdom of Magadha on the southern Ganges (Bihar), and the Vaiśāli *gana sangha* controlled by the Vrijji clan in the northern foothills. Magadha's strategic position near the Gangetic delta gave the first boost to the royal treasure. King Bimbisara (ca. 550 BCE) enriched it further by replacing the earlier system of voluntary tributes with taxation. This and other measures created a wealthy landowning class and an underclass of peasant cultivators who were either *śudras* or *chāṇḍālās* outside the caste system.[46] As polygamy was allowed for elite *varna* men, Bimbisara made matrimonial alliances with neighboring states whose princesses brought him large, often territorial, dowries. He married Kośaladevī, sister of king Pasenadi of Kośala, who brought him revenues from the rich town of Kāśī; his second wife, Cellanā, was a Licchavi princess from the wealthy oligarchy of Vaiśāli, and his third was Madra, a princess from Punjab. Bimbisara was probably killed by his son Ajātaśatru, who annexed the kingdom of Kośala, whose revenues enriched his treasury. Magadha was later ruled by a low-caste barber's son, Mahāpadma Nanda (ca. 450 BCE), who met the Buddha. Magadha was also the later nucleus of the Mauryan Empire (322–184 BCE), founded by Chandragupta (322–298 BCE), a non-*dvīja* from a tribe of peacock trainers.[47] Chandragupta's lower-caste ancestry may explain why he later became a Jaina monk. Yet his initial forays into governance were shaped by his *brāhman* mentor, Kauṭilya, who wrote the *Arthaśāstra* as a guidebook on kingship and statecraft. Eponyms revamped the *Arthaśāstra* in the early classical era for monarchs eager to emulate Chandragupta's skill in governance.

While *dvīja* women's ritual authority diminished in the later Vedic centuries, some elite royal women were revered as semi-divine and thus had indirect access to power. *Taittirīya* and *Śatapatha* scriptures contain some misogynist verses, but others describe a dozen elite women as the kingdom's jewels (*ratnins*), such as the *rājan*'s chief consort (*mahiṣī*) and second wife (*parivṛkti*). The *Taittirīya Samhīta* (1.8.9) and *Taittirīya Brāhmana* (1.7.3) ranked the highest *ratnins* as the *brāhman, rājan,* and *mahiṣī*. In the *Śatapatha Brāhmana* (5.3.1), the highest *ratnin* was the army chief (*senāpati*), followed by *brāhman, rājan,* and *mahiṣī*. In these kingdoms, the *mahiṣī* was revered as the embodiment of earth goddess Aditi (Mahi), mother of the gods, and the precursor of Lakşmi, goddess of bounty. The *mahiṣī*'s house was the venue for Vedic rites invoking Aditi's beneficence in agriculture and dairy farming, which enriched the kingdom.[48] While the *Taittirīya* texts rank the *parivṛkti* as a secondary *ratnin*, she was not given this honor in the *Śatapatha Brāhmana*. Below the *mahiṣī* were male *ratnins*, including village chiefs (*vaiśya-gramānī*), and *vaiśyas* valued as taxable farmers, traders, and artisans in new townships. The texts also refer to *śudra* soldiers (*senānī*), bards (*sūtas*), and carvers/artisans (*kṣattṛ*) as lesser *ratnins*.[49] These ideals were challenged in daily life, however, as wives without sons and menial *śudras* were often scorned. Moreover, as polygamy reduced the power of most wives, intrigue was fairly common.

B. Matrimonial treaties in mahājanapadas

In this dynamic era, some larger *janapadas* absorbed weaker states. By 600 BC, there were sixteen major states (*mahājanapadas*) with multiethnic rural, urban, and arboreal communities, many with an acquired Sanskritic veneer. The sixteen *mahājanapadas* were Kāśī (modern Varanāsī), whose early ruler was a Jaina saint; Kōśālā (eastern Uttar Pradesh), whose kings held sway over Kāśī; Aṅga (eastern Bihar in lower Ganges); Magadha (Bihar; Patna and Gayā); the Vajjī/Vṛjjī confederacy (*viz.*, the Licchavis, Videhas, and Jnatrika clans) in Vaiśālī; the Malla kingdom (north of Vṛjjī); Cedi (near the Jamuna river); Vamşa near the Jamuna (capital Kauśambi); the Kuru kingdom (modern Delhi); the Pañchāla kingdom on Yamuna-Ganges Doab (capital Ahhīcchatra); Matsya (south of Kuru); Śurasena kingdom (capital Mathura); Assaka (on Godavari river); Avanti in Malwa-Gujarat (capital at Ujjain; Dwāraka); Gandhāra (modern Kashmir and Pakistan); and Kambhōja (near modern Afghanistan).[50]

Buddhist sources describe the most powerful as those straddling fertile rivers and important trade routes. These were the Gangetic kingdoms of Magadha, Kōsala, and Kāsī and the *gana-sanghas* of the Vṛşnīs of Avanti (Mālwa-Gujarat) and the Vṛjjīs (Bihar and Nepal). Smaller egalitarian oligarchies merged into larger confederacies resembling kingdoms, whose wealthy leaders styled themselves as *kşatṛiyas*. Examples include the Buddha's Sākya clan/state in the Nepal foothills and Chandragupta Maurya's clan of Mōriyas from north Bihar. Land ownership and occupational diversity brought prosperity for some but poverty for others. Monarchies like Magadha and oligarchies like the Licchāvi *gana-sangha* both benefitted from slave/serf labor. In contrast, the Videha and Vaiśāli kingdoms fragmented into oligarchies, perhaps as their leaders rejected *brāhman* influence upon a military polity, as well as the wasteful use of cattle, timber, and resources to exhibit royal pomp.[51]

Women became pawns in the contests among polygamous kings and oligarchs.[52] Conflicts often ended in a matrimonial alliance, in which a royal bride's dowry (*nahāna cuṇṇamūla*) included moveable assets like jewelry controlled by her and gifts to her husband of territories that either enriched or extended the boundaries of his kingdom. The *Vedas, Mahābārata*, and *Rāmāyana* all endorsed polygamy as the natural accoutrement of kings.[53] While monarchs contracted numerous matrimonial treaties, queens were expected to remain loyal and chaste so that their sons were accepted as legitimate heirs to the throne.

This is seen in the history of war and reconciliation between Magadha, Kōsala, and the Vṛjjī confederacy, although leaders and subjects paid homage to the peaceful Buddha.[54] King Bimbisāra (543 BCE) established the first large kingdom of Magadha, and his successor was his son Ajātaśatru. Bimbisara annexed the Anga kingdom to gain access to the Ganges delta. He fortified his capital at Pātaliputra, and he had an invincible standing army with chariots and catapults as weapons. Bimbisāra's war against Kōsala's king Pasenadi (Prasenjit: Skt.), overlord of five *janapadas*, ended with a matrimonial peace treaty through which he married Kōsaladevi, Pasenadi's sister. Kōsaladevi's substantial dowry consisted of jewels and the affluent town of Kāsi and its revenues. Bimbisāra's second queen, Cellanā, a princess of the Lichchavi-Vṛjjī oligarchic confederacy, brought a territorial dowry that extended his boundaries to Nepal. His third senior queen was Kşema of the Mādra clan, who brought him territories in Punjab. When Bimbisāra was starved to death by his unscrupulous son Ajātaśatru (d. 461 BCE), Kōsaladevi committed suicide. Pasenadi reclaimed Kāsi, another war ensued, and there was still another treaty, which allowed Ajātaśatru to marry Vijirā, Pasenadi's daughter, whose dowry included revenues from Kāsi. Magadha and Kōsala waged a joint offensive against the Vṛjjī oligarchy, leading to a marriage treaty that let Ajātaśatru annex the Vṛjjī state.[55] Magadha was the nucleus of the later Mauryan Empire, which extended across most of the subcontinent.

Notes

1 *Śatapatha Brāhmana,* 1.3.2: 14–15. See F. Max-Muller, ed., and J. Eggeling, trans., *Śatapatha Brāhmana According to the Text of the Madhyandina School (Sacred Books of the East),* Vol. 12 (1882), New Delhi: Motilal Banarsidass, June 1988, 78–79. These verses are quoted thus by Hermann Kulke and Dietmar Rothermund, *A History of India,* London and New York: Routledge, 1999 (3rd ed.), 40–42, 340 (*n* 3):

> *Śatapatha Brāhmana* (1.3.2: 14): And thus a king who has established himself among a numberless people, subdues them even from a single dwelling; (1.3.2: 15): Now, if he were to offer it with the *upabhrit* (left hand), those subjects (of the king) would assuredly become separated from him, nor would there be either an eater or what is to be eaten. When, on the other hand, he pours (the butter) together and thus offers it with the *guhû* (the right hand), thereby the people pay tribute to the Kshatriya. Hence by what he takes in the *upabhrit,* the Vaiśya (man of the people), under the rule of the Kshatriya, becomes possessed of cattle; and when he pours (the butter) together and offers it with the *guhû,* thereby the Kshatriya, whenever he likes, says, 'Hallo Vaiśya, just bring to me what thou hast stored away!' Thus he both subdues him and obtains possession of anything he wishes by dint of this very energy.

2 Ram Sharan Sharma describes how the clansmen's share (*bhāga*) became the chieftain's tribute/tax (*balī*), *vide.,* Ram Sharan Sharma, *Aspects of Political Ideas and Institutions in Ancient India, op. cit.,* 228–229.

3 F. Max-Müller, ed., and J. Eggeling, trans., *Śatapatha Brāhmana, op. cit.* The prose verse is: 7.1.4: 'The Fathers have prepared this place for him! for Yama is the Kshatra (nobility, or ruling power), and the Fathers (deceased ancestors) are the clansmen; and to whomsoever the chief (kshatriya), with the approval of the clan, grants a settlement, that (settlement) is properly given: and in like manner

does Yama, the ruling power, with the consent of the Fathers, the clan, now grant to this (Sacrificer) a settlement on this earth'.

4 Ainslee T. Embree, ed., *Sources of Indian Tradition, Volume 1: From the Beginning to 1800, op. cit.*, 43–45.

5 *Riṣī* Yājñavalkya's words to his wife Maitreyī appear at the end of this Sanskrit verse: *BU* 2.4.5: 'The Self, my dear Maitreyī should be truly realized, heard of, reflected upon, and meditated upon. By the realization of the Self alone, my dear, through hearing, reflection and meditation, all this is known'. ('*Ātmā vā arai driṣṭavyaha śrotavyo mantavyo nidhi dhāsitavyo, Maitreyī, Ātmanovā arai darśanena śraṇena matyā vijnānenedam sarvam viditam*'.). *vide.*, Ramakrishna Math, ed., *The Brihadaranyaka Upaniṣads,* with original text and word-by-word meanings, 144–146. The *Bṛhadāraṇyaka Upaniṣad* may be one of the earliest (ca. 800 BCE), as it is taken from the *Śatapatha Brāhmana.*

6 The *Chāndogya Upaniṣad's* first verse (*ChU* 1.1.1.) is: '*Omityetad akṣara mudgīthamupāsīt*' ('One must first chant the syllable Om before meditation'). *vide., Swami* Swahananda, ed., *Chāndogya Upaniṣad,* with Sanskrit text and annotated translation, Chennai: Sri Ramakrishna Math, 1980 (1st ed. 1956), 5.

7 Swami Swahananda, ed., *Chāndogya Upaniṣad, op. cit.,* 58–59, 96. The first esoteric verse cited here (*CU* 1.7.7) states that Om is the deity Udgītha residing in the Sun, and the person who sang pure devotional verses (sāman) would become the deity. The second verse cited here (*CU* 2.1.1) simply declares that meditation upon Om brought goodness or Sāman, while anything untrue and imperfect was Asāman (*CU* 2.1.1).

8 The major *Upaniṣads* are the *Brihadaranyaka, Chāndogya, Īśāvāsyo, Aitereya, Kauṣitāki, Taittirīya, Kena, Katha, Māṇdukya, Praṣna,* and *Muṇdāka.*

9 The *Īśāvāsyopaniṣad's* first verse reads: '*Īṣavāsya midam sarvam yatkiń cha jagatyām jagat; tena tyaktena bhunjītā; mā gridhaha, kasya svidhanam*'. Swami Sarvananda, Isavasyopanisad, Chennai: Sri Ramakrishna Math, 2015 (20th ed.; 1st ed. 1998). Like most of the Ramakrishna Math publications of the *Upaniṣads,* there is a word by word translation from Sanskrit, with the insights of the sage monks who brought out the work.

10 The Sanskrit verse from *Aitareya Upaniṣad* is: *AU* 1.1: '*Ātmā vā idameka evāgra āsīnnānyat kitchińa miṣat; sa īkṣata lokānnu srijā iti; ambho marīchīr ramāpoadoambhah*'. See Swami Sarvananda, *Aitareyopaniṣad,* Chennai: Sri Ramakrishna Math, 2001, 29.

11 Swami Swahananda, ed., *Chāndogya Upaniṣad, op. cit.,* 276–281, for sage Haridrumata Gautama's reply, *vide* 281.

12 Romila Thapar, "The First Millennium B.C. in Northern India (Up to the End of the Mauryan Period)", in R. Thapar, ed., *Recent Perspectives of Early Indian History,* Bombay: Popular Prakashan, 1995, 80–141, *vide,* 88–89, 110–111; R. Thapar, *Early India: From the Origins to AD 1300, op. cit.*, 146–155, 184–185.

13 Sanskrit text, with word-by-word translation is given in Swami Swarupananda, trans., ed., *Shrimad Bhagavad Gita,* Calcutta: Advaita Ashrama, 1976 (12th ed.).

14 These two Sanskrit verses from the *Bhagavad Gītā* are:

> *(BG 9:26): Patram puṣpam phalam toyam yo me bhaktyā prayacchati;*
> *tadaham bhaktyu pahritamaśnāmi prayatātmanah.*
> *(BG 9.29): Samoaham sarva bhuteṣu na me dveṣyo asti na priyah;*
> *Ye bhajanti tu mam bhaktyā mayi te teṣu chāvyāham.*

15 For the most insightful exposition of the *gana sanghas,* see R. Thapar, *Early India: From the Origins to AD 1300, op. cit.*, 146–150.

16 Ainslee T. Embree, ed., *Sources of Indian Tradition, Volume 1: From the Beginning to 1800, op. cit.*, 43–45.

17 Embree, *ibid.*, 43–199.

18 The *Dharma Sūtras* in Sanskrit are available as PDF files at: www.hinduonline.co/DigitalLibrary.html, under Scriptures/Sutra. See apastamba_dharma_sutra.pdf; baudhayana_dharma_sutra.pdf.; gautama_dharma_sutra.pdf.; vasishta_dharma_sutra.pdf. See also P. Olivelle's notable critical translation, *Dharmasūtras: The Law Codes of Āpastamba, Gautama, Baudhāyana, and Vasiṣṭha, op. cit.* Also see his historical analyses: P. Olivelle, ed., *Between the Empires: Society in India 300 BCE to 400 CE, op. cit.*; P. Olivelle, *Language, Texts and Society: Explorations in Ancient Indian Culture and Religion, op. cit.*

19 *Aitareya Brāhmana* (1.14, 23). See Martin Haug, trans., ed., *Aitareya Brāhmanam of the Rigveda: Rites of the Vedic Religion*, Bombay: Govt. Central Book Depot, 1863, 33–34; Sudhindra Nath Vasu (reprint), Bahadurganj, Allahabad, 1922, streamed by the University of Toronto Press, 2008, at this website: https://archive.org/stream/aitareyabrahmana04hauguoft/aitareyabrahmana04hauguoft_djvu.txt. Also see R. Anantakrisna Sastri, ed., *Aitareya Brāhmana*, Vol. I, Travancore: University of Travancore Sanskrit Series CXLIX, 1942 at: https://archive.org/stream/aitareyabrahmana014460mbp.

20 The *Yajur Veda* has two sections, namely the Kṛiṣna (Dark) section, in which *Taittirīya Brāhmana* appears, and a Śukla (White) section. Subramania Sarma, ed., *Taittirīya Brāhmana,* at: www.sanskritweb.net/yajurveda/tb-1-05.pdf

21 *Bṛihadāranyaka Upaniṣad*, ed., Chennai: Sri Ramakrishna Math, 2000 (2nd ed.), 1–4.

The first of six sections, the first verses of the *Aśva-Brāhmana* (1.1) are: 'Om. The head of the sacrificial horse is truly the dawn, its eye is the sun, its vital breath is air, its open mouth is the fire Vaiśvānara' ('*Om. Uṣā vā aśvasya meghasya śirah; sūryaśchakśuh vātah; prāṇah, vyāttamagnir Vaiśvānarah*').

22 Henry Clarke Warren, *Buddhism in Translations: Passages Selected from the Buddhist Sacred Books and Translated from the Original Pāli into English* (1st ed. 1896 by Harvard University Press), New York: Athenaeum, 1982 (11th rpt.), 101–103. See also T.W. Rhys Davids and J.E. Carpenter, eds., *Dīghā Nikāya,* 3 vols., 1899–1911, London: P.T.S.

23 See Ram Sharan Sharma, *Aspects of Political Ideas and Institutions in Ancient India, op. cit.,* 28, 50, 64–68. The *Digha Nikaya* includes the sermon *Ambaṭṭhasutta*, a tale of creation, and a secondary story on the first state. Still another sermon, the *Atānatiya Sūtta,* describes the primal Kuru clan thus: 'There do men live calling no goods as their own, nor as their chattels any women kind'.

24 Ram Sharan Sharma, *Aspects of Political Ideas and Institutions in Ancient India, op. cit.*; R. Thapar, *Early India: From the Origins to AD 1300, op. cit.,* 11–125, 146–156; R. Thapar, *Aśoka and the Decline of the Mauryas, op. cit.*; Hermann Kulke and Dietmar Rothermund, *A History of India, op. cit.*, 54–57; Ramashankar Tripathi, *History of Ancient India,* New Delhi: Motilal Banarsidass, 1942 (9th ed. 1999), 82–114; Kumkum Roy, *The Emergence of Monarchy in North India: Eighth-Fourth Centuries BC as Reflected in the Brahmanical Tradition,* New Delhi: Oxford University Press, 1994. Also see P.C. Bagchi, "Religion and Politics in the Arthaśāstra of Kautalya", in Ram Sharan Sharma, ed., *Aspects of Political Ideas and Institutions in Ancient India, op. cit.,* 253–274.

25 K.A. Nilakanta Sastri, ed., *Age of the Nandas and Mauryas*, New Delhi: Motilal Banarsidass, 1997 (2nd ed.). This collection includes chapters by: See K.A.N. Sastri, ed., *Age of the Nandas and Mauryas,* for essays by H.C. Raychaudhuri, "India in the Age of the Nandas", ch. I, 9–42; K.A.N. Sastri, "India in Early

Greek and Latin Literature", ch. III., 81–91, 112–120; K.A.N. Sastri, "Mauryan Polity", ch. V, 171–201; S.K. Chatterji and V. Raghavan, "Language and Literature", ch. X, 325–338, 341–342.

26 At least three modern historians reaffirm this fact. See Romila Thapar, *Aśoka and the Decline of the Maurya, op. cit.,* 12–13, which cite the Buddhist scriptural *Vamsatthapakāsinī* (1.5) as stating that Chandragupta's family of Moriyas lived in sub-Himalayan forests rich in peacocks (*mayur*). Also see H.C. Raychaudhuri, "Chandragupta and Bindusara", in K.A.N. Sastri, ed., *Age of the Nandas and Mauryas, op. cit.,* 132–170, *vide* 143. Raychaudhuri cites the Jaina canon *Pariśiṣṭaparvan* (8.231), which describes Chandragupta's father as the Moriya tribal chief in Pipphalivana and his mother as a daughter of a peacock trainer ('Mayūraposhaka'), thus reaffirming Buddhist references to Moriyanagar/ Pātaliputra as Chandragupta's home. Also see Ramashankar Tripathi, *History of Ancient India,* quoting Roman historian Justin who described Chandragupta as a 'new man' (*novus homo*). An early work is Purushottam Lal Bhargava's *Chandragupta Maurya,* Lucknow: The Upper India Publishing House, Ltd., 1935, 28.

27 Such texts reflect the social norms of the author or eponymous author. The *Arthaśāstra's* first volume (1.1–3) lauds the *Rig, Sāma, Yajur,* and *Atharva Vedas* as the source of enlightenment. *AŚ* 1.4–8 describe the four *varnas* and professions thus:

> (*AŚ* 1.1.4) states that the first three *Vedas* established the *varna dharmas ('eṣa trayīha dharmaṣa caturṇām varṇānām ākśamānāṇam ca svaha dharmah sthāpanād aupakārikah').*
> (*AŚ* 1.1.5) states that the *brāhman's dharma* entailed Vedic study, wisdom, devotion, performing sacrifices, gifts to the gods, and receiving of gifts ('*svdharmo brāhmaṇasya adhyaynam adhyāpanam yajanam yājanam dānam pratigṛahśca*').
> (*AŚ* 1.1.6) states that the *kṣatṛiya's dharma* was to acquire skills for work, do rites, give to the gods, live according to law, and protect subjects ('*kṣaṭriyasyah adhyayanam, yajanam, dānam, śastrah ājīvo bhūta rakṣaṇam ca'*);
> (*AŚ* 1.1.7) states that the *vaiśya's dharma* was to learn the sacred rites, give to the gods, farm, tend cattle, and trade ('*vaiśya hadhyayanam yajanam dānam kṛiṣih pāṣupālye vānijya ca*');
> (*AŚ* 1.1.8) states that the *śudra's dharma* was to serve the three twice-born (*dvījas) varnas* and to be poets and dancers ('*śudrasya dvijātih śuśrūṣa vārtā kāruh kuśīlavah karma ca*'). Yet the author speaks respectfully of *śudras* as '*kūśīlavah*', the title given to the hunter-sage Vālmiki, who composed the sacred *Rāmāyana.*

28 On matriarchal and patriarchal clans, see Charles Drekmeier, *Kingship and Community in Early India,* Palo Alto: Stanford University Press, 1962, 75–76.

29 Swami Swahananda, trans., *Chāndōgya Upaniṣad,* Chennai: Sri Ramakrishna Math, 1980, 244–245.

30 On matriliny among the Yadavas, see R. Thapar, *Ancient Indian Social History: Some Interpretations,* Hyderabad: Orient Longmans, 1978 (rpt. 2004), 286–316, *vide.* 304–306.

31 Ram Sharan Sharma, *Aspects of Political Ideas and Institutions in Ancient India, op. cit.,* 201–202, 357–359.

32 For a lucid discussion of the furrowed field and royal domains, see D.N. Jha, *Ancient India In Historical Outline,* New Delhi: Manohar, 1998 (revised, enlarged ed.), 97–98.

33 Ram Sharan Sharma, "How Feudal Was Indian Feudalism?" in Hermann Kulke, ed., *The State in India, 1000–1700,* New Delhi: Oxford University Press, 1995, 48–55, vide., 57. Sharma suggests that by 7th c. ACE, *vaiśya* peasants were so impoverished that their rank fell almost to that of *śudras.*

34 The Sanskrit *Dharma Sūtras* are available as PDF files at: www.hinduonline.co/DigitalLibrary.html, under Scriptures/Sutra. See apastamba_dharma_sutra.pdf; baudhayana_dharma_sutra.pdf.; gautama_dharma_sutra.pdf.; vasishta_dharma_sutra.pdf. See also P. Olivelle's notable critical translation, *Dharmasūtras: The Law Codes of Āpastamba, Gautama, Baudhāyana, and Vasiṣṭha, op. cit.* Also see the notable historical analysis by Patrick Olivelle, ed., *Between the Empires: Society in India 300 BCE to 400 CE, op. cit.*; P. Olivelle, *Language, Texts and Society: Explorations in Ancient Indian Culture and Religion, op. cit.*

35 Mary McGee, "Ritual Rights: The Gender Implications of *Adhikāra*", in Laurie L. Patton, ed., *Jewels of Authority,* New Delhi: Oxford University Press, 2002, 32–50.

36 See Sita Anantha Raman, *Women in India: A Social and Cultural History, op. cit.*, 36–37.

37 Arthur Berriedale Keith, trans., *The Taittirīya Samhita,* Cambridge, MA, 1914; New Delhi: Motilal Banarsidass, 1967 (rpt.), 293–294.

38 F. Max-Muller, ed., and J. Eggeling, trans., *Śatapatha Brāhmana, According to the Text of the Madhyandina School (Sacred Books of the East)*, Part I, Vol. 26 (1885), Chapter 4, 367, Delhi: Motilal Banarsidass, 1988, at this website: www.sacred-texts.com/hin/sbr/sbe12/sbe1213.htm.

39 F. Max-Muller, ed., and J. Eggeling, trans., *Śatapatha Brāhmana,* Part V, Vol. 44 [1900], Chapter 14, 441. The translation is at this website: www.sacred-texts.com/hin/sbr/index.htm.

40 Wendy Doniger O'Flaherty, *Tales of Sex and Violence: Folklore, Sacrifice, and Danger in the Jaiminīya Brāhmana,* Chicago: University of Chicago Press, 1985, 18–20, 85–96.

41 Monika Chawla, "Rights of Female", in *Central India Law Quarterly,* Vol. 18, No. 1, 2007, 443–511, *vide.,* 452–462.

42 Stephanie Jamison, "Women 'Between the Empires' and 'Between the Lines'", in P. Olivelle, ed., *Between the Empires: Society in India 300 BCE to 400 CE, op. cit.*, 191–214, *vide.,* 192–193. See also Stephanie Jamison, *Sacrificed Wife/Sacrificer's Wife: Women, Ritual, and Hospitality in Ancient India,* New York: Oxford University Press, 1996, 30–50.

43 Sita Anantha Raman, *Women in India: A Social and Cultural History, op. cit.*, 34–64.

44 See *Aitareyopaniṣad, op. cit., vide.,* Introduction, 1–5; Swami Swahananda, trans., *Chāndōgya Upaniṣad, op. cit.*; *Bṛhadāraṇyaka Upaniṣad,* Ramakrishna Math, 2000.

Mahidāsa Aitareya's mother was a *śudra* named Itarā, and his father was a *brahman.* He was the author of the *Aitareya Brāhmanā, Aitareya Āranyaka,* and *Aitareya Upaniṣad.* As a boy, Aitareya was shunned from his father's ritual, whereupon he invoked his mother's tutelary earth goddess Mahi; *vide, Aitareyopaniṣad,* Introduction, 1–5.

The *Chāndōgya Upaniṣad* relates Aitareya's teachings (*CU* 3.16–17) and the story of Satyakāma Jābala (*CU* 4.4.2–5). When Satyakāma asked his mother Jābala who his father was, she replied that she did not know, as Satyakāma was conceived when she was a servant in a *dvīja* household. Despite this handicap, Satyakāma's brilliance was recognized by a great sage who instructed him in the *Vedas.*

The *Bṛhadāraṇyaka Upaniṣad* contains discourses between sage Uddalaka Āruni and two women, namely his wife Maitreyī (*BU* 2.4.1–2.4.6; 4.5.1–15), and his brilliant, inquisitive student Gārgi (3.6.1–2; 3.8.1–12).

45 The story appears in the *Chāndogya Upaniṣad* (4.4.5). See Swami Swahananda, ed., *Chāndogya Upaniṣad, op. cit.*, 277–281.

46 For Romila Thapar's brilliant discussion of how *varna* ranks became embedded in early India's class system, *vide.,* R. Thapar, *Early India: From the Origins to AD 1300, op. cit.*, 150–156.

47 See Ramashankar Tripathi, *History of Ancient India,* Delhi: Motilal Banarsidass, 1999 (9th ed.; 1st ed. 1942), 109–110; R.C. Majumdar, H.C. Raychaudhuri, and Kalikinkar Datta, *An Advanced History of India, Part I: Ancient India*, London: Macmillan, 1958 (2nd ed.), 62–63; and D.N. Jha, *Ancient India: In Historical Outline,* New Delhi: Manohar, 1998 (revised ed.; 1st ed.1977), 78–110.

48 *Śatapatha Brāhmana* (5.3.1:4): 'And on the following day, he goes to the dwelling of the Queen, and prepares a pap for Aditi; for Aditi is this Earth, and she is the wife of the gods; and that (queen) is the wife of that (king): hence it is for Aditi. And she, the Queen, assuredly is one of his (the king's) jewels: it is for her that he is thereby consecrated, and he makes her his own faithful (wife). The sacrificial fee, on her part, is a milch cow; for this (earth) is, as it were, a milch cow: she yields to men all their desires; and the milch cow is a mother, and this (earth) is, as it were, a mother: she bears (or sustains) men. Hence the fee is a milch cow'.

49 Ram Sharan Sharma, *Aspects of Political Ideas and Institutions in Ancient India, op. cit.,* 143–148. See also K.A.N. Sastri, ed., *Age of the Nandas and Mauryas, op. cit.* (rpt. 1997).

50 See John Keay, *India: A History,* New York: Grove Press, 2000, 42–45. See also Ramashankar Tripathi, *History of Ancient India,* 1999, *op. cit.*, 82–85, 89–96.

51 Ram Sharan Sharma, *Aspects of Political Ideas and Institutions in Ancient India, op. cit.,* 64–68, 130–132.

52 N.N. Bhattacharya, "Property Rights of Women in Ancient India", in L.K. Tripathi, ed., *Position and Status of Women in Ancient India,* vol. I, Varanasi: Benares Hindu University, 1988, 62–72. See also Romila Thapar, "The First Millennium B.C. in Northern India (Up to the end of the Mauryan Period)", in R. Thapar, ed., *Recent Perspectives of Early Indian History, op. cit.*, 80–141, *vide,* 110–111; and R. Thapar, *Early India: From the Origins to AD 1300, op. cit.,* 146–155.

53 For example, *Rig Veda* (8.19.36), and the *Mahābhārata (Ādi Parvan,* 157.36), among other texts cited by Harsh Narain in, "The Near Incorruptibility of Woman: An Almost Forgotten Chapter of Indian Culture", in L.K. Tripathi, ed., *Position and Status of Women in Ancient India, op. cit.*, 109–118.

54 The landed elite of Buddhist oligarchies like the Licchhāvi confederacy depended on the labor of slaves and serfs. See Ram Sharan Sharma, *Aspects of Political Ideas and Institutions in Ancient India, op. cit.*, 130–132.

55 R.C. Majumdar, H.C. Raychaudhuri, and Kalikinkar Dattar, *An Advanced History of India, Part I: Ancient India, op. cit.*, 58–61.

4

JAINA AND BUDDHIST CANON, STATES, AND WOMEN

I. Heterodoxy and the state

While patriarchy was a scripturally ordained feature of Indo-Āryan society, early Vedic clans followed amorphous customs. These norms evolved in the later Vedic era, which witnessed territorial, genetic, and social expansion of Sanskritic clans. The clans extended their sway from the Indus and Punjab into the Yamuna-Ganga Doab (ca. 1000 BCE), southwest into Rajasthan and Gujarat and east along the Ganges. Around 800 BCE, their domains crystallized into large *janapadas*, which included monarchies (*rājya*) and oligarchic confederations (*gana sangha*). The formation of these political states had dramatic religious and social effects. These were increased *brāhmanical* orthodoxy visible in the *Brāhmana* liturgies that commemorated *kşatŗiya* victories and ascension; the dissensions of seers who composed the *Upanişads*; diverse heterodox dissenters who formed sects; and increased subordination of women, *Śudras*, and local tribes.

While elite *kşatŗiya* rulers and *brāhmans* used conquests to spread Sanskritic norms, in a subtle reverse osmosis, pre-Āryan Dravidian/Tibeto-Burman/Austric gene pools, languages, and cultures created a hybrid Sanskritic society with extended families. This appears in the adoption of some matrilineal/matriarchal customs, such as the maternal uncle's importance in a family and the use of the matronymic. Examples of the latter appear in the epic *Mahābhārata*, in which the divine hero Ķrişna is often hailed as Devakīputra (son of Devakī), and the princely hero Arjuna is often called Kaunteya (son of Kunti).

It also appears in the Sanskritization of some pre-Āryan beliefs, such as the cycle of birth and death (*samsara*) caused by human actions (*karma*), which are evident in the *Upanişads*, some composed by gifted *Śudras*. The *Upanişads* also drew attention to the redemptive power of meditation (*tapasya*) and *yoga*, pre-Sanskritic practices first etched on a Harappan seal of god Śivā the *yogi* amid trees and animals. These seers disagreed with *Brāhmana* fire rituals, but as they accepted Vedic deism and founded monistic belief in the unity of the individual and cosmic souls (Ātman-Brāhman), the *Upanişads* were soon included into the *Vedas*.

Other dissidents were heterodox renunciants who practiced meditative *yoga*, but their conclusions were different. Heterodox ascetics broke free of the *Vedas* and refuted deism and *brāhmanical* fire rituals for royal ascensions and victories. Important heterodox sects included Buddhist agnostics; Jainas who denied a cosmic Being, but believed in a soul (*jīvā*) in all living beings; Chārvākā atheist materialists (700 BCE); and atheist fatalists like the Ājīvikās (500 BCE). Unlike the extreme Chārvākas and Ājīvikās, the founders of Jainism and Buddhism emphasized ethical morality (*dhamma/dharma*) in society, compassion for all beings, and humane solutions to human problems.

This chapter focuses on Jainism and Buddhism, founded by elite *kṣatṛiyas* from *gana sanghas* whose subjects included pre-Āryan groups. The ethical emphases in Jainism and Buddhism must have appealed to ordinary people who were either *śudras*, those outside the *varna* order, or pre-Āryan tribes in forests and hillsides. Jaina and Buddhist sects gave a greater meditative space for women, although women's domestication was now rigidly enforced in most orthodox and heterodox Sanskritic societies. *Upaniṣadic* seers and the sage Vyāsā, the primary author of the *Mahābhārata*, disliked *Brāhmana* ritual fire sacrifices, as these conflagrations consumed forests and tribal denizens. This is depicted in the *Mahābhāratā* tale of the burning of the Khandva forest, but the epics were prized as embodiments of Vedic culture.[1]

In contrast, Jainas and Buddhists broke away from Vedic religion, chose a renunciant's life, or lived in political states where heterodox, lower-caste, and tribal groups were less subjugated. As many Jainas lived among Buddhists and some Hindus, these groups shared a common language and belief in ethical *dharma* (Skt.)/*dhamma* (Pāli) as the foundation (Skt. root '*dhr*') of civil society. If Hindu mores seeped into heterodox societies, in turn, Jaina and Buddhist emphasis upon nonviolence (*ahimsa*) seeped into Hindu societies. All groups agreed that women's primary function was within the household, but Jaina and Buddhist women had greater opportunities to become renunciants.

A. Jainism

Jainism was formally established by Vardhamāna Mahāvīra ('Great Hero'; 540–468 BCE), also known as the 'Jina' (Conqueror). Mahāvīra was born into the elite *kṣatṛiya* clan of Jňātrikās in the *gana sangha* in Vaiśāli, and his mother Triśala belonged to the powerful Licchavi oligarchy.[2] Mahāvīra's home was near Magadha, a kingly state that later became the center of the heterodox Mauryan Empire (324–184 BCE). Jainas believe that ascetics who meditate deeply can attain enlightenment and become *kevalins*. Male and female Jaina *kevalins* pre-dated Mahāvīra, the last of twenty-four Jaina preceptors ('ford crossers': *tīrthankaras*). The first *tīrthankara*, Rishabha (ca. 750 BCE), was a Sramana or Nirgrantha ('bondless ascetic') who objected to *brāhmanical* fire sacrifices that exalted *kṣatṛiya* kings but destroyed forest tribes and animals. Rishabha was a Sramanā, possibly an early Digambara ('Sky-Clad') sect whose monks were nude.

Despite Jainism's strong ascetic tradition, there was also a vibrant lay community whose men and women worked in various occupations. There now emerged two sects, that is, the Śvetāmbara ('White Clad') of lay and ascetic members and the Digambara ('Sky Clad') sect, whose monks were nude. Śvetāmbaras believe that the nineteenth *tīrthankara* was a female *kevalin* named Malli, an event that is viewed as extremely rare. Jaina myths state that in a previous life, Malli was a wicked king, whose rigid penances led to his next birth as a woman *kevalin*.[3] Digambaras refute this tale, and they claim that Malli was a man called Mallinatha. The twenty-third *tīrthankara*, Pārsvānāth, was a Śvetāmbara who encouraged women ascetics. As renunciants take vows to give up all worldly desire, including sexual intercourse, Jaina and Buddhist male and female ascetics (*bhikku and bhikkunī*) belong to separate orders.[4] As Śvetāmbaras are clothed, they accept women *bhikkunī* more readily, and some renunciants shave their heads to downplay gender distinctions. Mahāvīra was a Digambara monk, yet he was the first to initiate an order of Jaina nuns. Digambara monks strictly avoid women to avoid breaking their vow of celibacy. Jainas refute the existence of a supreme Spirit, but their basic tenet is that all living beings have an inner soul (*jīva*). They also hold the belief that enlightened renunciants (*kevalin*) have a suprasensory perception of *jivas* in the environment. Jainism has three principles ('Three Jewels'), *viz.*, Right Views, Right Actions, and Faith, and five rules, *viz.*, nonviolence (*ahimsa*), truth (*satya*), non-stealing (*asteya*), and two extra rules for renunciants, that is, celibacy (*brāhmachārya*) and non-attachment to worldly goods (*apārigraha*).[5] The belief that the world has myriads of *jīvas* led Jainas to emphasize nonviolence (*ahimsa*) as their supreme *dharma*, a doctrine that has shaped political policies even in the modern era. As Jainas were forbidden to harm or kill even small organisms around them, Jainas rarely became soldiers or farmers who tilled the earth, but many entered mercantile professions. As believers in *ahimsa*, Jainas became vegetarians and took rigorous fasts to cleanse their *jīvas*. While regular householders broke their fasts after a specified period of time, many monks and nuns fasted for longer periods, some even until death.[6]

Chandragupta Maurya (324–301 BCE), the brilliant general who founded the Mauryan Empire, later abdicated, became a Digambara monk, and retired to Karnataka. In the Mauryan–early classical era, Jainas spread west into Gujarat and south into Karnataka and the Tamil regions, living under the aegis of Buddhist and Hindu kings. In the medieval era, some regions were ruled by benign Muslim monarchs who valued Jaina merchants and bankers. Most Jainas were clearly not all renunciants but ordinary householders who practiced *ahimsa* through kindliness. The early Jaina canon includes the *Āchārānga Sutrā* (Book of Good Conduct), whose ethical guidelines probably influenced kings who valued Jainas as nonviolent, respectable subjects. Yet as Jainas did not have a temporal code like the *Arthaśāstra* written by a *brāhman* for a heterodox emperor, many heterodox rulers probably governed and meted out justice with this Mauryan code. The Jaina *Āchārānga Sūtra* and *Kalpa Sūtra* are in Prakrits, which are derived from Sanskrit and local languages. The doctrine of *ahimsa* is seen in the *Ācārānga Sutrā* (1.1):

> Injury to the earth is like striking, cutting, maiming, or killing a blind
> man . . . a man should not sin against the earth. . . . There are many souls
> embodied in water . . . he who injures the lives in water does not understand
> the nature of sin or renounce it. . . . By wicked or careless acts one may
> destroy fire-being, and moreover, harm other beings by means of fire. . . .
> He who understands the nature of sin against animals is called a true sage
> who understands karma . . .[7]

B. Buddhism

Siddharta Gautama, also known as the Buddha ('Enlightened One'; 563–484 BCE), was born a *kṣatṛiya* of the Shākya clan in a *gana sangha*. Like Mahāvīra, Siddhartha was thus raised in an oligarchy that had numerous indigenous tribal and lower caste subjects, which may explain why the early Buddhist canon describes his compassion as a youth. The Shākya *gana sangha* was situated in the hills of Nepal and northern India, near the large kingdoms of Kośala (Bihar) and Magadha on the eastern Ganges. Magadha was originally governed by elite *kṣatṛiya* groups, until it became a kingdom under Bimbisāra (b. 543 BCE). Bimbisāra's ambitious son Ajātaśatru (d. 461 BCE) starved his father to death to ascend the throne, whereupon Bimbisāra's wife Kosaladevi, sister of king Pasenadi of Kosala, committed suicide. Pasenadi reclaimed his sister's dowry of revenue from the town of Kāsi; this triggered a war between Kosala and Magadha. A new matrimonial treaty allowed Ajātaśatru to marry Pasenadi's daughter Vijirā, and two allies jointly invaded the Vṛjjī *gana sangha*, which Magadha now annexed.[8] Although such kings expressed respect for the Buddha, clearly their political actions were not based on ethical *dharma/dhamma*.

In contrast, the Buddha's empathy for the suffering of humans and animals is described in the Theravāda canon. Disturbed by the overwhelming presence of sorrow, the twenty-nine-year-old Siddhartha left his wife and children in their aristocratic home for Gayā (in Bihar) to meditate upon sorrow. There this spiritual aspirant (*arhant*) sat under a pipal tree in Lumbini Gardens until he attained insights into sorrow's causes and cure. Early Buddhist canon describes his solution as the 'Middle Way' between indulgence and complete renunciation. He emphasized compassion as the fundamental precept while humans perform their ethical duties (*dhamma:* Pāli). Siddhartha preached his psychological solutions in his first sermon in the Deer Park in Vāranāsī, after which he was called the Buddha ('Enlightened One') and Tathāgatha ('He Who Has Attained').

This first sermon described Four Noble Truths. The first Truth is that sorrow (*dukkha*) is universal; the second Truth is that sorrow stems from ignorance that the world is transient (*anicca*) and that there is no soul (*anatta*); the third Truth is that there is a 'cure' for sorrow; and the fourth Truth is the cure of the Noble Eight-Fold Path. Buddha's teachings now set the Wheel of Law (*dhamma chakka*) into motion, thus establishing Theravāda Buddhism. Although Buddha did not believe in a Creator-Spirit, unlike the Ājīvikā atheists, this early agnostic psychologist brushed negativity aside to focus upon a pragmatic 'cure' for sorrow. This curative message appealed to those without power, as well as to Magadha's next dynasty of lower-caste Nandas. Theravāda *Samyutta Nikaya* (5.421), from the canon *Sutta Pitaka*, describes The Middle Way:

> ('*Samyutta Nikaya* 5.421): Thus I have heard. Once the Lord was at Vāranāsī, at the deer park called Isipatana. There he addressed the five monks: There are two ends not to be served by a wanderer. What are these two? The pursuit of desires and the pleasure which springs from desire, which is base, common, leading to rebirth, ignoble, and unprofitable; and the pursuit of pain and hardship, which is grievous, ignoble, and unprofitable. The Middle Way of the Tathāgatha avoids both these ends. It is enlightened, it brings clear vision, it makes for wisdom and leads to peace, insight, enlightenment, and Nirvāna. What is the Middle Way? . . . It is the Noble Eightfold Path–Right Views, Right Resolve, Right Speech, Right Conduct, Right Livelihood, Right Effort, Right Mindfulness, and Right Concentration.[9]

Theravāda canon in Pāli consists largely of the *Tripitaka* (Three Baskets), whose sections are the *Vinaya Pitaka* (Discipline) codebook for ascetics (*bhikkus/bhikkunis*), the *Sutta Pitaka* of Buddha's Discourses given in a conversational style, and the *Abhidhamma Pitaka* (Additional Doctrines). The most significant is the *Sutta Pitaka* whose five main sections were meant for all adherents of Buddhism. The most important sections are the

Digha Nikāya (Long Discourses), *Majjima Nikāya* (Medium Discourses), *Samyutta Nikāya* (Short Discourses), the section *Khuddha Nikāya* (Minor Group) with poems, and the *Jātaka* (Birth Tales) with historical references to the Buddha. While the canon is socially and psychologically important, as the sections did not describe temporal laws on governance, it is probable that most Buddhist kings chose the *Arthaśāstra*, which had served the first heterodox imperial Mauryan regime.

Women in early Buddhism

As Siddhartha's mother died when he was an infant, he was raised by his foster mother and aunt, Mahā-Pajāpatī. The Buddha is recorded as having compared unselfish motherly love to the compassion of a true sage.[10] Mahā-Pajāpatī made three appeals to Buddha, asking him to sanction an order of women ascetics (*bhikkunīs*), but he refused, probably fearing that women's presence near *bhikkus* would tempt monks to break their vow of celibacy. Finally, she and 500 women walked barefoot across miles to his doorstep for a final appeal. They included widows whose husbands had died in devastating war; others were mistreated by polygamous husbands and patriarchal family; some mourned their child's death or the lack of a supporting family and hence came to Mahā-Pajāpatī for help. The women had painful, bleeding feet; wore saffron robes; and had shaved their heads like male *bhikkus*. The Buddha now consulted his gentle cousin, monk Ānandā, who convinced him that women should be initiated as *bhikkunīs*. Ānandā asked pointedly if the Buddha believed that women could be *arhants* and attain *nirvana*, and the Buddha then replied that they could. Ānandā praised Mahā-Pajāpatī for having raised Siddhartha with love, subtly indicating that women's maternal compassion was that of sage monks. Buddha then initiated the first order of *bhikkunīs*, but he stipulated that nuns had to follow 'eight weighty laws'. Monks were ordered to respect women's menstrual needs, but nuns would be subordinate to monks, and even young monks could remove nuns for slight transgressions; female sexuality and morality would be suspect; *bhikkunis* were forbidden to use 'magical' potions for childbirth or to abort children. Ānanda's dialogue with Buddha was described later by a sympathetic Theravāda monk:

Vinaya Pitaka: *Culla Vagga (10.1):*
(Ananda): Consider, Reverend Sir, how great a benefactress
Maha-Pajapati the Gotamid has been. She is the sister of the mother
of The Blessed One, and as foster-mother, nurse, and giver of milk,
she suckled The Blessed One on the death of his mother. Pray,

Reverend Sir, let women retire from household life to the houseless one,
under the Doctrine and Discipline announced by the Thathagatha.

(Buddha): If, Ananda, Maha-Pajapati the Gotamid will accept eight weighty regulations, let it be reckoned to her as her ordination.[11]

The *Therigātha* (Hymns of the Elder Nuns) is another text that sheds light on the first *bhikkunī/therīs* who composed these hymns. The *Therigātha* hymnal possibly dates from the Buddha's lifetime, but it was only inscribed ca. 70 BCE. These 522 hymns rejoice over Buddha's compassion and ethical messages, and they were first sung by seventy-two minstrel nuns. By the time that the hymns were recorded, the songs had undergone some changes, but their message is poignant. The *Therigātha* indicates that women had a subordinate role in both orthodox and heterodox societies of early India but that they found comfort and refuge in the Buddha's teachings. The Buddha may have hesitated to induct nuns, but his compassion was never in doubt.[12]

Buddhist Sangha and later sects

The community of early monks and lay folk was called the Sangha (community), a term that possibly reflects Buddha's early life in the Shakya *gana sangha* or semi-republic. Buddha urged his *bhikku* monks to spread his message, and over time, the expanding community needed new guidelines on who was to be a member. These defined rules on admitting new members, rules for *bhikkus* and eight extra 'weighty' rules for *bhikkunis*, simpler rules for lay folk, and those for teaching monks.[13] After Buddha's death, growing divisions finally led to three broad groups of believers, who all agreed on Buddha's fundamental precepts but with some new interpretations. His teachings became the basis of Theravāda Buddhism. The Mauryan emperor Āśoka Maurya (268–231 BCE) was the most influential early proponent of Theravāda. Āśoka carved Buddha's teachings and his own edicts on nonviolence on rocks and pillars in Pāli and local languages but using regional scripts known to the local populace across his empire. These were the Persian Kharoshti script in the northwest and Brahmi script, from which Sanskrit Devanagari and Tamil evolved on the subcontinent. Āśoka introduced Theravāda Buddhism into Srī Lanka, from where it spread to Southeast Asia. In the early classical era, the two factions of the Mahāsanghikā and Sarvāstivādin merged into the Mahāyana Buddhist sect. Mahāyana Buddhist teachings were adopted by the Graeco-Bactrian king Menander after his dialogues with monk Nāgasenā (ca. 1st c. ACE), which were recorded in the *Questions of Milinda*. Mahāyana was also the religion of the Buddhist Kuśāṇa emperor Kaniṣka (ca. 100 ACE), who hosted a highly commended conference on Buddhism across his empire, which extended from the Indian subcontinent's northwestern regions into Central Asia. This period witnessed an outburst of Buddhist art and literature.

While Theravāda and Mahāyana Buddhists all believe in the Middle Way and Eightfold Path, there are some notable differences. Theravādins highly value the *Tripitaka*'s discourses between Buddha and his followers, and they believe that the Buddha was unique when he attained Nirvāna ('Nothingness'). Mahāyana texts emphasize the Buddha's essential practices rather than the early canon, as well as his great compassion. Mahāyana Buddhists believe that Buddha was the first of potentially future compassionate 'Buddhas' (*bodhisattvas*) who delay their own Nirvāna in order to save others on earth. This led to a widespread, theistic reverence for the Buddha amongst followers of both sects, but amongst the Mahāyanists, there developed a unique faith in *bodhisattvas*, whose carved images occur in Gāndhāra in the northwest, across the Gangetic plain, and elsewhere on the subcontinent. Theism appears in the Mahāyana scripture *Aṣṭasāhasrikā Prājñāpāramitā* (22.403):

> The bodhisattva is endowed with wisdom of a kind whereby he looks on all beings as though victims going to the slaughter. And immense compassion grips him. His divine eye sees. . . . innumerable beings, and he is filled with great distress at what he sees, for many bear the burden of past deeds which will be punished in purgatory, others will have unfortunate rebirths which will divide them from the Buddha and his teachings, others must soon be slain . . . So he purs out his love and compassion upon all those beings . . .[14]

In the classical centuries (200 BCE–200 ACE–600 ACE), especially after emperor Kaniṣka organized his famous conference, Mahāyana Buddhism spread into C. Asia, China, Korea, and Japan. In South Asia and Asia, the climate of cultural heterogeneity led to fresh philosophical ideas in Buddhism. On the subcontinent, Sanskrit replaced Pāli as the royal court language, as seen in the edicts of the Śaka king Rudradāman and the imperial Guptas (320–550 ACE), who were Hindus but encouraged Buddhism. Meanwhile, in the south, Dravidian kings hosted Tamil literary conferences (Sangam) where works of aphorisms, poetry, and epics were exhibited (200 BCE–500 ACE). Sanskrit and Dravidian languages borrowed from each other, thus weaving linguistic-cultural threads into a multiethnic fabric, a pattern replicated over the next millennia.

Notes

1 On the burning of the Khandva forest, fire rituals, and Buddhist and Jaina responses, see Madhav Gadgil and Ramachandra Guha, *This Fissured Land: An Ecological History of India,* Melbourne: Oxford University Press, 1993, 78–84.

2 Ainslie T. Embree, ed., *Sources of Indian Tradition, Volume 1: From the Beginning to 1800, op. cit.*, 49–51.

3 Padmanabha S. Jaini, *Gender and Salvation: Jaina Debates on the Spiritual Liberation of Women*, Berkeley and Los Angeles: University of California Press, 1991, 14–15, 105–106, 217. Also see Nalini Balbir, "Women in Jainism", in Sita Arvind Sharma, ed., *Women in India: A Social and Cultural History, op. cit.*, 70–107.

4 Padmanabh S. Jaini, ed., *Collected Papers on Jaina Studies*, New Delhi: Motilal Banarsidass, 2000, 3–11, 11–27; Padmanabha S. Jaini, *Gender and Salvation, op. cit.*, xvi–xx, 1–35, 52–59, 72–73, 82–92.

5 *Ācharānga Sūtra* (1.4.1; 1.1) translated by A.L. Basham, in Ainslie T. Embree, ed., *Sources of Indian Tradition, Volume 1: From the Beginning to 1800, op. cit.*, 58, 64–66.

6 Sita Anantha Raman, *Women in India: A Social and Cultural History, op. cit.*, 75–78.

7 Ainslie T. Embree, ed., *Sources of Indian Tradition, Volume 1: From the Beginning to 1800, op. cit.*, 65–66.

8 R.C. Majumdar, H.C. Raychaudhuri, and Kalikinkar Dattar, *An Advanced History of India, Part I: Ancient India, op. cit.*, 58–61.

9 Ainslie T. Embree, ed., *Sources of Indian Tradition, Volume 1: From the Beginning to 1800, op. cit.*, 100–101.

10 For a longer discussion of women in Buddhist texts and sculptures, see Sita Anantha Raman, *Women in India: A Social and Cultural History, op. cit.*, 86–97; Nancy Barnes, "Women and Buddhism in India", in Sita Arvind Sharma, ed., *Women in India: A Social and Cultural History, op. cit.*, 38–69; Nancy Auer, "The Case of the Vanishing Nuns: The Fruits of Ambivalence in Ancient Indian Buddhism", in Nancy Falk and Rita M. Gross, eds., *Unspoken Worlds: Women's Religious Lives*, Belmont, CA: Wadsworth Publishing Company, 1989, 155–156.

11 Henry Clarke Warren, *Buddhism in Translations: Passages Selected from the Buddhist Sacred Books and Translated from the Original Pāli into English, op. cit.*, 441–447. For a longer discussion of women in Buddhist texts and sculptures, see Sita Anantha Raman, *Women in India: A Social and Cultural History, op. cit.*, 86–97.

12 Susie Tharu and K. Lalitha, eds., *Women Writing in India, 600 BC to the Present, Vol.1.*, New York: Feminist Press, 1991, 65; Susan Murcott, *The First Buddhist Women: Translations and Commentary of the Therigatha*, Berkeley: Parallax Press, 1991, 115–117.

13 John M. Koller, *The Indian Way: An Introduction to the Philosophies and Religions of India*, Upper Saddle River, New Jersey: Prentice-Hall, Pearson, 2006 (1st ed., 1982), 154–160.

14 The *Aṣṭasāhasrikā Prājñāpāramitā* (22.403), translated and cited by Ainslie T. Embree, ed., *Sources of Indian Tradition, Volume 1: From the Beginning to 1800, op. cit.*, 160.

5

DHARMA SŪTRAS

I. *Dharma* and *artha*: temporal meanings (600–300 BCE)

As seen in their nomenclature, the early law codes were traditionally dichotomized as sacred texts on *dharma* (religious/ethical laws) or as texts on *artha* (material wealth/mundane affairs). This led some early scholars to highlight the ritual aspect of the *dharma* codes over their sociopolitical underpinnings. Yet the chief purpose of all *dharma* authors, even those who described ritual duties, was to define laws and royal justice in the mundane world. In late Vedic era *janapadas* with complex economies and diverse populations who assimilated and rejected some Sanskritic norms, the terms *dharma* and *artha* assumed potent political meanings.[1]

Once commensurate with a just Cosmic Order (Ṛta) in the *Rig Veda*, *dharma* (Sanskrit root '*dhr*': to support) was further elaborated upon in the later Vedic scriptures, the *Upaniṣads* (800–300 BCE). The early *Chāndogya Upaniṣad* advocated belief in the Vital Breath (*Prāna*) as Truth in the universe and urged individuals to meditate on kindly righteousness (*sāman*) as the superior virtue in daily life (*ChU* 2.1.2).[2]

The *Mahābhārata* and *Rāmāyana* describe *dharma* as the individual's sacred duties based on gender and *varna*. While women's *dharma* revolved around husband, family, and household rites, that of *brāhmans* was to conduct rituals and advise kings, that of *kṣatṛiyas* to protect subjects and serve justice, that of *vaiśyas* to enrich the kingdom, and that of *śudras* to labor for it. In the *Bhagavad Gīta*, the *Mahābhārata*'s scriptural addendum, *dharma* signified selfless actions within such duties. With slight variations, Buddhist and Jaina texts in Pali equated *dhamma* with ethical acts irrespective of one's *varna* at birth.

The terms *dharma* and *artha* also took on political meanings in the first temporal codes, the *Dharma Sūtras* (600–300 BCE), and in the *Arthaśāstra*. *Dharma* now meant the ethical laws of states, as well as the sacred duties of individuals. *Artha*, or earthly wealth, now also connoted the material resources of the state. In the *Arthaśāstra, artha* signified the administrative, military, and juridical organs of the Mauryan Empire and the material welfare of subjects. The *janapada* was now idealized as an institution supporting the ambitions of the *rājan*, if he observed righteous laws (*dharma*) and if he promoted the welfare (*artha*) of his subjects.

Composed across a millennium across regions, *dharma* and *artha* codes have different emphases, but they share some important features. Their authors were all male *brāhmans* whose chief purpose was to delineate temporal laws and procedures (*vyavahāra*) for kingdoms. This differed from contemporary sages of the *Upaniṣads*, whose goal was spiritual freedom (*mōkṣa*). Although the first *Dharma Sūtra* codes were sketchy on *vyavahāra*, this was elaborated further in the *Arthaśāstra*, which became the blueprint on royal governance and temporal law for even the orthodox code *Manu Smṛitī*. After centuries of foreign rulers and heterodox kingdoms, Manu glamorized *kṣatṛiya* kings who had *brāhman* advisors. Yet he ignored the important historical truth that although immigrant kings were not *dvījās* but *mlecchas* without caste, most of them adopted the temporal hallmarks of *kṣatṛiya* kingship. By the early Guptan era, this royal ideal was firmly entrenched in most liberal monarchs, irrespective of their origins. Thus, neither Yājňavalkya and Nārada chose to restate it, but they focused instead upon defining the rules of *vyavahāra* to ensure justice in the kingdom.

Second, all these code writers endorsed the *varna* order, though their motives were probably more political than religious belief in the cycle of *karma*. The *dharma* authors praised *kṣatṛiya* kings with *brāhman* advisors as the best guarantee of sociopolitical stability. The Hindu *Purānas*, Buddhist canon, and Jaina scripture all trace the genealogies of kings.[3] The *Purānas* describe Kauṭilya as a wily *brāhman* who masterminded the accession of the non-*dvīja* Chandragupta, while the heterodox canon draws attention to his low-caste origins and military skills superior to that of humdrum *kṣatṛiyas*. The *Arthaśāstra* was revised by later *brāhmans* who upheld *varna* as the economic framework of kingdoms, while the *Dharma Śāstra* writers reiterated its ideals on kings and women. Olivelle effectively shows that despite Manu's disdain for heterodoxy, he used the *Arthaśāstra*'s legal terms almost verbatim in the *Manu Smṛitī*.[4]

Third, in an era when rape routinely accompanied war and sexual mingling redefined gene pools, all the authors not only endorsed patrimonial kingship but male polygamy to ensure princely heirs. Kings routinely sealed political alliances with polygamous, polyglot marriages, but a king's death often resulted in a violent scramble among numerous claimants for the throne. This was resolved when the later *Dharma Sūtras* defined filial legitimacy and pared women's property and marriage rights, to set a pattern for future codes. While non-*kṣatṛiya* kings could circumvent the accident of birth, fewer women overcame gender restrictions on power.

The male writers include paternalists whose codes for liberal or humane kings gave women some rights (Āpastamba, the first Kauṭilya, Nārada), fairly benign patriarchs who had some distrust of women with power

(Yājñavalkya, Gautama, Viṣnugupta who completed Kauṭilya's code), and outright misogynists (Baudhāyana, Vasiṣtha, Manu). All these men were undoubtedly born into, and shaped by a patriarchal society, but as the first and last codes were more humane to women, misogyny appears to thrive during political instability.

II. *Dharma Sūtras*: kings, women, and *varna*

Amid social and sectarian challenges, erudite *brāhmans* sought to preserve Vedic traditions in secondary scriptures (*Kalpa Sūtras*) derived from the *Vedas* for *dvīja* males. The corpus comprised the *Śrauta Śūtras* on public rites; the *Gṛihya Sutras* on *dvīja* household rites (*ācāra*), sacred duties (*dharma*), and life stages (*āśrama*), with women as secondary participants; and the *Dharma Sūtras*. The *Dharma Sūtras* codified patriarchal customs into righteous temporal laws (*dharma*).[5] The authors listed sins and penances supervised ritually by *brāhmans* and crimes adjudicated by kings whose *rāja dharma* required them to oversee justice. The term *dharma* now clearly meant the righteous laws of states, as well as the moral duties of individuals.

The four main *Dharma Sūtras* are attributed to Āpastamba (ca. 550 BCE), Gautama, Baudhāyana, and Vasiṣṭha (ca. 300 BCE). Āpastamba and Baudhāyana also authored a *Śrauta* and a *Gṛhya Sūtra*, which suggests that they were contemporaries, but as Baudhāyana quoted Gautama (*BDS* 1.2.7), this chronology is unclear. Olivelle suggests that as Gautama and Vasiṣṭha bore the names of ancient sages, eponymous authors possibly added to the original texts.[6]

Other historical facts are clearer. Between Āpastamba and Vasiṣṭha, the royal state had grown significantly more powerful, and women had been legally subordinated. The territorial boundaries of *janapadas* extended from the northwest to the east, from the Himalayan foothills to the Vindhyas. Amid state territorial contests, the *Dharma Sūtra* authors tried to safeguard succession by defining which sons had the legitimate right to paternal property and the throne. This led them to deny women the right to inherit both landed property and crown domains. Second, after the Persian emperors Cyrus and his grandson Darius (550–486 BCE) conquered regions from Afghanistan to the Indus Valley, there began the first influx of westerners into the subcontinent. This trickle became a torrent after Alexander's brief invasion (326 BCE) and through the open trade policies of the Mauryans (324–184 BCE), Śakas (80 BCE), Kuśānas (100 BCE–100 ACE), Śātavāhanas (ca. 50 BCE–200 ACE), and Guptans (275–525 ACE). Third, Gautama's *Dharma Sūtra* lists diverse groups of mixed ethnicity/*varna*. As he and Baudhāyana cautioned *dvījas* against sexual intermingling with *śudras* and foreigners, their laws were more 'puritanical' on women's marriage.

Interestingly, although Vasiṣṭha frowned on female rights to paternal property, he was lenient on levirate marriage for widows. Gautama, Baudhāyana, and Vasiṣṭha endorsed male polygamy, which reduced women to pawns in matrimonial treaties between kings.

The louder the voices praising female chastity and caste exclusion in Sanskritic society, these remained ideals, never the reality, as gene pools changed continuously in India's long history. Women did have sex across caste and community ranks; the *dharma* codes allowed polygamous, elite caste men to marry women from other castes; foreign soldiers did rape local women; foreign visitors did have sex with local women; immigrant kings did marry Indic princesses as an essential clause of peace treaties with local kings. Differences in the codes reflect these historical contexts, as well as the authors' individual styles.

A. Patrimonial kingship

The *Dharma Sūtra* codes were composed for a society and state dominated by Sanskritic norms of patriarchy and *varna*, and the authors carefully described the rules for *dvījas* on household rites and life stages. Yet, unlike their contemporary seers of the *Upaniṣads*, their primary purpose was temporal, rather than spiritual. They paid homage to the king's military authority (*kṣatra*) by defining his royal duties (*rājā dharma*) to defend, govern, tax, and serve justice, as prescribed in the *Brāhmanas*. Reflecting the growth of the state between Āpastamba and Vasiṣṭha, the codes became more elaborate on the ideals of kingship, *vyavahāra*, and legal witnesses. While Āpastamba briefly touched on these topics, Vasiṣṭha highlighted the role of *brāhman* advisors to the royal state. Yet even Vasiṣṭha was sketchy on royal governance when compared to Kauṭilya's *Arthaśāstra* on the Mauryan Empire.

All the authors were convinced that patrimonial *kṣatṛiya* kings with *brāhman* advisors guaranteed political stability. They thus legally authorized *kṣatṛiya* kings to wage war, construct forts, maintain internal order, mete out justice, and raise taxes at their convenience. This prerogative gave kingdoms a distinct advantage over oligarchies, where key decisions were debated and undertaken by the assembly. Moreover, when *janapadas* extended their domains, they absorbed indigenous, semi-autonomous inhabitants as agricultural and menial laborers. The codes legally transformed the *varna* order into a less flexible economic hierarchy, in which some *śudras* and many *chandālas* formed the lowest ranks of workers.[7] Last, as Vedic rites and *varna* were being rejected by heterodox sects popular among marginalized groups, the authors ordered *dvījās* to perform orthodox rites. While all the *Dharma Sūtra* authors advised *kṣatṛiya* kings to lodge *brāhmans* at court (*ĀDS* 2.25.8–9; *GDS* 10.7–8; *BDS* 1.18.2–7), Vasiṣṭha declared that *brāhman* scholars must make up the majority in the royal assembly.

Āpastamba declared that the king owned all public roads and that wayfarers must give way, except for the *brāhman* who owned his stretch of the road at that time (*ADS* 2.11.5). Baudhāyana (*BDS* 1.18.16), Gautama (*GDS* 10.36–38), and Vasiṣṭha (*VDS* 16.19) declared that the king was heir to all lost and unclaimed property, except that belonging to a *brāhman*. This ruling gave the king latent rights over all property in his domain, except during the lifetime of the male owner or of his male heirs.

B. Paternal property: who inherits?

For the *Dharma Sūtra* authors, the question of which son inherited paternal property/lands was related to which legitimate son inherited the throne and its domains. Their laws show that they considered lineage of primary importance, followed by the rights of the king. The first *Dharma Sūtra* author, Āpastamba, refuted the claim of primogeniture, and he gave all sons equal rights to paternal property. In the absence of sons, property was inherited by ancestral male relatives, teachers, students, and, in their absence, a daughter or the king (*ADS* 2.14.1–5).

As a southerner from Andhra, Āpastamba was familiar with Dravidian customs, including matriliny. He gave importance to the 'married pair' (*ĀDS* 2.1.7–10) who performed Vedic rites together for the prosperity of the family. Āpastamba decreed that such wealth was owned jointly by the couple and that the wife could use it freely in her husband's absence (*ADS* 2.14.16–20). This line suggested that the widow had inheritance rights over such wealth. At the end of his treatise, he reiterated that: 'The husband and wife have joint control over their property' and that those who tended it had some rights to benefit from it (*ADS* 2.29.3–4). He also decreed that if a man died without male family members to inherit his property, his wealth could be taken by his teacher and his family, or his student, or his daughter, or the king.[8] Gautama stipulated that a man without sons could appoint his daughter as his son (*GDS* 28.18–20). If he did not have a daughter, upon his death, his property would be given to his patrilineal male relations or his matrilineal male relations and then only by his widow if she 'procured a son' (*GDS* 28.21–23) to manage the property. Gautama advised wives to speak with caution and to bow to the husband on matters of law. A widow without sons had to seek the elders' approval to contract a levirate remarriage with her husband's brother or his male ancestral relative. Through this relationship, she could conceive up to two sons who could inherit her deceased husband's property (*GDS* 18.1–4).

Baudhāyana and Vasiṣṭha entirely denied the widow's right to inherit or even to act as a caretaker for her minor son. They cited the *Taittirīya Samhita*'s dictum that a woman must be protected by the father, husband, and the son (*BDS* 2.3. 15–16, 43–46; *VDS* 5.1–3). These laws validated patrimonial kingship, and they prevented dowager queens from ascending the throne. Chawla shows that these codes influenced even colonial legalists, who cited Baudhāyana to deny widows spousal property.

C. *Women's property (*Strīdhana*)*

As a *brāhman* scholar of the Yajur Veda, Āpastamba adhered to Indo-Āryan practices on paternal and female property (*strīdhana*). In the later Vedic era, paternal property was largely equated with land and female property with moveable assets. He briefly instructed a man to 'adorn his daughter with jewelry to the best of his ability' (*ADS* 2.11.17) for her financial security. A few verses later, he emphasized women's right to control jewelry and money gifted by relatives and that, as *strīdhana* was maternal property, it was bequeathed by women to their daughters in perpetuity (*ADS* 2.14.9). Yet as a southerner familiar with Dravidian matrilineal customs, Āpastamba also stipulated that the 'married pair' jointly owned property. He also conceded that women and *śudras* had skills unknown to *dvīja* men, and this knowledge formed a part of the *Atharva Veda* (*ĀDS* 2.29.11–12). He reaffirmed this in a final line, which states that certain types of knowledge lay outside the *Vedas*: 'According to some, one should learn the remaining laws from women and people of all classes' (2.29.15).[9]

On *strīdhana*, Baudhāyana stated tersely that: 'Daughters should take their mother's jewelry and anything else customarily given to her' (*BDS* 2.3.43). Gautama's decree was the most elaborately phrased: 'The wife's property goes to her daughters who are unmarried or indigent. A sister's dowry goes to her uterine brothers after her mother dies, or according to some, even before' (*GDS* 28.24–26). Vaśiṣṭha briefly dismissed female property in this single line: 'The daughters should take their mother's wedding gifts' (*VDS* 17.46). These authors reduced *strīdhana* just to moveable assets, but they also declared that it lay outside male control, as its main purpose was to provide financial security to women. This apparent generosity simply reinforced gender distinctions by warning women not to aspire for paternal lands or dynastic succession. These authors uniformly honored chaste mothers, wives, and sisters, but they did not regard women as viable contenders to the throne.

D. *Women, sexuality, and marriage*

The royal state had dignified chief queens as *ratnins* as embodiments of the earth goddess Aditi, as agriculture and dairy farming enriched its economy. Despite such idealization of elite women, royal polygamy curtailed the scope of women's actual authority. While polygamy assured the *rājan* of several male heirs, this custom also resulted in a raucous scramble for the throne upon his death. The authors debated over filial legitimacy and who was a legitimate male heir to paternal property, as well as which son could perform funeral rites for his parents.

Āpastamba upheld monogamy for the husband whose wife had borne his children, but the three later writers endorsed male polygamy. All the authors exalted women's chastity before and after marriage, but Āpastamba censured those who encouraged a widow to remarry. He declared that the deceased husband would have seen later suitors for his widow as strange 'outsiders'. Āpastamba did not endorse the custom of levirate remarriage, in which a widow was married to the brother of her deceased husband, and he described this relationship as an unbearable 'hell' (*narak*) to the couple (*ADS* 27.2–7). Gautama allowed levirate remarriage to enable a widow to bear a son as an heir and to perform her rites. She could also adopt a male blood relative of her deceased husband as a son to manage her husband's property (*GDS* 18.4–7). However, a remarried widow's sons could not inherit the property of her deceased first husband.

Their laws were clearly intended to prevent a wife's illegitimate sons or sons from a later husband from inheriting the paternal property of her deceased husband. There are pointed references to female sexual compulsions and to mixed-caste groups right after a description of kingship (*ADS* 2.13.6; *BDS* 2.3.34–35; *GDS* 4.16–28; *VDS* 17.9). They indicate the authors' concern that illegitimate or non-*dvīja* sons would seize the throne. As the political stakes were potent, contemporary kings probably appealed to scholarly *brāhmans* to compose laws to validate male succession, define filial legitimacy, and restrict women's inheritance and marriage rights. The dominant principle of legitimate filial rights to paternal lands was extended to the rights of legitimate princes to the throne and its domains. The authors cited the *Vedas* for scriptural validation. This appears in Āpastamba's decree:

> (*ADS* 2.13.5, 7): A son belongs to the man who fathers him – so says a *Brāhmana*. . . . Diligently guard this progeny of yours, lest strangers sow their seeds in your field.

This was echoed by Baudhāyana (*BDS* 2.3.35) and Vasiṣṭha (*VDS* 15.9). The question of who was a legitimate male heir and paternal rights loomed large in the authors' minds. Gautama argued in favor of a biological father's primary rights to a child born out of wedlock, but he also gave the husband some rights if he raised the child (*GDS* 18.9–14). Gautama, Baudhāyana, and Vasiṣṭha denounced sexual relations between *dvīja* women and *śudra*, *chāndāla*, and tribal men. Gautama declared unequivocally that if a *brāhman* woman had sex with lower-caste men, the king should have dogs devour her, kill her lover, and declare their child a *chāndāla* (*GDS* 18.20–21; 21.9; 23.14–15; 4.23.14). Baudhāyana was so obsessed with the sexual purity of *brāhman* men that he forbade cohabitation with *chāndāla* or Nishada women, incest, and/or adultery with the wife of a *guru* (*BDS* 2.4–5). He sternly forbade adultery for all castes, but he allowed *dvīja* men to sleep with women performers, even those with a minstrel husband (*BDS* 2.4.1–5).

Surprisingly, Vasiṣṭha's punishment for murdering *brāhmans* was gruesome. The killer had to light a fire into which he was forced to ritualistically offer his 'hair, skin, blood, flesh, sinews, bones' until death overtook him (*VDA* 20.25–26). In a similar incendiary manner, *śudra* and *vaiśya* men were burnt alive for having sex with a *brāhman* woman, whose penalty was to be shaved and paraded naked on a donkey. All wives ranked lower than husbands, but the penalty for killing a *brāhman* woman, especially to one who had bathed after her menstrual period (*ātreyī*), was the same penalty given to the killer of a *kṣatṛiya* or a *vaiśya* ('*brāhmanim chātreyīm hatvā savanagato cha rājanya vaiśyo; VDS* 20.34). The penalty for killing a *kṣatṛiya* woman was equal to that given to a killer of a *vaiśya* man, and so forth (*VDS* 20.35–36).

Since the birth of a legitimate son was almost the primary reason for marriage, the authors of the *Dharma Sūtras* considered abortion as deadly a sin as killing a *brāhman*, using the same term (*bruṇahan*) for both crimes. After a discussion between students Kaṇva, Kautsa, and Vārṣyāyaṇi on the rules of eating to prevent being outcast, Āpastamba quoted 'a Purāna' to decree certain acts that rendered a person heinously impure (*aśuchi*). These included eating with one who aborts a foetus ('An abortionist rubs his sin on the man who eats his food', *ADS* 1.21.12–19), a crime equal to killing a *brāhman* (*ADS* 1.24.6–9). Baudhāyana equated the sin of aborting a fetus with that the sin of a father who fails to get his daughter married three years after her puberty (*BDS* 4.1.12). Gautama decreed that *dvījas* lost caste by eating food from a *śudra* except in desperate times, and by eating food that was 'looked at by an abortionist' (*GDS* 17.5,11). Vasiṣṭha sternly condemned the abortionist as a '*brāhman* killer' (*bruṇahan)* since the foetus had grown from male semen, it could develop into a male *brāhman* embryo (*VDS* 20.23–24).[10]

III. *Dharma Sūtras*

A. *Āpastamba's* Dharma Sūtra

Āpastamba described royal duties succinctly, and only at the end of his code. He declared the importance of a safe royal residence and of a defensive fort from which soldiers could maintain internal order by apprehending drunks and rapists (*ADS* 2.25.2–7, 14–15, 2.26.4–8). Āpastamba decreed the king had the right to tax all state revenues. He exempted *brāhmans* and the infirm from taxes, as also *śudras* who could not own land (*ADS*

2.26.9–15). He reminded the king that, as *rāja dharma* included justice, he had to rehabilitate raped women and to punish rapists, adulterers, and men who allowed female relations to remarry (*ADS* 2.26–2.27.1–13). Āpastamba briefly described *vyavahāra* and witnesses (*ADS* 2.27–29), but he was expansive on sexual and caste sins and ritual penances supervised by *brāhmans* (*ADS* 1.15–29).

Āpastamba was also the only *Dharma Sūtra* author to disapprove of male polygamy. He declared that, 'So long as his wife participates in religious rites and bears children, a man may not take another wife' (*ADS* 2.11.12). However, if a wife were barren, the husband could remarry in order to have progeny and for a wife to share his sacred rites. Obviously, once the wife was set aside, she lost her ritual *adhikāra*. Āpastamba listed six types of marriage, the finest being the sanctified (*brāhma*) ritual. In this marriage, the bride's father first enquired about the groom, then entrusted his daughter to him as the bearer of future children, as his companion and helper when performing holy rites. In the seer's (*ārṣa/ṛiṣī*) wedding, the groom paid a bride price to the father-in-law; in the divine (*daiva*) wedding, a father gave away his daughter in rites by a priest; in the *gandharva* marriage, a loving couple eloped; in a demonaic (*aśura*) wedding, the groom paid the bride price as best he could; and in the 'fiendish' (*rākṣasa*) marriage, a group of men raped the woman (*ADS* 2.11.17–20, 2.1–2). In keeping with Vedic mores, Āpastamba lauded chastity in both sexes, but he also rejected levirate widow remarriage (*niyoga*) as conducive to depravity. The penalty was exile for a *dvīja* who slept with a *śudra* woman but castration and forfeit of property if he slept with a *dvīja* woman. The harshest punishment was execution, reserved for a *śudra* who slept with a *dvīja* woman (*ĀDS* 2.26.18–24; 2.27.1–13).

Āpastamba's laws and advice to monarchs on justice and clemency applied primarily to Sanskritic society, but his code does not reflect his fear that illegitimate sons would ascend the throne. He advised kings to be merciful to a defeated enemy, as the noble ones (Ārya) did not mistreat soldiers after they had discarded weapons and pleaded for mercy by folding their hands. He also stated that it was against the king's sacred *dharma* to beat and enslave criminals. Instead, he advised that the king instruct the guilty about their duties or *dharmas*, to perform ritual penances, and to thus atone for sins (*ADS* 2.10.10–11).

B. Baudhāyana's Dharma Sūtra

The next three *Dharma Sūtras* contain more details on royal governance and *vyavahāra*. At the same time, Baudhāyana's lengthy guidelines on *dvīja* rituals for men and his monastic anathema to female sexuality suggest that his code can be dated after Āpastamba's text. Baudhāyana begins the first of four books by declaring the Vedic origins of *dharma* as law and the importance of ten *brāhman* scholars in the legal assembly (*BDS* 1.1.1–16) in the kingdom. After describing the geographical extent of lands inhabited by Āryas, Baudhāyana outlined the life stages (*āśrama*) of *dvījas*, with emphasis on the ritual duties of students and householders, *varna* occupations (*BDS* 1.10.20–34), ancestry, and male inheritance rights (*BDS* 1.11.1–31). After a discussion on *varna* occupations and various mixed castes (*BDS* 1.16–17), Baudhāyana's first book defined the king's duties to tax and defend (*BDS* 1.18.1–16). Like Āpastamba, he decreed that a defensive fort was imperative, as its soldiers waged war and maintained internal order. On taxes, he was more precise than Āpastamba, as he decreed that the king had a right to one-sixth of all revenues. The first book also discussed *vyavahāra*, qualifications for legal witnesses (*BDS* 1.18.17–20; 1.19), and the laws on marriage and inheritance (*BDS* 1.20–21). The next chapter describes penances for murder, theft, sex between the *varnas*, legitimate sons, heirs to paternal property, female property, and adulterous women (*BD* 2.1–4).

Baudhāyana, Gautama, and Vaśiṣṭa frankly distrusted women's sexual and political influence, but their views on *śudras* were more complex. While acknowledging the importance of *śudra* workers for the kingdom, they imposed severe penalties for performing jobs outside one's *varna* occupation. This stricture was probably intended to prevent the eventuality of non-*brāhman* priests and kings. Although they frowned on sex between *dvījas* and *śudras*, as this was fairly common, they recorded diverse groups of mixed ancestry.

Baudhāyana's long treatise reaffirms Vedic traditions, caste occupations, paternal traditions, death and birth rituals, and mixed-caste groups. He then described the king's duties but then returned to rules on marriage and inter-caste sex for the four *varnas* (*BDS* 1.20–21). Baudhāyana listed eight styles of marriage, out of which only four were accepted for *brāhmans,* that is, the *brāhma, prajāpatya* when a girl was adorned and given to the groom, the *ārṣa/ṛiṣī*, and the *daiva* or divine. The other four styles of union were acceptable for the other *varnas,* that is, the demoniac or *rākṣasa*, elopement or *gāndharva*, fiendish or *aśura*, and ghoulish or *paiśācha* (*BDS* 1.20.1–9). The author was severe in his penalties for murder and theft, but also for promiscuity, masturbation, sex with elders, and incest (*BDS* 2.1.13–15; 2.4.11–15), as these could result in progeny. He thus defined the inheritance and ritual rights, or the lack thereof, of legitimate, adopted, and purchased sons (*BDS* 2.3.3–42). Harsher to women than Āpastamba, he declared tersely: 'Daughters should take their mother's jewelry and anything else customarily given to her. It is not possible for women to act independently'. Citing the *Taittiriya Samhita*'s aphorism that women must be protected by the father, husband, or son, he concluded: 'Women are considered to be devoid of strength to inherit property' (*BDS* 2.3.43–46). Yet Baudhāyana decreed milder penances for adulterous women than for men, and he rejected corporal punishment on the principle that menstruation cleansed women of sins (*BDS* 2.4.4–5). Like Āpastamba, he allowed men to divorce a barren wife (*BDS* 2.2.6), but unlike Āpastamba, Baudhāyana recommended levirate remarriage (*niyōga*) for childless widows (2.4.7–10). If his sternest words for men were on their adultery, his sternest words for women were on their apparent inability to manage property. His section on filial rights suggests that he feared female sexuality less than he dreaded a queen upon the throne.

C. *Gautama's* Dharma Sūtra

Gautama also began by defining the duties of *dvījas* as students and householders, with rules on chastity, marriage, and sons. He frequently alluded to diverse mixed-caste groups, presumably as sons of dual ancestry could claim a share of paternal property and even the throne (*GDS* 4–5). Gautama was more expansive on royal governance than Āpastamba or Baudhāyana, as he examined kingship in four sections, first briefly (*GDS* 8.1) stating the importance of *brāhman* scholars of the law and *kṣatṛiya* kings and soldiers. Returning to this same topic, he later elaborated on the important roles in the state of *vaiṣyā* farmers, pastoralists, merchants, and *śudra* workers and artisans (*GDS* 10). Gautama described the king's duty to protect, wage war, collect booty, and levy a one-sixth tax on revenues (*GDS* 10.7–48). The next three chapters on royal governance exalt the king as 'one who rules above all except *brāhmans* whose advice enforced the laws, and they authorize the king to dispense justice with *brāhmans* who understood legal treatises and scriptures. Gautama defined some laws; *vyavahāra*; requirements for legal witnesses; and punishments for murder, assault, debt, theft, and property damage. His philosophical arguments in favor of strong punishments for the last three crimes indicate that the state and its subjects were fairly affluent (*GDS* 11–13).

Like Āpastamba and Baudhāyana, he began his treatise by delineating the rules on sexuality, women's marriage, and property for *dvījas*. Listing eight types of *dvīja* marriages (*GDS* 4.4–7), Gautama described the bride as 'adorned with jewelry' (*alankṛte*) in the noble (*brāhma*) and divine (*daiva*) marriages. That in which the couple vowed to fulfill all *dharmas* together was the *prajāpatya*, while in the marriage of sages (*ārṣa*), the groom gave cows and bulls to the bride's father.[11] Such gifts made the new bride an asset to her husband's family. Less respectable were *gāndharva* elopement, the *rākṣasa* union when the groom paid the bride's parents, the *aśura* when a woman was forcibly abducted, and the *paiśācha* rape of an unconscious woman.

Gautama praised the roles of *brāhman* and *kṣatṛiya* in the kingdom, with a shorter discussion on *vaiśya* and *śudra* contributions (*GDS* 6.1–25, 7–8,

10.2–11.32). He listed mixed caste/ethnic groups, such as *chāndalās* and Yāvanās (Graeco-Persians), indicating that *dvījas* had sexual contact with lower castes and with westerners. Yet he decreed that sex with a *śudra* woman made one outcaste, listing this with more horrific crimes like incest, murdering a *brāhman*, theft, drinking liquor, fetal abortion, and performing rites for *śudras* (*GDS* 20–21). A section on women's property and marriage describes the care of children born out of an adulterous relationship and the widow's right to a levirate marriage (*GDS* 18).

D. *Vasiṣṭha's* Dharma Sūtra

Vasiṣṭha's *Dharma Sūtra* is the most expansive on kingship and *vyavahāra*. His references to written documents in trials (*VDS* 16. 10, 14–15) indicate that this is the last of the four extant *Dharma Sūtras*.[12] He began by stating the laws on monogamy and polygamy (*VDS* 1.24–38). He offered a paean to *brāhmans*, whom he exempted from tax, and another to *kṣatṛiya* kings who levied taxes (*VDS* 1.39–46), as the king was guaranteed the right to collect one-sixth of all revenues (*VDS* 2.39–45). This is followed by a discourse on caste professions, ethics for *dvījas* and women, and sins against *varna* (*VDS* 2–4). Vasiṣṭha not only declared that kings ruled with *brāhman* advisors, but he stipulated that seven out of ten men in the royal assembly had to be *brāhman* scholars of the *Vedas*, secondary scriptures, and laws (*VDS* 3.20). A few chapters later, he resumed the subject of kingship and *vyavahāra* by elaborating on property disputes and legal witnesses (16.1–37). He emphasized that truth was essential to a trial, as it upheld the honor of the ancestors and safeguarded the witness from becoming outcaste. Yet Vasiṣṭha also allowed men to lie on some occasions, including during marriage, in a sexual encounter, when life and property were at stake, or when helping a *brāhman* (*VDS* 3.20). He reaffirmed the laws on male inheritance, filial legitimacy, and women's marriage and remarriage (*VDS* 17). With a short, but significant, interlude on mixed caste groups (*VDS* 18), he gave a final paean to the king as protector and owner of all lands with the sole right to collect tolls (*VDS* 19.1–2, 17–48). He also elucidated the laws on taxation, dynastic succession, crimes, and religious sins (*VDS* 19–20).

His early chapters praise the learned *brāhman*, offer a guideline for all *dvījas*, and generally admonish *śudras*. He praised the *brāhman* whose advice brought prosperity to the kingdom. He also emphasized the importance of good conduct and the study of the *Vedas* to the *brāhman*, who was otherwise akin to a *śudra* (*VDS* 3.1–2). Vasiṣṭha exalted the duties of *dvījas* as students, householders, and hermits (*VDS* 7–14) and their diverse occupations (*VDS* 2.5–4). He also prohibited to *brāhmans* and *kṣatṛiyas* jobs such as usury and the sale of meat, milk, and sesame. Yet Vasiṣṭha allowed *brāhmans* to till the field with the plow, work that he compared to the male sexual act. This may partly explain why the iron plow became a male instrument in this era. He decreed that *śudras* were ritually impure at all times (*VDS* 6) and that the *brāhman* who taught the *Vedas* to a *śudra* became an outcaste. However, after specific ritual penances, the *brāhman* could be readmitted into his caste (*VDS* 15).

Vasiṣṭha's biases against *śudras* and women appear early in his treatise and through the major part of his code. In his first chapters, he described sins causing ostracism for a *dvīja*. The most heinous crimes were having sex with an elder's wife, imbibing liquor, murdering a *brāhman*, stealing gold from a *brāhman*, while a *brāhman* or other *dvīja* would be outcaste for marrying a *chandāla* or for teaching the *Vedas* to a *chandāla* (*VDS* 1.19–23). In this chapter, he declared the laws on marriage and unequivocally endorsed male polygamy (*VDS* 1). He sanctioned three wives to *brāhmans*, two for *kṣatṛiyas*, and one each for *vaiśyas* and *śudras*. Like Baudhāyana, Vasiṣṭha denounced female infidelity, and he was especially incensed since the groom usually paid a bride's price of a cow or bull to her father (*VDS* 1.24–38). In a later chapter, Vasiṣṭha suggested that women were made to please men:

> (*VDS* 6.4): Like a pretty wife to her husband who is blind, what happiness can all the *Vedas* together with all the supplements and sacrifices bring to a Brahmin who is bereft of good conduct?[13]

The text appears to have been the work of more than one author. This is evident in the discussion of menstruation. At first, Vasiṣṭha tersely described women as ritually impure during their monthly flow of blood (*VDS* 5), but in the end of his treatise, he passionately declared that menstruation cleansed women of all sins, including infidelity (*VDS* 28). The earlier author was as sexually puritanical as Baudhāyana, while the later author was more permissive. Like Baudhāyana, Vasiṣṭha forbade women control over their sons, paternal lands, and crown domains (*VDS* 5). Thus, when describing the process by which a man could adopt a son as his heir, Vasiṣṭha categorically excluded the wife from helping to make this decision (*VDS* 15.5). To prove that women were inept and weak, he also cited the misogynist *Vedic* verse (*VDS* 5.3):

> (*VDS* 5.3): The father guards a girl in childhood, the husband guards her in her youth, and the son takes care of her in her old age, as women are not independent.[14]

The authors of the three later *Dharma Sūtras* regarded women as financially inept. Thus, in a single line, Vasiṣṭha restricted female property to moveable assets (*VDS* 17.46), a view vehemently endorsed by Manu (*MS* 5.148) and that was echoed in the later classical centuries by Yājñyavalkya (*YS* 1. 85), but not by Nārada. The royal state grew in strength and territories between the codes of Vasiṣṭha and Kauṭilya, and dynasties vied over territorial control. As kings were the legal owners of all realm lands, the distinctions between private and royal domains became blurred. The solemn implications for women's inheritance rights are evident in Vasiṣṭha's seventeenth chapter. In these verses (*VDS* 17.4–5), he cited a *Rig Vedic* prayer to the god Agni (*RV* 5.4.10), asking for fame and progeny (*prajā*) who made men immortal (Skt: '*jātavedo yaśo asmāsu dhehi prajābhir aghne amṛtatvam aśyām*'). As patriarchy heightened in the late Vedic era, Vasiṣṭha defined the rules on filial legitimacy and on missing husbands. He denied widows a share of spousal property but sanctioned levirate marriage so that widows would have a son to manage this estate. His decree on pre-puberty marriage for girls ensured progeny for *dvījas*, but it also prevented girls from studying the *Vedas*, since pre-menstrual marriages pulled girls from school into domesticity and early sexual life, which led to more offspring, which in turn enlarged the clan. In the late Vedic climate of heightened patriarchy, Vasiṣṭha chose to translate this as a request only for sons:

> (*VDS* 17.4–5): Through a son one gains the worlds; through a grandson
> one attains eternal life; and through the son's grandson one gains the crest
> of the sun.[15]

Vasiṣṭha decreed that six acceptable forms of marriages, the first four unions, that is, the *brahma, daiva, ārṣa,* and *gandharva* recognized by earlier writers. Yet, unlike his predecessors, he accepted two others, to which he gave dignified names. The *asura* abduction of a woman was now termed a *kṣatṛiya* union, as this *varna* was respected for being forceful, and the *rākṣasa* union in which a groom paid the bride's family was termed the *mānuṣya* (*VDS* 1.28–38). These terms indicate changing social mores, as *kṣatṛiyas* were forgiven for carrying off women, and bought brides was a custom now seen as acceptable in the climate of growing prosperity.

This code indicates the author's contempt for women and all castes below *brāhmans*. He thus decreed that a *śudra, vaiśya,* or *kṣatṛiya* be burned alive for sexual intercourse with a *brāhman* woman, who was to be punished by being paraded naked on a donkey (*VDS* 21.1–4). Yet, in the final chapter (*VDS* 28), an eponymous Vasiṣṭha did a moral somersault with a kinder approach. Five verses glorify women as primordially so pure that they were first gifted to the gods before marriage to an earthly husband and state that women could be outcaste only for killing their husband or a *brāhman* or for aborting a fetus (*VDS* 28.7). He forbade a husband to abandon an unfaithful wife:

> (*VDS* 28.1–5): 1) Women cannot be corrupted by lovers, nor a pure *brāhmans* by ritual fire, nor water by urine or faeces. 2) Whether she strayed on her own to seek pleasure, or if she was sent away, whether raped violently, or taken by robbers, a wife who has been unchaste must not be abandoned. 3) No law allows a wife to be abandoned; wait for her to menstruate, she will be cleansed by her monthly flow. 4) Women have their own means for cleansing, no harm will come to them, as month after month they are cleansed of sins and protected. 5) Women are first enjoyed by the gods Soma and Gandharva, before they go to men; this prevents their corruption, that is the law.[16]

Notes

1 Patrick Olivelle proposes that the term *dharma* was most closely associated with rituals of kingship. See P. Olivelle, "The Power of Words: The Ascetic Appropriation and Semantic Evolution of *dharma*", in P. Olivelle, ed., *Language, Texts and Society: Explorations in Ancient Indian Culture and Religion, op. cit.*, 121–135, vide, 131–132; P. Olivelle, ed., *Dharma: Studies in Its Dharma – Studies in its Semantic, Cultural and Religious History*, New Delhi: Motilal Banarsidass Publishers, 2010.

2 The Sanskrit verse in the *Chāndogya Upaniṣad* 2.1.2 states: '*Tadutā pyāhuh sāmnainumupāgāditi sādhunaimupāgātithyeva tadāhura sāmnaina mupāgātitya sādhunai nupāgādityaiva tadāhu.*' See Swami Swahananda, ed., *Chāndogya Upaniṣad, op. cit.*, p. 97.

3 R. Thapar, *Aśoka and the Decline of the Mauryas, op. cit.*, 13–18, 25–26, 182–187. She cites three sets of sectarian sources: 1) the Buddhist *Mahāvamśa* and *Dīpavamśa*; 2) the Hindu *Vāyu*, *Brahmānda*, *Matsya*, and *Viṣnu Purānas*; 3) the Jaina *Pariśiṣṭaparvan* of sage Hemachandra.

4 See Patrick Olivelle, "Manu and the 'Arthaśāstra': A Study in Śāstric Intertextuality", in *Journal of Indian Philosophy, op. cit.*, 281–291.

5 A pathbreaking study is by Patrick Olivelle, trans., ed., *Dharmasūtras: The Law Codes of Āpastamba, Gautama, Baudhāyana, and Vasiṣṭha, op. cit.* Also see Robert Lingat, *The Classical Law of India,* translated from the French by J. Duncan Derrett, Berkeley: University of California, 1973.

6 On relative dates and other issues, see P. Olivelle, trans., ed., *Dharmasūtras: The Law Codes of Āpastamba, Gautama, Baudhāyana, and Vasiṣṭha, op. cit.*, xxi–xxxiv; Robert Lingat, *The Classical Law of India, op. cit.*, 21–24, 60–62, 74. Āpastamba and Baudhāyana belonged to the *Taittirīya* school of the Black *Yajur Veda*. Lingat dates Baudhāyana earlier than Āpastamba. Olivelle dates Āpastamba's code earlier, as he did not list the mixed *varna* groups, as did the other *Dharma Sūtra* authors. Olivelle (p. xxvii) also believes that Āpastamba and possibly Baudhāyana came from Andhra's region between the Godavari and Krishna rivers. He deduces this from Āpastamba's reference to the practices of northerners (*udīcya*): 'to pour water taken from the water pot into the hands of seated Brahmins' (*AS* 2.17.17).

7 P. Olivelle, trans., ed., *Dharmasūtras: The Law Codes of Āpastamba, Gautama, Baudhāyana, and Vasiṣṭha, ibid.*, 68–72, 96–101, 159–163, 290–302. Also see P. Olivelle, "Explorations in the Early History of Dharmaśāstra", in P. Olivelle, ed., *Language, Texts and Society: Explorations in Ancient Indian Culture and Religion, op. cit.*, 174–175.

8 *Āpastamba Dharma Sūtra*, 2.14.3–5 states: 'In the absence of male ancestral family, the teacher, teacher's family, or his student, then the daughter, or the king can take the inheritance' (*'tad bhāv āchāryārbhāve antevāsī hatvā tadaryeṣu dharma kutyeṣu vōpō jyet; duhita vā; sarva bhāve rājā dāyam harate'*). For Sanskrit texts, see: http://hinduonline.co/DigitalLibrary, subheading Sutra, then Dharma Sutra, *op. cit.* Also see P. Olivelle, trans., ed., *Dharmasūtras: The Law Codes of Āpastamba, Gautama, Baudhāyana, and Vasiṣṭha, op. cit.*, 57.

9 *Āpastamba Dharma Sūtra*, 2.29.11–12 states: *'Sāniṣṭaya vidyā stṛī śūdreṣucha śrāthar varnasya vedasya śeṣa ityupādhiśanti'* ('In conclusion, the knowledge amongst women and *śudras* are a lesser part of the *Vedas*'). The final line 2.29.15 states: *'Strībhya sarva varnebhyascha dharmśeṣān pratīyādityeka ityeke'* ('It is said that one can learn the laws known to women and the other castes'). *op. cit.*, 72–73.

10 P. Olivelle, trans., ed., *Dharmasutras, vide., ADS*, 30–34, 363; *GDS* 108, 114; *BDS* 228–229; *VDS* 304. Vasiṣṭha equated abortion with the murder of a *brāhman* (*bruhanan*) as the foetus comes from male semen, it could develop into a male *brāhman*. This appears in his verse *VDS* 22: *'Bruhanan vaĵñyāmo brāhmanam hatvā bhavatyavijñyātam cha garbham'*; *VDS* 20.23: *'Avijñyātā hi garbhah pumāmso bhavanti tasmāt pumskṛityā juhvatīti'* (An abortionist is like the killer of a *brāhman* as the foetus born from male semen could be male).

11 The last three types of marriage were 1) elopement (*gāndharva*); 2) when the groom bribed the girl's father with money (*aṣura*); 3) rape (*rākśasa*).

12 For literary references to Vasiṣṭha's code, see P. Olivelle's introduction, in *Dharma Sūtras: The Law Codes of Ancient India*, New York: Oxford University Press, 1999, xxv–xxxiv.

13 P. Olivelle's translation, *vide., Dharmasutras, op. cit.*, 265.

14 *Vasiṣṭha Dharma Sūtra* states: *VDS* 5.1: 'A woman cannot act independently, as she is under the authority of a man' (*asvtantra stṛī puruṣapradhānā*); (5.2): 'A woman who is neither a girl running naked nor in her menstrual period, it is stated is ambrosia' (*anagni kānudakyā vāmṛtamiti viĵnyāte*; (5.3): 'Now they also quote (*athāpyudā haranti*): "Her father takes care of her in her childhood; her husband takes care of her in her youth; and her son takes care of her in her old age. A woman is not fit to act independently (*pitā rakṣati kaumāre bhartā rakṣati yauvane, putrascha sthavire bhāve na stṛī svātantryamartīti*)." ' *Vide*, Sanskrit *Dharma Sūtras*, at this updated website: http://hinduonline.co/DigitalLibrary; English translation and edition by P. Olivelle, *Dharmasutras, op. cit.*, 264.

15 *Rig Veda* 5.4.10. The Sanskrit text is: *'yas tvā hṛdā kīriṇā manyamāno 'martyam martyo johavīmi; jātavedo yaśo asmāsu dhehi prajābhir aghne amṛtatvam aśyām'*. R.T.H. Griffith's translation is: 'As I, remembering thee with grateful spirit, a mortal, call with might on thee Immortal, Grant us high renown, O Jātavedas, and may I be immortal by my children'. He uses the word children for *'praja'*. See *Rig Veda* in Sanskrit, and R.T.H. Griffith, trans., *op. cit.* Olivelle translates *'praja'* as sons, based on Vāsiṣṭha's interpretation of the word, P. Olivelle, *Dharmasutras, op. cit.*, 293.

16 *Vāsiṣṭha Dharma Sutra*, 28.1–5. Transliteration of Sanskrit verses read: 1) *'na stri duṣyati jāreṇā; na vipro devakarmaṇā, nāpo mutrapurīṣeṇā*; 2) *svayam*

piprati pannā vā yadi vā vipravāsitā, balātkāropa bhuktā vā chōrahasta gatāpi vā; 3) *na tyājyā dūṣitā nārī, nāsyāstyāgō vidhiyate, puṣpakālamupāsīt ṛtu kālena śudhyati;* 4) *strīyaha pavitramtulam naite duṣyanti karhichit; māsi māsi rajohyāsām duṣkṛtānyapakarṣati;* 5) *pūrvam striyaha surairbhuktāh soma gandharvavahinabhih; gacchānti mānuṣānpanchān etā duṣyanti dharmatah*'.

Part III

MAURYAN–CLASSICAL ERA

Arthaśāstra and *Manu Smṛiti*

6

MAURYAN EMPIRE AND *ARTHAŚĀSTRA*

I. Magadha: political antecedents

Ajātaśatru's (d. 461 BCE) descendents were ousted by the Śisunāgas (ca. 413–463 BCE), who in turn gave way to the Nanda dynasty. Several different sources indicate that the founder Mahāpadma Nanda was not a *kśatiya* but that he had superior martial skills. The Hindu *Purānas* dismiss him as a *śudra*, but Jaina texts describe him further as the son of a barber and a courtesan (*gaṇikā kuşijanma*). Roman historian Curtiss also states that Mahāpadma was the son of a starving barber, who convinced the Śisunāga queen to appoint him guardian of her children and later murdered her husband and usurped his throne.[1] The Nandas used their massive army and chariot force to wage war to expand their kingdom. This is verified by the Hāthigumpha inscription of a neighbor, the Jaina king Khāravela of Kalinga (Orissa). Magadha's success can be attributed to substantial timber, copper, and iron resources, while agriculture and trade flourished in the Gangetic delta. As an eastern *mahājanapada*, Magadha was also secure from turbulent foreign invasions experienced by northwestern states like Gāndhara, Punjab, and Mālwa.

II. Mauryan Empire (321–184 BCE)

Sources include the *Arthaśāstra*'s early volumes;[2] Aśoka's stone pillar and rock edicts;[3] coins; Buddhist architectural sites like Sārnath, Rāmpurva, and Sānchi; Megasthenes's *Indika* in fragments quoted by Greek or Roman writers;[4] the Hindu *Purānas*; Buddhist and Jaina scriptures; classical Sanskrit literature;[5] and the Junagarh inscription of king Rudradāman (ca. 150 ACE) stating that a Puşyagupta was governor of Gujarat in Chandragupta Maurya's empire.

Magadha was the nucleus of the Mauryan Empire, whose capital Pātaliputra (Patna, Bihar) was built at the confluence of the Ganga and Son rivers. Although its origins are clouded in legends, some elements appear to be historically true. The *Purānas* state that when the *brāhman* Chānakya

(Kauṭilya) recognized the potential of young Chandragupta, he arranged for his studies at Nalanda in Gāndhāra. This story may explain Chandragupta's presence in the northwest shortly after Alexander of Macedon invaded India (326 BCE). After conquering Darius III of Persia, Alexander entered Bactria and then crossed the Indus. The Roman historian Justin states that Alexander then met a youth named 'Sandrocottas', who was probably Chandragupta Maurya.[6] Shortly after Alexander's abrupt departure, Chandragupta apparently seized the opportunity to assert his authority over local kings with the help of his mentor Kauṭilya. Shortly afterward, Chandragupta rushed east, overthrew the last Nanda king, and proclaimed himself emperor of Magadha (ca. 321–297 BCE). Magadha was the nucleus of the Mauryan Empire, which later extended across the subcontinent.

In 304 BCE, Chandragupta defeated Seleucus Nikator, the Greco-Bactrian king (*satrap*), who ceded Gāndhāra, Kabul, and Kandahar to the Mauryans. Chandragupta later conquered Gujarat, Avanti (Madhya Pradesh), and Sopara on the Konkan coast. By the end of his reign, Magadha was no longer simply a large *mahājanapada* but an empire stretching across northern India. Kauṭilya probably advised his emperor to sign a peace treaty after war, as described in his seminal work on statecraft, the *Arthaśāstra* (*AŚ* 7.1). Chandragupta and Seleucus sealed a memorable pact opening up cultural contacts between east and west. Seleucus Megasthenes was his ambassador to Pātaliputra, where Megasthenes wrote *Indika*.

Later Roman writers cited the *Indika* on Mauryan administration and economy, palace life in Pātaliputra, and prince Bindusāra. Others viewed its society through a European lens, as their exotic accounts resemble later colonial 'orientalist' writings.[7] Some scholars have debated over the 'right to intermarriage' (Ltn: *epigamia*) clause in the treaty. Stabo states that as the victor, Chandragupta received territories and the right to marry a Seleucid princess. In return, he gave Seleucus 500 elephants and other friendly gifts, such as aphrodisiacs. Some modern scholars have mistaken this to propose that Chandragupta's wife was a Bactrian princess and that his sons were partly Greek. The treaty certainly ushered in cultural exchanges. Due to the long term stay of Greek officials like Megasthenes and their noblewomen in Pātaliputra, the Mauryans established a special department for their needs.[8] While it is probable that some Mauryans married foreign women, there is no evidence that Chandragupta's consort was Greek. Moreover, the Jaina text *Pariśiṣṭaparvan* clearly states that his chief queen was an Indian named Durdharā, the mother of his heir Bindusāra (297–272 BCE).[9]

In this period, numerous heterodox sects flourished in India, many with ascetic orders of monks, with others including nuns. As the Mauryan emperors' ancestors were non-*dvījas*, a fact confirmed by different sources, they preferred the heterodox sects of the Jainas, Buddhists, and Ajīvikas and the use of Prakrit over Sanskrit. The Buddhist text *Vamsatthapakāsinī* states that Chandragupta's father was a chief of the Mōriya tribe (Pali: *mōra*; Skt.: *mayura*) in Pipphalivana (Pātaliputra) and that his mother's father was a peacock trainer (*mayura poshaka*) in sub-Himalayan forests.[10] The Jaina *Pariśiṣṭaparvan* confirms that the Mōriyas were not elite caste *dvījas*.[11] The Roman historian Justin describes Chandragupta as a plebian, 'new man' (*novus homo*).[12] The emperor became a Jaina, and his final years were spent as a monk in Saravanabelagola, Karnataka. Despite his heterodox beliefs, Chandragupta and his followers respected other sects, apparently following Kauṭilya's *Arthaśāstra* (I.19), which advised kings to 'personally attend to the business of gods, of heretics, of Brāhmans learned in the Vedas, the care of sacred places'. Chandragupta's son Bindusāra supported Ajīvika ascetics at his court, while his son Aśoka became an ardent Buddhist. Aśoka later sent his son and daughter as Buddhist emissaries to Srī Lanka, while his descendents also favored heterodox sects.

Classical western sources refer to Bindusāra as Amitrochates (Skt.: *amtraghāta* or slayer of foes). This gifted general's biggest feat was to conquer the Deccan beyond the Krishna-Tungabhadra rivers, thus extending the empire to the boundaries of the Dravidian Pāndya, Chōla, and Keralaputra kingdoms. Buddhist sources state that Bindusāra's chief consort was Dhamma/Subhadrāngi, the daughter of a *brāhman* in Champā, who became the mother of his sons Aśoka and Vītaśoka. Bindusāra had numerous sons from his other wives.

Aśoka (272–232 BCE) initially exhibited his father's military zeal by quelling a rebellion in Taxila. When appointed governor of Ujjain (Madhya Pradesh), he lived in the town of Vidīsa with a Buddhist woman named Devī, who became a force in his life. Although the couple never married, they had a son named Mahinda and a daughter called Sanghamittā. Aśoka left this family behind in Vidīsa and returned to Pātaliputra. After Bindusāra's death, there ensued a fierce power struggle between Aśoka and his numerous stepbrothers. Aśoka emerged the victor, and when crowned as emperor, he appointed his uterine brother Vītaśoka-Tissa as vice-regent. A later Buddhist legend states that Aśoka brutally massacred ninety-nine of his brothers to ascend the throne, as he was not a Buddhist at this time. While it is probable that he murdered those with a strong claim, the legend appears to be exaggerated. Perhaps the authors wished to show that even so a dissolute murderer could reform by adopting the Buddhist path. However, Aśoka's reformation occurred only after his war of attrition against Kalinga (Orissa), a province whose mineral wealth matched its resistance to imperial rule. Upon seeing all the devastation that he had wreaked, Aśoka became an ardent believer in *dhamma* (Pali; Skt: *dharma*) as compassion, peace, and nonsectarian justice, which shaped his imperial vision. He now sent his children Mahinda and Sanghamittā to Srī Lanka as his Buddhist emissaries.[13]

The historical remains include Aśoka's sixteen edicts inscribed on large pillars, several rock edicts, minor pillar edicts, and cave inscriptions, as well as stone and metal pillars without inscriptions at Buddhist tomb monuments (*stūpas*) to monks, notably at Sārnāth, Rāmpura, Pātaliputra, and Sānchi. Calling himself Piyadassi (Beloved of the Gods), Aśoka paternally advised subjects on how to pursue *dhamma*. The edicts were in local languages like Prakrit or Tamil written in the Brahmi script or in the Aramaic in the northwest. Non-inscriptional monuments include the famous limestone Sārnāth Lion Pillar engraved with the wheel of law (Pali: *dhamma chakka*; *Skt.: dharma chakra*) and the imperial insignia of a virile bull. As the emperor was the *chakravartin* ('he who sets the wheel of law into motion'), these visual messages of majestic justice were understood even by the illiterate.[14] Inscriptions tell us that he had a large bureaucracy, as described in the *Arthaśāstra*, but a newer cadre of officials (*mahāmattas*) guided subjects on *dhamma*. Rock Edict 13 describes his sorrow at unleashing carnage in Kalinga:

> When he had been consecrated eight years, the Beloved of the Gods, king Piyadassi, conquered Kalinga. A hundred and fifty thousand people were deported, a hundred thousand were killed and many times that number perished. Afterwards, now that Kalinga was annexed, the Beloved of the Gods very earnestly practiced *Dhamma*, desired *Dhamma*, and taught *Dhamma*. On conquering Kalinga the Beloved of the Gods felt remorse, for when an independent country is conquered the slaughter, death, and deportation of the people is extremely grievous to the Beloved of the Gods, and weighs heavily on his mind. What is even more deplorable to the Beloved of the Gods, is that those who dwell there, whether brāhmans, Śramanas, or those of other sects, or householders who show obedience to their superiors, obedience to mother and father, obedience to their teachers and behave well and devotedly towards their friends. . . . relatives, slaves, and servants, all suffer violence, murder, and separation from loved ones.[15]

Yet peace proved elusive to Aśoka's successors. When his consort Asandhimittā died, leaving him Kunāla as his heir, the aging emperor appointed a secondary wife, Kāruvāki/Tissarakhā, as chief queen. Buddhist sources describe Tissarakhā as conniving, as she prodded her son Tīvara to blind Kunāla. Yet victorious Kunāla was crowned as Suyaśas ('he of great fame'), and like his father, he lavishly endowed the Buddhist Sangha (232–224 BCE). Kunāla's heir Daśaratha (224–216 BCE) favored the Ajīvikas. His other son, Samprati/Śāliśuka (216–206 BCE), was a Jaina who gained control over the western regions. The last Mauryans were Devavarman (206–199 BCE), Śātadhanvan (199–191 BCE), and Bṛhadratha (191–184 BCE).[16]

III. *Arthaśāstra*: kingship and women

Due to its longevity, the Mauryan Empire witnessed numerous changes, but some features remained constant. These hallmarks were closely linked to the *Arthaśāstra*'s ideals of patrimonial kingship coupled with legal justice (*dharma*).[17]

The *Dharma Sūtras* legally validated male succession, which the *Arthaśāstra* reaffirmed, along with polygamy for the Mauryan Empire, a pattern followed by later codes for other empires. Mauryan genealogical lists of sons and brothers who ascended the throne indicate that this was a patrimonial empire. Yet, as polygamy was a common practice to ensure more than one male heir, royal fraternal struggles were inevitably common. This caused Aśoka's murderous quarrels with his stepbrothers and strife between Kunāla's sons. Elite men certainly held the political reins, but queens could exert indirect power. This could be either benign, as when Aśoka's unofficial wife Devī directed him to adopt Buddhist nonviolence, or malevolent, as when his last consort Tissarakhā incited their son Tīvara to blind his rightful heir Kunāla.

Yet such chaotic tyranny could be averted or reduced if rulers followed the *Arthaśāstra*'s guidelines on kingship and justice. This code glorified the benevolent king who upheld justice as his *dharma*, an ideal resonating in the epics *Rāmāyana* and *Mahābhārata*. Although composed in a patriarchal, stratified society, the *Arthaśāstra*'s laws promoted the ideal of benign, imperial justice, which must have appealed to the maturer Aśoka. As it also defined legal procedures (*vyavahāra*) more precisely than the *Dharma Sūtras*, we can conclude that the *Arthaśāstra* was a major factor of Mauryan imperial success.

Second, the emperors' non-*dvīja* ancestry and heterodox beliefs shaped policies on righteous justice as *dharma/dhamma*. Although not *kşatŗiya* by birth, they projected *kśatŗiya* ideals of martial kingship, and proved that they were better warriors than humdrum *kśatŗiyas*. They also astutely gauged that dynastic survival depended on their inclusion of all subjects under one judicial umbrella. It is probable that as a non-*dvīja*, Chandragupta knew that he needed a *brāhman* spokesman to advocate universal justice. Kauţilya then wrote the *Arthaśāstra* because his non-elite caste emperor had experienced the sting of exclusion.[18] The author did not gloss over social distinctions, but his laws were more humane to women and non-*dvījas* than Vaśiştha's *Dharma Sūtra*. The *Arthaśāstra* told the king and priests to avoid caste bigotry:

> The king must dismiss a priest who, when ordered, refuses to teach the Vedás to, or to perform a sacrifice for a sincere person without caste (*ayājya*).
>
> (*AS* 1.10.2)[19]

Furthermore, this culturally diverse empire could have been governed only with a vast administrative and military apparatus, as described in the first four volumes of the *Arthaśāstra*. Officials closely monitored society and economy, while subjects probably tolerated such intrusion, as they were assured of justice as *dharma*. A politically astute Aśoka later revamped this bureaucracy and redefined *dharma* as nonsectarian, compassionate justice (*dhamma*). As the emperor (*chakravartin*) who 'set the wheel of law into motion', his edicts spoke of *dhamma* in local languages, and his monuments were etched with the 'wheel of law' (*dhamma chakka*), an image understood by all. Rock Edict #5 describes officials who worked to inculcate *dhamma:*

> Among servants and nobles, *brāhmans* and wealthy householders, among the poor and the aged . . . they are working for the welfare and happiness of those devoted to *Dhamma* and for the removal of their troubles,. . . . they are busy everywhere, here and in all the women's residences, whether my own, those of my brothers and sisters, or those of other relatives.[20]

A. Date, author/s, and synopsis

The *Arthaśāstra*'s earliest sections were composed in the Mauryan era by Kauṭilya, whose name appears often in the first volume (e.g., *AS* 1.1.19). Our analysis of women's rights in the *Arthaśāstra* confirms that it is the work of more than one author, as it has several layered responses to women as the 'other' gender. An early stratum of benign laws respect female property and marriage rights, but later sporadic verses exude suspicion of women's sexual and other motives. The *Arthaśāstra* model of kingship became the normative ideal for later kings. In the early classical era (180 BCE–200 ACE), elite *dvījas* attributed Mauryan imperial success to the *Arthaśāstra*, which was regarded as the proven scientific treatise (*śāstra*) on statecraft. Scholarly *brāhmans* then updated this code to suit Śāka, Kuśānā, and other kingdoms during these centuries. The final revision was made by Viṣnugupta (ca. 150 BCE), two centuries before *Yajñyavalka*'s *Smṛitī* (250 ACE). As the *Arthaśāstra*'s legal features appear in the *Smṛitīs* of Manu, Yājnyavalkya, and Nārada, one can suggest that the first Mauryan mastermind was not Chandragupta but Kauṭilya.

R. Shamasastry's first English translation (1915) attributed all fifteen volumes to Kauṭilya in the Mauryan era, based on the archaic Sanskrit and on textual references to the later Vedic economy. This was endorsed by nationalist scholars like K.A.N. Sastri, as it validated their vision of a historically unified India. Norwegian Indologist Konow (1945) concurred with this view, and he cited the first and last verses of the *Arthaśāstra* (*AS* I.1.1;

15.1.73), which state that it was a compendium written by Kauṭilya, after Chandragupta overthrew Nandā tyrants:

> By mainly condensing those arthaśāstras composed by earlier teachers about winning and guarding the earth, this arthasastra has been made; (*AS* 1.1.1) This treatise has been made by him who in indignation quickly extracted the treatise and the sword and earth gone before the Nanda king.
>
> (*AS* 15.1.73)[21]

Thapar has described Kauṭilya as 'the theorist of the politico-economic Mauryan state' (1961; 2002) and as the author of the early volumes (Books II–IV). However, she believes that inconsistencies in the *Arthaśāstra* indicate revisions in the classical era, notably by Viṣnugupta (ca. 250 ACE),[22] whose name appears in a concluding line after the last verse (see previously):

> Having seen discrepancies in many ways on the part of the writers of commentaries on the Sástras, Vishnu Gupta himself has made (this) Sútra and commentary.
>
> (*AS* 15.19.73)[23]

Some early scholars dated the *Arthaśāstra* entirely to the classical era, a view less accepted today. German Sanskritist Jolly first believed it was a classical work, but he later retracted by stating that it was a Mauryan code (1923) that influenced the *Yājñyavalkya Smṛitī*.[24] Trautmann (1971) argued that several scholars wrote the *Arthaśāstra* in the classical era.[25]

Olivelle's linguistic analyses have shed light on the early codes' historical contexts and their terminology on litigation (*vyavahāra*), most notably in the *Dharma Sūtras, Arthaśāstra*, and *Manu Smṛiti*.[26] He has shown that the *Arthaśāstra*'s terms on *vyavahāra* occur almost verbatim in the *Manu Smṛiti* (Chs. 8–9).[27] He has also sequenced the texts by stylistic developments, as the earliest *Dharma Sūtras* by Āpastamba is in prose, the later *Baudhāyana* and *Vasiṣhta Sūtras* include verses (*ślokās*), and the *Arthaśāstra* is entirely in *ślokās*, a style followed in the *Manu Smṛiti*, the *Yājñyavalkya Smṛiti*, and the *Nārada Smṛiti*.[28] Olivelle and McClish have recently suggested a new date for the *Arthaśāstra*. They state that Kauṭilya was the primary author but that the *Arthaśāstra* was composed between the Mauryan and Kuśāna empires (ca. 100 BCE–100 ACE). Their thesis is based on the text's reference to copper and silver coins (*AŚ* 3.16.37–42) but not to gold coins, first issued by the Kuśāna Vīmā Kadphises (1st–2nd ACE).[29] While this theory validates a pre-Kuśāna date, it does not exclude a Mauryan date (pre-184 BCE), as the *Arthaśāstra*'s description of a vast, complex bureaucracy is commensurate with the Mauryan Empire. Thapar's theory seems to be the most accurate, although it is as yet unconfirmed.

In the *janapadas* of the later Vedic era, *dharma* connoted sacred and temporal laws, morality, and the social duties of each *varna*. The king's *dharma* (*rāja dharma*) was to rule fairly, adjudicate laws, and defend his kingdom. The *Dharma Sutras* had first defined the duties of all *dvījas* before specifying those of kings, and they gave priority to defense. In contrast, the *Arthaśāstra*'s first volumes describe the 'disciplined king'; internal governance; royal women (*AŚ* 1); courtesans and artisans; spies (*AŚ* 2); laws on marriage; female and male property; remarriage; male polygamy; legal evidence and procedures (*vyavahāra*) (*AŚ* 3 & 6); crimes like rape, abduction, and molestation; the treatment of female suspects in jail (*AŚ* 4); and inheritance rights of princesses and other women (*AŚ* 1 & 5). The *Arthaśāstra* describes a vast kingdom with complex laws enforced by a centralized bureaucracy. It had separate departments for agriculture, animal husbandry, commerce, espionage, artisanal industries, and entertainment, whose workers included women, and for the mint, infantry, weaponry, and war chariots, whose workers were male. This study of kingship and laws affecting women focuses on the first four volumes, with selective references to gender from later volumes (*AŚ* 5, 6, 8, 11) and on foreign policies in peace and war, areas in which few women had substantive authority in the early kingdoms. These early volumes are largely Kauṭilya's skeletal work, fleshed out by later writers.

B. Royal governance

Kauṭilya emphasized that the focus of his text was temporal governance rather than spiritual enlightenment, since wise, legal governance would ensure prosperity and happiness for all members of society. The *Arthaśāstra*'s first volume on kingship declares that the benevolent ruler's first duty was to promote the material welfare of his subjects. At the same time, it cautions him not to be 'careless' by ignoring the presence of traitors. To ensure the 'unsullied loyalty' of ministers, officials, priests, princes, wives, the king was told to hire male and female spies' (*AŚ* 1.10–12; 17, 20) and to send envoys abroad to ferret out potential enemies. These sections have led to some scholarly comparisons between the *Arthaśāstra* and Machiavelli's *The Prince*, the late medieval European work on political duplicity. This simplistic comparison reduces the *Arthaśāstra* to a cynical treatise on *realpolitik* while ignoring its basic premise that kings had a sacred duty to care for subjects. The *Arthaśāstra* was later respected as a scientific treatise on statecraft, serving justice for all, including women and *śudras*, based on the norms of that era. Despite Manu's disdain for heterodoxy, he borrowed legal terms and royal ideals from the *Arthaśāstra*; Viṣnugupta later expanded Kauṭilya's code, while Yājnyavalkya and Nārada incorporated its humane features into their *Dharma Śāstras*.

Kauṭilya first invoked the learned gurus as witnesses to his work as a temporal treatise (*AS* 1.2.1–12). He defined four beneficial forms of knowledge, namely 1) mundane evidence (*ānvīkśhikī*) derived from the schools of logic (Samkhya), discipline (Yoga), and human affairs (Lokayata); 2) the scriptural *Rig*, *Sāma*, and *Yajur Vedas* (*trayī*) defining righteous duties as *dharma*, the four occupational *varnas*, and the four life stages or *āśramā*; 3) the science of economics (*varta*) generating wealth from agriculture, cattle farming, and trade; and 4) political science on the royal scepter and laws (*daṇda-nītī*) based on expediency and strength. The *Arthaśāstra* proclaims that the king had to be vigilant when pursuing *dharma*, which would grant him heavenly bliss.

The theme of morality based on *varna* and *āśrama* (*varnāśramadharma*) occurs in several verses bearing Kauṭilya's name. It also occurs in the third volume on laws (*AŚ* 3.1.38 a–b–c–d & 3.1.39 a–b), which stipulate that the king was the guardian of righteous laws (*dharma*), the four social *varnas*, and the four life stages (*āśrama*) of individuals. It emphasizes that royal decrees (*rāja śāsāna*) superseded all laws, legal procedures and evidence (*vyavahāra*), and precedent (*carita*).

> *AŚ* 3.1.38 a-b-c-d: 'As the upholder of all justice, it is the king's duty is to enforce the duties of the four *varnas* and four *āśramas*' ('*Catur varnāśramasyāyam lokasyācāra rakśaṇāth; Naśyatām sarva dharmāṇām rājā dharma pravartakah*').
>
> *AŚ* 3.1.39 a-b: 'The four legs of justice are laws, legal procedures, precedent, and royal decrees' ('*dharmaścha vyavahāraścha charitram rāja śāsanam*').[30]

This idea was the king's duty to guard the social norms of *varnāśramadharma* echoes in other late Vedic texts like the epics and *Bhagavad Gītā* (*BG* III.24, 35), composed in kingdoms with culturally diverse communities. The *Arthaśāstra* (*AŚ* 1.3.13–17) states that while everyone had some moral qualities, each had duties based on *varna* and *āśrama*. The king had to rule fairly and uphold *varnāśramadharma*, or there would be social confusion (*loka sankarād*):

> (*AŚ* 1.3.13–17): 13) Non-violence, truth, purity, mercy, lack of malice and cruelty are everyone's moral duties; 14) Doing ones own righteous duties (*svadharma*) leads us to heaven (*svarga*) and bliss (*anantya*); 15) but social chaos ensues if we break these rules; 16–17)The king must not allow people to deviate from their duties, as this brings happiness in this world, and in the next. To do ones

> duties by the rules of *varna* and *āsrama* is the Ārya custom. If society obeys these laws, it will be protected by the triple *Vedas*, and it will progress, and not perish.[31]

The next chapter reaffirms royal responsibility for *varnāśramadharma* (*AŚ* 1.4.7–16), as this led to a stable economy and society. Kauṭilya first presented his teacher's opinion that the king's scepter must be raised (*udhyata daṇda*) to intimidate and to punish severely those who opposed him (*tīkśha daṇda*) (*AŚ* 1.4.5–6). Kauṭilya then rejected this view by declaring that the wise king inflicted mild punishments (*mṛidu daṇda*) to uphold righteousness and the *dharmas* of individuals based on *varnāśrama* (*AŚ* 1.4.7–16):

> *AŚ* 1.4. 7–8) Not so, says Kauṭilya. He who wields the sceptre (*daṇda*) to punish cruelly, is repugnant to the folk; 9–10) He who punishes mildly, when deserved alone is respected; 11–12) This will instill righteousness (*dharma*) in people, and it will increase wealth (*artha*) and pleasure (*kama*). But when the king punishes unfairly due to his greed, anger, ignorance, such acts will excite the fury of even respected forest dwellers (*vānaprasthān*) and ascetics (*parivrājkān*), not to mention householders (*gṛhasthān*); 13–15) Yet, without any punishment, chaos and injustice will ensue, as in the tale of the fishes. Without the king's protective sceptre, the strong will swallow the weak; but when protected, the weak will resist; 16) The sceptre protects people of four *varnas* in four life stages (*āsrama*) so they can do their respective duties.[32]

This first volume contains three chapters on the disciplined king (*AŚ* 1.6; 1.7; 1.19) and others on policies towards officials, spies, princes, and wives. The *Arthaśāstra* instructed the king to inspire his subjects by conquering his passions, since righteous acts would be rewarded in this life and in the next (*AS* 1.6.5–12). To drive home this message, Kauṭilya listed kings whose indulgence in lust (*kāma*), anger (*krodha*), greed (*lobha*), ego (*māna*), arrogance (*mada*), and over-excitement (*harṣa*) had cost each his family, wealth, throne, and life. Thus, king Bhoja tried to rape a *brāhman* girl; Janamajeya seethed with hatred for *brāhmans*; vain Rāvanā kidnapped Sīta in the *Rāmāyana*; and egotistical Duryodhana would not share his kingdom in the *Mahābhārata*.

The wise king was proficient in the social sciences, and he sought the advice of elders to bring prosperity to his kingdom. He never harmed women, and he shunned the six sensory enemies even in dreams; yet he enjoyed wealth (*artha*) and earthly pleasures (*kāma*) justly earned by him (*AŚ* 1.7.1–3). The last *sloka* tersely directed him to heed the advice of ministers because: 'The chariot of kingship (*rājatva*) does not run with a single wheel' (*AŚ*

1.7.9). The *Arthaśāstra*'s next three chapters reiterate this by advising him to choose loyal, brave, learned, resourceful men whom he knew to be ministers, advisors, and priests (*AS* 1.8.27–29). At the same time, the text warns the king not to trust naively, as duplicitous officials could overthrow him. The *Arthaśāstra* advised the king to divide his day into working segments, in which to supervise finances, collaborate with ministers and army chief, and assess the work of spies. He also reserved time for prayer; consultations with priests, teachers, and physicians; and relaxation. He held daily court for subjects, and he was warned never to keep them waiting, as royal arrogance would incite public anger that would bring his downfall (*AŚ* 1.19.26–28). This definitive chapter begins with solemn aphorisms (*AŚ* 1.19. 1–5), and it ended with others (*AŚ* 1.19.33–36):

> (*AŚ* 1.19.1) An energetic king instills energy into his subjects; (1.19.2) his lethargy spreads lethargy; (1.19.3) that will eat up his achievements; (1.19.4) causing dissension that will lead to his downfall. (1.19.5) Hence, the king must always be alert.[33]
>
> *AŚ* 1.19.33 a–b) A king's highest discipline is his vow of action; his most sacred rite is to perform his duty; 1.19.34 a–b) His happiness lies in the happiness of subjects, his welfare in theirs; he should please his people, rather than please himself; 1.19.35 a–b) The king must always fulfill his duties, as action is the root cause of all prosperity, and lethargy of all misfortune; 1.19.36 a–b) Inactivity will end prosperity, but the fruits of action are wealth and happiness.[34]

Such phrases on royal responsibilities echo in a later volume (*AŚ* 6.1.15–18), probably the work of a later author emulating Kauṭilya's style:

> *AŚ* 6.1.15–18): A wise king can make even the poor and miserable elements of his sovereignty happy and prosperous, but a wicked king will surely destroy the most prosperous and loyal elements of his kingdom. Hence a king of unrighteous character and vicious habits will, though he is an emperor, fall a prey either to the fury of his own subjects or to that of his enemies. But a wise king trained in politics, will, though he possesses a small territory, conquer the whole earth with the help of the best-fitted elements of his sovereignty, and will never be defeated.[35]

C. Women in the Arthaśāstra

The *Arthaśāstra* is rich in its references to queens, courtesans, wives, workers, spies, and traitors. It also specifies the rights of married, pregnant, and divorced women, young girls, widows, and even those arrested for crimes.

As a treatise on the royal state, it describes kings before subjects and, similarly, queens and royal courtesans before the laws for ordinary women. The first chapter on royal women is a male-centric exegesis on protecting the kingdom by safeguarding the women's palace (*AŚ* 1.20) and the king himself (*AŚ* 1.21). This gendered perspective echoes in guidelines on hiring the king's courtesans (*AŚ* 2.27). As the *Arthaśāstra* begins with the royal state, we begin with its chapters on royal women, courtesans, and spies (*AŚ* 1.10–12; *AŚ* 11.1), then move to laws on marriage, property, and punishments for all women (*AŚ* 3; *AŚ* 4) and male attitudes in volumes from the early classical era (*AŚ* 5; *AŚ* 6).

Queens and courtesans

The *Arthaśāstra* describes the royal residence of queens, relatives, offspring, royal midwives and servants (*AŚ* 1.20–21), and courtesans who entertained and guarded the king (*AŚ* 2.27). As the king spent a considerable portion of his day in the women's palace, Kauṭilya describes it as a 'house for enjoyment with many doors' (*aneka kakśya mohanagṛiham*). Yet it was also the source of considerable royal anxiety, as, if captured by an enemy, the kingdom would be jeopardized (*AŚ* 1.20.2). There was also an abiding 'fear of duplicitous cohorts' (*vikalpeta sahādhāyi bhayate*) of the king who could seditiously connive with disgruntled subjects within the women's abode (*AŚ* 1.20.3). Taking a cue from the *Dharma Sūtras*, the *Arthaśāstra* thus stipulated that the palace be strategically placed, constructed like a fire-proof treasury house, defended by a moat, and built with parapets for soldiers to spy its environs. Its cellars (*bhūmigṛiham*) had niched altars to protective gods (*chaityā kāştadevatā*) but also secret passages with rambling snakes to deter lurking enemies. To protect the royal family, peacocks, parrots, cats, mongoose, and deer roamed freely, eating vipers' lethal poisons (*AŚ* 1.20.1–7). Elite, resident midwives administered herbal antidotes if needed, while family women and trusty servants ensured that the king's meals were not poisoned. Queens lived near their children in luxurious rooms, amid fragrant plants and reservoirs. Loyal soldiers, and eighty male, fifty female, and eunuch spies roamed the palace. Aside from these, there were chambers for the crown prince and for the king to meet his counselors (*AŚ* 1.20.10–13). Kauṭilya advised the king to visit the queen only after she was cleansed and screened by her maid (*AŚ* 1.20.14), justifying these precautions by citing cases when miscreants had enticed relatives to murder kings. Sexual politics and intrigue were clearly bedfellows, as seen in these lines (*AŚ* 1.20.14–17):

> (*AŚ* 1.20.14): The king must see the queen in her chambers after a maid has cleansed her thoroughly; 15) since only in the queens' chambers did infamous Bhadrasenā's brother hide (to kill him); where Kārūşam's son hid under his mother's bed; 16) where a

> queen gave poisoned honey to Kāśi Rājan; where Vairantya's queen smeared her anklet with poison, Sauvīra's queen smeared her girdle, Jālūthan's lover smeared her mirror; where vile Vidūrathan's queen hid a weapon in her braids. 17) Therefore, let us proceed cautiously as if amongst enemies.[36]

This male perspective echoes in the sections on the king's safety (*AŚ* 1.21) and his courtesans (*gaṇikā*) (*AŚ* 2.27). They first identified various poisons; the manner in which they were given to the victim; telltale mannerisms of poisoners; and the need to hire trustworthy doctors, cooks, and servants (*AŚ* 1.21.4–10). Loyal maids and male servants attended to the king's bath, and ascertained if his 'fragrances, apparel, garlands' were free from taint (*AŚ* 1.21.13–14). They also guarded his musical instruments and jewels and the regalia of his horses, chariots, and elephants that were stored in the women's palace (*AŚ* 1.21.15–17). While royal women had indirect power, ordinary women were marginally empowered by working in various capacities for the state. They included the king's guards, cooks, maids, warehouse servants, and spies, hired on the assumption that women servants were often less corruptible than men.

Among these were the highly paid ranks of royal entertainers-courtesans (*gaṇikās*). The *Arthaśāstra* (*AŚ* 2.27) describes the duties of *gaṇikās*, their three ranks, high wages, matrilineal customs, and jobs after retirement. Many *gaṇikās* belonged to established courtesan families, but others were recruited simply because of their 'auspicious beauty' (*saubhāgyalankāra*), youth, and musical or other talents (*AŚ* 2.27.1–6). The state purchased young girls of eight and older from their families to serve as the king's musicians (*kuśīlavakarma*). The title of *gaṇikā* indicates their musical (*gāna*) profession, but as they were paid slaves (*dāsis*) of the king, they were also known as *gaṇikā-dāsis*. Mature *gaṇikās* sang and played instruments, juggled, enacted dramas for the king and his guests, or served as royal regalia bearers and bodyguards. High-ranking *gaṇikās* presented a striking presence beside the throne holding the king's ceremonial umbrella, fan, and golden pitcher (*AŚ* 2.27.4). When he went out to mete out justice, perform rites, or hunt, they accompanied him in palanquins, while women guards wielding weapons surrounded him. As a senior *gaṇikā* possessed personal information on his habits and movements, the *Arthaśāstra* stipulated that a second *gaṇikā* be hired as a counterfoil. When a high-ranking *gaṇikā* grew older, she was installed as a nurse matron (*mātrika*), while those of lesser rank or beauty became cooks or warehouse servants (*AŚ* 2.27.8). This section can be attributed to Kauṭilya, as it tallies with Megasthenes's vivid account of *gaṇikās* in the Mauryan Empire:

> Crowds of women surround him, and outside of this circle spearmen are ranged. The road is marked off with ropes, and it is death,

> for man and woman alike, to pass within the ropes. Men with drums and gongs lead the procession. The king hunts in the enclosures and shoots arrows from a platform. At his side stand two or three armed women. . . . Of the women, some are in chariots, some on horses, and some even on elephants, and they are equipped with weapons of every kind as if they were going on a campaign.
>
> (Megasthenes's *Indika*)[37]

Although the courtesan was protected against sexual and physical abuse, the king owned her body and life, such paid servitude evident in the name *gaṇikā-dāsi*.[38] A *gaṇikā* had to submit accounts of her expenses to the supervisor or face fines and dismissal. The *Arthaśāstra* recognized the matrilineal rights of a *gaṇikā*, as it stipulated that she could entrust jewels and property only to her mother or sister, and she could not sell or dispose of her earnings. When a *gaṇikā* died or was absent for a long period, her property was given to her daughter or sister, and her mother had the sole authority to find another *gaṇikā* to replace her (*AŚ* 2.27.8–12). Yet there were restrictions on her use of her property. If she worked for or had sex with other men, she forfeited her earnings to the king. Ironically, although she had the right to bequeath her wealth to her daughters, a *gaṇikā* was the king's *dāsi*, and he could loan or gift her away to his friend or political ally. If she refused to oblige a client, before or after taking his wages, she was severely thrashed; if she killed him, she was cast into a fire or drowned. This gruesome scenario was mildly balanced by penalties for men who ill-treated courtesans. Men who raped, disfigured, assaulted, or abducted a *gaṇikā* or stole her property received harsh beatings and fines. Those who hurt a *gaṇikā*'s mother received lesser penalties, but the most severe were given to men who raped a virgin (*kumāri*), a young courtesan (*rupadāsi*), or a *gaṇikā*'s daughter (*AŚ* 2.27.17–18).

Princes and princesses

Aside from the chapter on queens described previously, two others describe the threats posed by ambitious princes (*AŚ* 1.17–18) to the kingdom. As the first codes, the *Dharma Sūtras* legally endorsed Āryan customs of male succession, the superior rights of sons from a legitimate marriage, and filial division of paternal property rather than primogeniture. It did, however, stipulate that a man's sons by his *brāhman, kṣatṛiya, vaiśya,* and *śudra* wives had different rights to his property. Thus, the son by a *brāhman* wife received four shares, a son from a *kṣatṛiya* wife received three, a son from a *vaiśya* wife two, and a son from a *śudra* wife received one. Like Baudhāyana, Kauṭilya stated that when a man 'sowed his seed in the field of another', the child belonged not to him, but to the 'owner of the field', that is, the husband, a ruling that some kings may have relied upon for dynastic continuity. It also emphasized that a child belonged equally to both husband and wife. There then ensued an interesting discussion on the rights of an unmarried woman's son (*kanina*), the son of a woman who is pregnant during her marriage (*sahoda*), and the son of a remarried woman (*punarbhava*) (*AŚ* 3.6). It gives details on the varying inheritance rights of a *brāhman's* son, who got four shares if his mother was a *brāhman*, three shares if his mother was a *kṣatṛiya*, two shares if his mother was a *vaiśya*, and one share if his mother was a *śudra* (*AŚ* 3.6.17). As the *Arthaśāstra* endorsed these principles as *prima facie* laws of a large empire, it set a precedent for many subsequent codes composed in later kingdoms.

Patrimonial kings were often polygamous, as it was widely believed that the ruler with many wives was assured of at least one male heir. As princes could demand a share of paternal territories, the ruler's death often fragmented his kingdom. This anxiety led kings to imprison unruly princes, princes to kill step-brothers, and queens to intrigue for their sons to inherit the throne. A wise king would appoint a worthy, eldest son by his chief queen as co-ruler and crown prince. Yet even this could be contentious, as some aging kings succumbed to a favorite queen's ambitions for her son. This is seen in the history of Aśoka and in the *Rāmāyana* legend about king Daśaratha. In the absence of a legitimate son, some kings adopted an illegitimate son born to a courtesan or the legitimate son of a daughter, brother, or male relative of their lineage.

The *Arthaśāstra*'s first chapter on princes begins with the stark statement that the king had more to fear from wives (*dāra*) and sons (*putra*) than from other enemies (*AŚ* 1.17.1). In a discussion, scholars suggested various options. One scholar believed that the king should spy upon and punish his sons, as sons resembled 'crabs' (*karkat*) that 'ate' their parents (*AŚ* 1.17.3–6). Another suggested imprisoning princes before they grew into rebels; a third replied that such constraints would teach a prince to ally himself with his father's enemy. Another proposed that princes be enticed to drink, as dissipation would render them too weak to overthrow the king.

Kauṭilya rejected these cruel options by declaring that it was 'death in life' to ruin a son and 'rot' the family wood. Instead, the king should pray for his pregnant wife, arrange a midwife for her care, and teach his son truth and moderation, as it was criminal to ruin an innocent mind (*AŚ* 1.17.22–28). If the prince was a loved, but unruly, single son, Kauṭilya asked the king to keep him under restraint (*prīyam ekaputra bandhiyat*) (*AŚ* 1.17. 40–41). If the son were worthy, the king had to instruct him on discipline and bravery, so that he could help his father, perhaps as his army chief (*AŚ* 1.17.42). Kauṭilya decreed that if the son were unruly, the king should appoint his daughter's son (*putrī kāputrān*) as his heir (*AŚ* 1.17.49). He then declared emphatically, 'Never should an unlawful, only son ascend the throne' (*AŚ* 1.17.51).[39]

A later volume on sovereignty reiterates this view (*AŚ* 5.6.24–40) in verses that bear Kauṭilya's name but with subtle differences suggesting an editorial hand. In a discussion with a man called Bharadvāja, Kauṭilya enacts an imaginary scene between a dying king and his ministers. As in the first volume, he declares that a king must never be unrighteous (*adharma*), and that he must appoint a worthy son as his successor (*AŚ* 5.6.31–33). In the first *ślokās*, the king presents three candidates: an unworthy prince (*sampannabhāve avyavasyanīn kumāran*), a princess (*rāja kanyā*), and a pregnant queen (*garbhiṇīm devī*). The king appeals to the ministers' honor, promising them great wealth and power for making righteous choices. At this point, however, the eponymous Kauṭilya began to favor the prince, and he completely ignored the princess and pregnant queen. The king thus asks his ministers to see the prince as his noble father's son, who could become noble himself with education and discipline (*vinaya karmāṇi cha kumārasya prayeta*). He also promises that a grateful prince would grant more wealth and influence to supporters (*AŚ* 5.6.34–39). Or they could appoint the son of a princess and a man from her caste (*kanyāyām samādajātīyāda*) as the royal heir (*AŚ* 5.6.40). These lines show that elite men were ready to grant women indirect rights through sons but that they disapproved of women ascending the throne in their own right. This political policy on royal women became a blanket law that denied all women direct rights to paternal property.

Women spies: loyalty and sedition

In this patriarchal society, women were neither ministers nor priests, but they were employed as royal bodyguards, entertainers, servants, and spies. To ensure the 'unsullied' loyalty of officials, and as a political strategy abroad, Kauṭilya's *Arthaśāstra* endorsed state espionage. Three chapters describe the large cadre of male and female spies who 'roamed' (*sanchārah*) through palaces, offices, and markets to ferret out traitors at home and the work of male envoys who identified the king's allies and enemies (*AŚ* 1.10–12). Interestingly, the first chapter on espionage first decrees that the king dismiss priests who refuse to teach the *Vedas* to *śudras* or to perform legitimate rites for them (*AS* 1.10.2). The chapter describes spies in disguise strolling through palaces, offices, and city, as they listen to rumors of disgruntled advisors, priests, princes, and queens plotting against the king. When investigating an official, a male spy would pretend to be his friend, but also listen to the official's colleagues who doubted his honesty (*AŚ* 1.10.6). A woman posing as an ascetic (*pravrājika*) could lure a shady official with false promises of favors from the queen to learn of his secret schemes. The verses state:

> *AŚ* 1.10.7–8: A woman spy in the guise of an ascetic highly trusted in the royal women's abode may try to bribe each chief minister by

> saying, 'The chief queen (*mahīṣī*) desires you, and she has arranged for you to enter her chamber. There are great opportunities for wealth and advancement'. 'This is the love-bribe', says Kauṭilya.[40]

These early verses on the use of mendicant, shaven nuns (*bhikśukī*) and monks (*bhikśu*) as spies are echoed in a later volume (*AŚ* 3.11.1,4,8). The later verses indicate that the author felt that ascetics were sexually active, despite their somber garb of celibacy. Jamison points out that the term *pravrājika* means 'woman who has gone forth' from home to be a mendicant.[41]

The details in the *Arthaśāstra* on recruiting and training spies indicate that they were indispensable to the kingdom (*AŚ* 1.12). Orphans, elderly folk, destitute women, and men without families were housed and fed and given a vocation by being taught languages, palmistry, sorcery, and medicine, while brutal men were taught the art of poisoning. Clever, destitute *brāhman* widows, ascetics, and aging prostitutes worked undercover as cooks, maids, dancers, and singers:

> (*AŚ* 1.12.4–5): An intelligent *brāhman* widow, destitute but eager to work, can be an ascetic respected in the women's palace, to move about amongst chief ministers, as can other shaven widows and ascetics of other castes.[42]

The eponymous author of a later volume advises the king that it was politically advisable to forge alliances rather than to wage war with other states with armed forces. He lists late Vedic states, such as the Kāmbojā and Surāṣtrā, whose leaders were farmers, traders, soldiers, and the Licchāvī, Vṛijjī, Mallaka, Mudraka, Kuru, and Pānchāla (*AŚ* 11.1.05) kingdoms. Archaeological findings include punch-marked copper coins common in early historical India, clearly indicating that these states were pre-Kuśāna.[43] At the same time, the author describes how rivals sowed dissension in an enemy state, not only as a defensive tactic but as a proactive policy. These few verses speak volumes about widespread political intrigue and the use of female sexuality to create mayhem in an enemy state. The women were lured by male pimps and given monetary rewards to serve as the king's pawns. The *Arthaśāstra* states that pimps first paraded dancers, acrobats, and jugglers (*bandhakiposakāh plavakanta nartaka saubhikā vā proṇihitāh*) to enthrall the enemy official and introduced him to 'supremely beautiful, young women' (*stṛībhiha paramarupa yauvanah*). In a subsequent secret assignation and violent struggle, the official would be murdered (*AŚ* 11.1.34).

Female sexuality played a key role in espionage dramas described in the next verses. A woman spy pretending to be a discarded lover would lure a foreign official to a secret place where he would be killed. A woman would allow herself to be abducted but then use poison to kill the seduced official; a woman ascetic would give poisonous love potions to another; a widow would appeal to a gallant foreign king with a sad tale of being cheated of money to gain access to his inner circle; prostitutes and pimps would entice an official to an assignation to murder him (*AŚ* 11.1.35–45).[44] Clearly women in ancient India were recruited for their sexual prowess and ability to glean enemy secrets, just as their modern *avatars* who are government moles now rely on electronic 'bugs'.

Laws relating to women

The *Arthaśāstra*'s volume on laws begins with a decree that three scholars of sacred laws (*dharmasthas*) and three ministers (*amātyas*) must supervise justice in towns and districts (*AŚ* 3.1.1).[45] This section focuses on laws and punishments for all women (*AŚ* 3 & 4), volumes that are Kauṭilya's skeletal work but probably embellished by others. Volume three describes the laws on female property (*strīdhana*), marriage, separation, widow remarriage, male polygamy (*AŚ* 3.2); spousal duties, marital discord, cruelty to wives, female promiscuity, and divorce (*AŚ* 3.3); husband's absences, widow remarriage (*AŚ* 3.4); rights of sons to paternal property, daughters to dowry and immoveable property (*AŚ* 3.5); filial inheritance based on parental castes (*AŚ* 3.6–7); debt liabilities (*AŚ* 3.11); treatment of workers, including women (*AŚ* 3.13); marriage contracts (*AŚ* 3.15); and slander of women and high castes (*AŚ* 3.18). Volume four concerns the social 'thorns' or crimes against artisans and workers, some being women (*AŚ* 4.1); prohibitions against torturing and rape of female suspects (*AŚ* 4.8), rape and abduction (*AŚ* 4.9–10), and molestation of young girls (*AŚ* 4.12). Selections from later volumes describe male and female spies, poisoners, and witches by the state (*AŚ* 5.1; 5.2; 11.1) and include a renewed discussion on the rights of princesses and their sons to the throne (*AŚ* 5.6). Some staid sections on the evils of drink, gambling, and women (8.2–4) were perhaps embellished after Aśoka's moral reformation.

MARRIAGE AND PROPERTY

Kauṭilya ranked seven procedures (*vyavahāra*) on marriage as prevalent Vedic customs, and these were accepted in most of the later ancient codes. Four highly honored forms of marriage were the *brāhma, prajāpatya, arśa,* and *daiva,* and three acceptable forms of marriage were the *gāndharva, aśura*, and *rākṣasa*. It also lists the eighth form, the *paiśācha*, which was highly reprehensible, but which could become legitimate if the groom performed acts of atonement. The most praiseworthy were the *brāhma*, in which a father gave his daughter wearing her dowry jewels in marriage to a groom; the *prajāpatya*, in which a couple undertook Vedic rites together; the *arśa*, in which a groom gave cows as a bride price (*śulka*) to her father; and the *daiva*, in which the father gave his daughter away to officiating *brāhman* priests (*AŚ* 3.2.1–5). Less acceptable were the *gāndharva*, in which a couple eloped; the *aśura*, when the groom demanded *sūlka* from the bride's father instead of giving it to her father; and the *rākśasa*, in which a man abducted a woman. The worst was the *paiśācha*: rape of a woman in deep slumber, but it could become legal if the man paid *sūlka* to her parents or to the woman whose parents were deceased (*AŚ* 3.2.6–12).

The *Arthaśāstra* legally endorsed other Vedic customs. The most important was to endow a bride with jewelry, which constituted female property (*strīdhana*) to be used in times of need for her subsistence. In the case of a husband's long absence, a wife could maintain herself, her son, and her daughter-in-law with her *strīdhana*. If he were present, the husband had the right to touch her *strīdhana* to support their family during calamities like famines and epidemics or to perform charitable acts. In a *brahma, prajāpatya, arśa*, or *daiva* marriage, he could borrow his wife's *strīdhana* for such purposes for three years, after which he had to pay her interest. In a *gāndharva* or *aśura* marriage, the husband was required to give his wife interest immediately on borrowing her *strīdhana*. In a *rākśasa* or *paiśācha* union, a husband's use of his wife's *strīdhana* was tantamount to theft (*AŚ* 3.2. 14–18).[46] A widow could live on her *strīdhana*, but she could not sell or give it away, as it was a trust for her children (*AŚ* 3.2.28–34). Although *strīdhana* was a woman's property, the *Arthaśāstra* stipulated that the husband had some control over his wife's *strīdhana*. The couple could live upon a man's property, but they could not fritter it away, as it was a trust for offspring. Similarly, neither wife nor husband could use up her *strīdhana*, as it was a trust for offspring. Upon the death of a chaste widow, her *strīdhana* was divided among sons and daughters, and in the absence of sons, daughters were the sole heirs. A childless widower was entitled to the *sulka* he had paid to his bride's parents, but he had to return her *strīdhana* to her family (*AŚ* 3.2.36–37).[47]

MALE POLYGAMY AND WIDOW REMARRIAGE

Other Sanskritic customs sanctioned by the *Arthaśāstra* were male polygamy and the remarriage of widows and abandoned wives through levirate marriage (*niyoga*) to a brother or kinsman of her former husband (*AŚ* 3.3. 35–42). Despite his cultural proclivities, however, Kauṭilya infused some kindness into his laws, which later writers respectfully retained, while they added misogynist verses. In a society dominated socially and sexually by men, Kauṭilya tried to rein in male promiscuous violence as unrighteous and harmful, and he tried to protect women's property as essential for their subsistence with honor. His code thus stipulated that a man could marry a second time, but only after he had waited for eight years for his first wife to bear him a son. If she bore a stillborn son, he had to wait for ten years to remarry; if she had a daughter, the waiting period was twelve years. Husbands who broke these laws were required to pay the first wife both *śūlka* and a *strīdhana* for subsistence. It was also a man's duty to endow his wives with a *strīdhana* if they had not received it from their parents (*AŚ* 3.2.35–42).

The code prohibited marital rape and sexual intercourse during a woman's menstrual period, and the state fined men heavily for breaking these laws. If a wife was menstruating, her husband was advised to sleep with another of his wives, based on the order in which he had married them. The first wife always ranked highest in a polygamous household. A wife could leave her husband if he lied about his affliction with leprosy or another illness, impotence, insanity, loss of caste, treachery to the king, or plans to flee the country. However, if a dutiful wife wanted a child, she could sleep even with a diseased husband. A barren, devout wife who wished to be celibate could not be forced into sexual intercourse (*AŚ* 3.2.45–48). Ironically, in the midst of such kind conciliations to women, a strident male voice interjected this line (*AŚ* 3.2.42): 'Woman's purpose is only to bear sons/offspring' (*putrārthā hi stṛiyah*). Although the male noun *putra* connoted both sons and all progeny, the later author clearly meant only sons.

The *Arthaśāstra* also endorsed widow remarriage (*niveśakāle*), specifically as the Vedic custom of levirate marriage. In such a union, a widow married her husband's brother or close kinsman chosen by her father-in-law in order to have children. The first verses stipulate that if a widow wished to remain celibate to lead a devout life (*dharma kāmā*), she was to receive all her *strīdhana* and also the *Śūlka* given by her husband to her family at their marriage. If she wished to remarry because she wanted a family (*kutumbakāma*), she was advised to marry the man chosen by her father-in-law, or she would lose all the gifts from this family (*AŚ* 3.2.22–24):

> *AŚ* 3.2.19: Upon her husband's death, a widow eager to lead a virtuous life must be given her dowry and jewelry, and the rest of her bride price; 20) if she does have these, they must be given to her with interest; 21) if she wishes to remarry, 22) she must receive what her father-in-law and husband once gave her; 23) if she does not marry the man chosen by her father-in-law, 24) she will lose what he and her husband once gave her.[48]

Although widows had a second chance at family life, the next verses indicate that patriarchal families had powerful monetary incentives to promote levirate. *Strīdhana* was technically a woman's property, but it was usually managed by the husband, and his family often regarded it as their extended wealth. The larger a bride's dowry, the more respect she received as a daughter-in-law, while a wife with a small *strīdhana* and a childless widow often faced censure and loneliness. Echoing this view, the *Arthaśāstra* stipulated that the property of a remarried woman to a man chosen by her father-in-law would be managed by her new husband. A wife could use her *strīdhana* for her needs, but she could not fritter it away, as it was a trust for her offspring (*AŚ* 3.2.25–27). Although the parents of a deceased man certainly mourned his death, levirate marriage of the widow to another son brought some benefits, as they retained control over her *strīdhana* and now could hope for male heirs. The remarried widow also derived comfort, as she was respected again as a wife capable of bearing sons, and she was not derided as a widow. The code gives details on a woman's *śulka* and *strīdhana* after her remarriage and on gifts from her deceased husband (*AŚ* 3.2.30–33). Interestingly, the *Arthaśāstra* indicates that widows could remarry more than once, as it speaks of widows with 'many husbands and offspring' (*bahu puruṣa prajānām putrānām*) (*AŚ* 3.2.31). However, each time, the remarried widow had to reserve her deceased husband's property only for his offspring.

MALE PROPERTY, FEMALE SEXUALITY

> The code defines the laws on male property, inheritance rights of sons and male kin, and the indirect rights of daughters and their sons (*AŚ* 3.5.7–10, 20–21). In the case of a man without sons, his moveable property (*dravyam*) was given to his brothers and male kin living with him, or to daughters born to him from his less noble *gāndharva, aśura,* or *rākṣasa* unions.
>
> (*AŚ* 3.5.9–10): If a man has no sons, his moveable property can be taken by his brothers who live with him, or by his daughters born of lower marriages (*i.e.*, other than four highest).[49]

However, his permanent, landed property (*ṛiktam*) accrued to a grandson born to a daughter from the four highest and most honored forms of *brāhma, prajāpatya, arśa,* or *daiva* marriages. The code clearly stipulates the daughter's rights to her father's moveable property, her indirect rights through her sons to his landed property, and the daughter's right to a dowry (*pradānikam*) as *strīdhana*, even if she was unmarried:

> (*AŚ* 3.5.21): 'Even if a daughter is unmarried, she is entitled to a dowry for her marriage.[50]

Women's rights to paternal property were also shaped by the *Arthaśāstra*'s laws on the rights of princesses to the throne and crown lands. As stated earlier, Kauṭilya began his discussion on royal succession in his first volume

(*AŚ* 1.17) by declaring that it was immoral (*adharma*) to appoint an undisciplined prince as the heir to the throne. This firm stance was modified in a simulated conversation between a dying king and his ministers in a subsequent volume (*AŚ* 5.6.30–40). The king first presents three candidates, an unruly prince, a princess, and a pregnant queen, but after this apparently dispassionate beginning, he changes his tune by favoring the prince. The king asks the ministers to view the unruly prince as his noble father's son, who could grow noble with discipline and education. Then, forgetting the princess and pregnant queen, the eponymous author offers a final option, namely the king's grandson, born to a princess and a man of her caste (*kanyāyām samāda jātīyāda*). The law restricted royal women's right to the throne and its domains, and this was extended by default to all women, who were denied direct rights to a father's landed or permanent property (*ṛiktam*).

The *Arthaśāstra*'s early sections gave the husband authority to manage his wife's *stṛīdhana*, and it defined the property rights of widows and her sons, while clearly stating the rights of chaste women. Three chapters (*AŚ* 3.5.7–10, 20–21; *AŚ* 3.6; *AŚ* 3.7) elaborated on the rights of sons and daughters to paternal property. The male author/s clearly wished to connect property rights with female sexuality, as the implications were serious for large, patrimonial kingdoms. Again, just as elite men wished to prevent a wife's illegitimate son from inheriting their property, polygamous kings jealously guarded thrones and crown lands from illegitimate princes. This exaltation of female chastity in later Vedic texts indicates the social trend that emerged after the Sanskritic elite acquired large land tracts and kingdoms dominated oligarchies. Just as ordinary men now viewed the wife's *strīdhana* as male personal property, kings like Ajātaśatru of Magadha regarded a queen's dowry of territories and revenues as their own crown lands.

The *Arthaśāstra* defines legal marital duties, the age of maturity for females and males, marriage, and female chastity (*AŚ* 3.3 & *AŚ* 3.4). It begins with a decree that girls were legally mature at twelve years after menstruation, while boys were legally adult at sixteen. If they broke laws after maturity, men received twice the penalties given to women (*AŚ* 3.3. 1–2). The husband was legally responsible for providing food and clothing to his wife, and, as polygamy was legal, if he remarried, he had to give his first wife monetary compensation. After these stern reminders to men on their duties, the author described how husbands could tame wives. If an angry, jealous, or cruel wife used intemperate language or was physically violent, the husband could slap her hands or hips with his hand, a rope, or a bamboo stick. However, if he exceeded this by more violent chastisement, he was punished with a heavy fine (*AŚ* 3.3.6–10).

A woman could leave her husband if she no longer loved him, but only if they were married by a rite other than the noble *brāhma, prajāpatya, arṣa,* or *daiva* union. Husbands and wives could divorce, but only with the consent of the spouse. A divorced wife had to return jewelry and gifts she had received from him; the husband had to pay a fine for dishonesty on sexual matters. If the man no longer desired his wife, he had to allow her to reside with her family or an ascetic woman (*AŚ*.3.3.11–19).

However, after such concessions to women, the eponymous authors who expanded the *Arthaśāstra* exuded suspicion of women and foreigners. The political vacuum after Mauryan imperial collapse (180 BCE) invited numerous invasions, which led to new empires and territorial struggles. The Mauryan model of grand kingship was reinvigorated by indigenous rulers like Kharavela of Kalinga and reshaped by Gautamiputra Satakarni, founder of the Śātavāhanā Empire in central India (50 BCE–150 ACE). Indo-Greek kings from Bactria and Pahlava rulers from Parthia encroached from the northwest, while Central Asian Śākas and Kuśānas (1st–2nd ACE) established large, often Buddhist empires. Arabs and Romans plied the coastline, docking at seaports to buy and sell products, while itinerant monks and traders plied the northwest routes, carrying goods and Buddhism to Central Asia, Tibet, and China.

In this dynamic era, sex across caste and ethnic lines became the norm that changed Indian gene pools, but it also stirred shivers of schizophrenic anxiety in patriarchal breasts, as various authors paid loud homage to chaste women in their works. The *Arthaśāstra*'s eponymous authors now chastised women for flirting, drinking, infidelity, and consorting with profligate men and women. They imposed high fines for intoxication, higher ones for public flirtation, and the highest for sexual intercourse. A verse forbids secret assignations between a woman and a man in shady places. In a heavily policed royal state, almost everyone was suspected as capable of treason. The authors were clearly suspicious of women's open display of sexuality in the public arena, which they felt was a cover for dangerous sedition. A woman accused of such an encounter was publicly whipped on the hips by a local, law-abiding outcaste (*chāndalā*) and then ostracized (*AŚ* 3.3.22–28). She could reduce the penalty by paying a heavy fine, but her best option was to stay chastely and safely at home. Ascetic women (*pravrajika*), once praised as nuns in the order started by the Buddha's mother (5th c. BCE), were now suspected as promiscuous women eager to flee from home. The *Arthaśāstra* lists them with widows who 'roam' as spies to seduce shady officials (*AŚ* 1.12.4) or are fined heavily for attempting to seduce loyal officials (*AŚ* 4.13.3).[51]

The third chapter (*AŚ* 3.4) reveals the author's conflict between stern patriarchy and compassionate justice. It begins with a tirade on female promiscuity, and it demarcates women's geographical limits outside the home. It forbids a woman to leave with a man and even with another female friend (*AŚ* 3.4.1–6). Kauṭilya cited his teacher's view that if a wife were constrained, beaten, and denied subsistence, she should shelter with her kinsmen or a woman ascetic. He then rejected this by arguing that virtuous but naïve women could be preyed upon by duplicitous people (*AŚ* 3.4. 9–12). He decreed high fines for those who stopped a woman from visiting her family or helping others during childbirth. Yet if a woman used such excuses to drink, cavort, or gad about, she would forfeit all her jewelry and *stṛīdhana* (*AŚ* 3.4.13–23).

The same chapter (*AŚ* 3.4. 24–42) shows the author's conflict between *dharma* as justice and distrust of female sexuality. It sanctions the remarriage of a woman if the husband abandoned her and lived elsewhere. As this section begins by listing lower-caste women before *dvījas*, one can surmise that such remarriages were more common among the lower castes. The code thus allows remarriage for a *śudra, vaiśya, kśatṛiya,* or *brāhman* woman without children if her husband is absent for one to four years and for a mother whose husband has disappeared for a year (*AŚ* 3.4. 24–27). A woman had the right to remarry if her husband failed to have intercourse with his virgin bride for seven months (*AŚ* 3.4.31). Other valid reasons were a woman's need for offspring, her destitution and that of her children, or the inability of her husband's family to financially support her (*AŚ* 3.4. 24–30). A woman could also remarry if her husband remained celibate or an ascetic who refused to have intercourse with a wife whom he had married in one of the four noblest styles of marriage (*AŚ* 3.4.37). After this humane ruling, the author ordered that a woman could marry her younger brother-in-law or male kinsman (*dāyādān*) in a levirate marriage. Yet if she chose another man, the *Arthaśāstra* decreed that couple would be punished for adultery, and those who aided them would be criminally culpable (*AŚ* 3.4. 42 a–b).[52]

Crimes and punishments

As empires required detailed laws and punishments for breaking the laws, the *Arthaśāstra*'s fourth volume describes crimes as the 'thorns' of the kingdom. Kauṭilya's vision of nonsectarian justice as *dharma* was expanded later by Aśoka's edicts, which made the king responsible for public welfare. However, there are anomalies in the code due to its multiple authors over centuries. Some sections are benignly respectful of women and protective of minor girls, while some others exhibit misogynist angst over female adultery and inter-caste sex.

Unlike the *Dharma Sūtras*, which largely advocated ritual penances (*prāyascitta*) and give fewer legal punishments for crimes, the *Arthaśāstra* precisely defined the amount of each fine and the level of punishment based on the seriousness of the crime. In one instance, perhaps as a concession to numerous bands of roving monks and hermits of various sects and castes in that era, it briefly recommends the option of doing *prāyascitta*. It states that hermits and ascetics without gold coins to pay fines could undertake fasts and penances for minor infringements but not for abducting women or theft, which were more serious crimes (*AŚ* 3.16.37–42).

Chapters forbade men to rape adult women, and a specific chapter prohibits sex with a minor girl. In this section, the author sternly reiterated his admonishment (*'na chaprākāyam akāmābhyām labhet'*) three times after intervals (*AŚ* 4.12.5, 13, 19). If a jailor denied a suspect under custody food and water, he paid a large fine, and for torture (*āpta doṣam*), he paid a higher fine, but the highest penalty was for the rape of a woman in custody, especially if she were pregnant, old, or ascetic. If the officer raped or tortured a *dvīja* woman, he was immediately hanged (*AŚ* 4.9.21–28). If men raped a teacher or tortured an enslaved worker, they were severely beaten. If a man committed incest with an aunt, teacher's wife, daughter, daughter-in-law, or sister, he lost his limbs, as did a woman who seduced a male slave or servant. However, the *dvīja* authors gave kinder penalties to the upper caste. For consensual sex with a married *brāhman* woman, a *kśatṛiya* paid the highest fine, a *vaiśya* lost all his property, but a *śudra* was burned alive on faggots (4.13.30–32).[53] Witnesses at court had to be worthy men, except for a few single women, but on the whole, females, lepers, and the outcaste (*chāndala*) were truly outcast from court proceedings (*AŚ* 3.11). People belonging to the four *varnas* could not be coerced into slavery, but they could sell themselves to pay debts, an early form of indenture. Laws prohibited high-caste men and women from thrashing slave workers, forcing them to carry manure and dung, or raping a female slave (*AŚ* 3.13), with high fines for such crimes.

All crimes had to be strictly weighed based on material evidence or *vyavahāra*. A woman who was pregnant or had just delivered a child received a milder punishment (*AŚ* 4.8), but if she murdered or maimed her husband, she was torn apart by bulls, even if she were pregnant (*AŚ* 4.11.19). Men were strictly forbidden to cheat a woman of her property, as this would make her subsistence difficult. This was gallantry of a sort, possibly because one author felt that poverty turned women into dangerous harlots. This section describes other social 'thorns' or crimes against artisans, merchants, and workers who enriched the economy. It defines the punishments for murder, mutilation, or the rape of ordinary women. It highlights the importance of witnesses and *vyavahāra* in court trials (*AŚ* 4.8–9), especially in cases involving sex with a girl before her puberty (*AŚ* 4.12).

Some sober discussions are interspersed with sexist lines reflecting the era's male attitudes. For example, a logical discussion on the rights of princes in the first volume (*AŚ* 1.17.35) includes a frightening warning to a youthful prince that his ability to have sons would be lost, if he was seduced by 'impure women disguised as Āryas who wait in lonely places at night' (AS 1.17.35). In a later volume, Kauṭilya's protagonist stated that kings could denounce erstwhile officials and allies, just as 'scorned women' often curse former lovers (*AŚ* 5.6.30). Another volume (*AŚ* 8.3.58–66) rehashes the issue of princely dissipation, when one person argued that gambling was worse than sexual infatuation. Kauṭilya disagreed, as a young man besotted with a woman usually forgot his duties. Another argued that drink was less destructive than sex, as women's 'childishness' induced a worse torpor than drink. The eponymous Kauṭilya then sagely recommended 'a change of wives in the harem', especially after a wife's pregnancy, when she was less interested in sex.

IV. Conclusion: justice for the *Arthaśāstra*

Scholarly dispassion requires one to state the truth, without foisting modern standards upon ancient texts. The *Arthaśāstra* was written for a patriarchal society and state in which women and non-*dvījas* were considered inferior. The authors and readers were elite men whose views on justice differed from present ideals of gender and class equality, although our vision can still be clouded, despite our new, improved glasses. Kauṭilya was a product of his ancient society, yet he tried to steer clear of religious biases. He emphasized his temporal purpose when he defined mundane laws for a diverse kingdom whose first rulers were heterodox. In that early era, the *Arthaśāstra* tried to grant women some sexual and property rights, and while it did not level the playing field for *śudra* workers, his laws were still more compassionate than Vasiṣṭha's *Dharma Sūtra*. Eponymous, orthodox writers retained Kauṭilya's benign rules on protecting minor girls, wives, and pregnant and old women, but decreed gruesome penalties for adultery and inter-caste sex.

Slavery and misogyny were accepted by many ancient and medieval civilizations, and they still thrive in modern societies, despite more enlightened ideals of human equality. Women suspected of infidelity were stoned and paraded naked while sitting backward on a donkey in medieval Europe or branded with an 'A' for adulteress in Pilgrim America, and they are still ostracized in misogynist cultures. Slavery flourished in ancient Egypt, Greece, and Rome; in modern European colonies in Africa and Asia; and in the southern United Sates. It still rears its ugly head as bonded labor in pockets of constitutional India and elsewhere, often wearing the duplicitous masks of technologically perfected economies.

Notes

1 H.C. Raychaudhuri, "India in the Age of the Nandas", in K.A.N. Sastri, ed., *Age of the Nandas and Mauryas*, *op. cit.*, 13–15. Raychaudhuri quotes McCrindle, *The Invasion of India by Alexander the Great,* Westminster, 1886, 220.

2 The first translation was by R. Shamasastry, *Kautilya's Arthaśāstra,* Mysore: Mysore Printing Press, 1967 (8th ed.; 1st ed., 1915). Shamasastry attributed a

Mauryan date, which was endorsed by Sanskrit scholar S. Radhakrishnan (1888–1975), India's first Vice-President (1952–62) and later President (1962–67). For the Sanskrit text, see Sanjeev Sabhlok, ed., *Chanakya (Kautalya)'s Arthashastra in Sanskrit,* with R. Shamasastry's trans., Melbourne, Australia, at this updated website: www.sabhlokcity.com/2012/09/chanakya-Kautalya-arthashastra-chanakya-niti-chanakya-sutras-full-text-sanskrit-and-translations/. Kauṭilya declared his authorship (*AŚ* I.1.19): 'So that happiness and victory may arise from these verses, Kauṭilya has composed this work of enlightenment' ('*sukha grihana vijayam artha pada niśchitam, kauṭilyena kṛtam śāstram vimukta granth vistāram*'). Early 20th century historians like K.A. Nilkanta Sastri endorsed Shamasastry's view that the *Arthaśāstra* was composed for the Mauryan Empire, *vide.,* K.A.N. Sastri, "Mauryan Polity", in K.A.N. Sastri, ed., *Age of the Nandas and Mauryas, op. cit.*, 171–191.

3 See R. Thapar, *Aśoka and the Decline of the Maurya, op. cit.,* 182–200. See also these colonial-era studies of some edicts in J. Burgess, E. Hultzsch, and A. Fuhrer, eds., *Epigraphica Indica: A Collection of Inscriptions of the Archaeological Survey of India, Corpus Inscriptionum Indicarum,* Vol. 1, G. Būhler, trans., "Aśoka's Twelfth Edict: Shāhbāzgarhi Version" in Punjab (1892; revised ed. 1983), pp. 16–20; E. Hultzsch, *Epigraphica Indica,* Vol. 3 (1894–95; revised ed. 1979), G. Būhler, "The Siddapura Edicts of Aśoka", in E. Hultzsch, ed., *Epigraphica Indica, op. cit.*

4 On classical Greek and Roman references to Megathenes's *Indika,* see K.A.N. Sastri, ed., *Age of the Nandas and Mauryas,* these articles, K.A.N. Sastri, "India in Early Greek and Latin Literature", in 81–120, *vide.,* 88–91; H.G. Raychaudhuri, "Chandragupta and Bindusara", 132–170, *vide.,* 132–139; P.C. Bagchi, "Religion and Politics in the Arthaśāstra of Kautalya", 285–308. Sastri quotes J.W. McCrindle's *Ancient India as Described by Megasthenes and Arrian* (1877), and *Ancient India as Described in Classical Literature* (1901).

5 R. Thapar, *Early India: From the Origins to 1300 AD., op. cit.,* 175–176; R. Thapar, *Aśoka and the Decline of the Maurya, op. cit.,* 182–200. She lists the *Vāyu, Brahmānda,* and *Matsya Purānas*; the Buddhist *Mahāvamśa, Dīpavamśa,* and *Vamsatthapakāsinī*; the Jaina text *Pariśiṣṭaparvan*; Viṣākhadatta's *Mudrarākṣasa* (ca. 4th c. ACE), a classical Sanskrit drama about Chandragupta's rise to power; and Kalhana's *Rājatarangini* (12th c. ACE), a Sanskrit chronicle of Kashmir. Their genealogical lists vary. Also see this notable work by Ramashankar Tripathi, *History of Ancient India,* Delhi: Motilal Banarsidass, 1999 (9th ed.; 1st ed., 1942), 162–182. Tripathi quotes Pāṇini's *Aṣṭhadhāyī,* the first Sanskrit grammar (ca. 500 BCE), and Bāna's *Harṣacharita* (ca. 700 ACE), a historical drama in Sanskrit about king Harṣa (606–647 ACE).

6 R. Thapar, *Aśoka and the Decline of the Mauryas, op. cit.* Thapar describes Kautilya as 'the theorist of the politico-economic Mauryan state' (p. 56), who composed the first sections including Vol. II of the *Arthaśāstra.* Thapar makes a persuasive argument that the *Arthaśāstra*'s references to silk, which was brought into India ca. 130 BCE from China, indicate that the code was revised in the classical era and that it was completed by Viṣnugupta (200 ACE), *vide.,* Appendix I, 217–225. See also R. Thapar, *A History of India,* Vol. 1 (Pelican: 1966), New Delhi: Penguin Books, 2000 (12th ed.); R. Thapar, *Early India: From the Origins to AD 1300, op. cit.,* 184–185. Patrick Olivelle and Mark McClish recently proposed a date between the Mauryan and Kuṣāna Empires, *vide.,* P. Olivelle and M. McClish, trans., *Arthaśāstra: Selections from the Classic Indian Work on Statecraft, op. cit.*

7 See K.A.N. Sastri's "India in Early Greek and Latin Literature", in K.A.N. Sastri, ed., *Age of the Nandas and Mauryas, op. cit.,* 81–131, *vide.,* 100–102, 117–119.

Sastri quotes Arrian, Megasthenes, Diodorus, and Curtius. The first western account was by Nearchus, the Cretan admiral who accompanied Alexander to India (326 BCE), but returned via the Persian Gulf. A Sicilian called Diodorus wrote *Bibliotheke* (ca. 50 BCE), in which he quoted Megasthenes's *Indika* (II.35–42). Strabo also quoted Megasthenes in his *Geography* (64 BCE–19 ACE). Roman scholar Pliny the Elder (23–79 ACE) also quoted Megasthenes in his *Natural History* (Book 6 on India). Arrian (2nd c. ACE), a Greek civil servant of the Roman Empire, wrote *Anabasis of Alexander*, an account of Alexander's campaigns, in which he cited Nearchus and Megasthenes's *Indika*. Roman historian Quintius Rufus Curtius (1st c. ACE) wrote of a history of Alexander in which he described Indians, Chandragupta, Pātaliputra, and women who accompanied the Mauryan emperor on palanquins. The Roman historian named Justin (a.k.a. Marcus Junianus Justinus or Justinus (3rd. c. ACE) described Chandragupta as a man of plebian ancestry (*novus homo*). Curtius and Megasthenes (Fragment XLI) both stated that an image of Herakles (Kṛiṣna) was carried in processions near Mathura.

8 H.C. Raychaudhuri, "Chandragupta and Bindusara", in K.A.N. Sastri, ed., *Age of the Nandas and Mauryas, op. cit.*, 132–170, *vide.*, 152, 154. The Greek word for an actual marriage is *kedos*, but Strabo and Appian both use the term *hypergamia,* meaning 'the right of marriage by state'. Raychaudhuri argues that 'there was no room in the family circle of Seleucus for any actual marriage relationship', yet it is strange that he believes that a marriage took place. See R. Thapar, *Aśoka, op. cit.*, 17. She states a Seleucid princess with her noblewomen may have come to Pātaliputra; some of whom were perhaps the wives of Mauryan officers. Neither historian states with certainty that Chandragupta's chief consort was Greek.

9 H.C. Raychaudhuri, "Chandragupta and Bindusara", in K.A.N. Sastri, ed., *Age of the Nandas and Mauryas, op. cit.*, 144–145, 151–160.

10 R. Thapar, *Aśoka, op. cit.*, 12 (fn 4), 17–18, 292–303.

11 H.C. Raychaudhuri, "Chandragupta and Bindusāra", in K.A.N. Sastri, ed., *Age of the Nandas and Mauryas, op. cit.*, 159–160. Raychaudhuri quotes J.W. McCrindle, *Ancient India as Described by Megasthenes and Arrian*, London, 1877 (rept. Calcutta: 1926), 70. An early work on the Mauryas is Purushottam Lal Bhargava's *Chandragupta Maurya, op. cit.*

12 Ramashankar Tripathi, *History of Ancient India, op. cit.*, 146; and D.N. Jha, *Ancient India: In Historical Outline*, Delhi: Manohar, 1998 (revised ed.; 1st ed., 1977), 92–94.

13 R. Thapar, *Aśoka, op. cit.*, 22–31. She cites the Ceylonese Buddhist chronicles, and Chinese pilgrim Hiuen Tsang (ca. 7th c. ACE) on the struggle between Aśoka and his brothers.

14 For a history of early monuments, see J.C. Harle, *The Art and Architecture of the Indian Subcontinent*, New Haven: Yale University Press, 1994 (2nd ed.), 22–27; Roy C. Craven, *Indian Art: A Concise History, op. cit.*, 34–49; R. Thapar, *Aśoka, op. cit.*, 179, 235, 269.

15 Edicts translated by R. Thapar and A.L. Basham, in R. Thapar, *Aśoka, op. cit.*, 255–256.

16 R. Thapar, *Aśoka, op. cit.*, 182–196.

17 Patrick Olivelle's studies of the *Arthaśāstra* and *Manu Smṛiti* include: P. Olivelle, trans., ed., *King, Governance and Law in Ancient India: Kautilya's Arthaśāstra: A New Annotated Translation, op. cit.*; P. Olivelle, "Manu and the 'Arthaśāstra': A Study in Sastric Intertexuality", in *Journal of Indian Philosophy, op. cit.*, 281–291; P. Olivelle, *The Law Code of Manu: A New Translation Based on the*

Critical Edition, op. cit.; P. Olivelle, trans., ed., *Manu's Code of Law: A Critical Edition and Translation of the Mānava-Dharmáśāstra with the Editorial Assistance of Suman Olivelle, op. cit.*; P. Olivelle, *The Law Code of Manu: A New Translation Based on the Critical Edition, op. cit.*

18 Although ideals on social inclusion today are wider than what prevailed 2,000 years ago, we may draw a broad and tentative analogy based on political psychology. Like non-*dvīja* Mauryan kings, today's elected officials from minority and upper-caste communities are often required to prove their democratic *bona fides* by upholding legal equity for all citizens, irrespective of gender, race, community, or class.

19 Kauṭilya declared his authorship in Vol. I (*AŚ* I.1.19), *vide.*, endnote 3 (see above). In his first 1915 translation, R. Shamasastry, trans., *Kautilya's Arthaśāstra, op. cit.*, attributed a Mauryan date, which was endorsed by scholar S. Radhakrishnan. Historian K.A. Nilkanta Sastri agreed that the *Arthaśāstra* was written for the Mauryan Empire, *vide.*, K.A.N. Sastri, "Mauryan Polity", in K.A.N. Sastri, ed., *Age of the Nandas and Mauryas, op. cit.*, 171–191. R. Shamasastry, *Kautilya's Arthaśāstra* (1915), *op. cit.* I have modified Sanjeev Sabhlok's translation of the Sanskrit verse *AŚ* 1.10.2 in the text. The transliteration reads: '*Purohitam ayājya yājanādhyāpena niyuktam amṛṣyamāṇam rājā avikśhipeta*'. See Sanjeev Sabhlok, ed., "Chanakya (Kautalya)'s Arthashastra in Sanskrit", as R. Shamasastry's trans. as a PDF file, *op. cit.*, at this website: www.sabhlokcity.com/2012/09/chanakya-Kautalya-arthashastra-chanakya-niti-chanakya-sutras-full-text-sanskrit-and-translations/.

Also see a later version by Sunil Daman, "Chanakya Arthashastra in English and Sanskrit", at this website: www.patheos.com/blogs/hindu2/2014/10/arthashastra-of-kautilya-by-r-shamasastry/ Chanakya Arthashastra in English and Sanskrit, October 2014, PDF.

20 R. Thapar, *Aśoka, op. cit.*, 252.

21 Sten Kononw, *Kauṭalya Studies*, Oslo: Komisjon Hos Jacob Dybwad, 1945. His transliteration reads: '*AS* 1.1.1) *Prithivyā lābhe pālane ca yāvanty arthāśāstrāṇi pūrvācāyaih prasthāpitāni prāyaśas tāni samhṛtyaikam idam arthaśāstram kṛtam*)'; and '*AS* 15.1.73) *Yena śāstram ca śāstram ca Nandarājagatā ca bhūh; amarsenoddhūṛtāni āśu tena śāstram idam krtam*'. Shamasastry's fine translation of the last verse of this text, which reads: '*AS* 15.19.73: 'This Sástra has been made by him who from intolerance (of misrule) quickly rescued the scriptures and the science of weapons and the earth which had passed to the Nanda king'.

22 Thapar's exemplary historical endeavors include Romila Thapar, *Aśoka and the Decline of the Mauryas, op. cit.* In this work, Thapar describes Kautalya as 'the theorist of the politico-economic Mauryan state' (p. 56), who composed the first sections including Vol. II of the *Arthaśāstra*. She argues persuasively that references to silk, first brought into India ca. 130 BCE from China, indicate that the code was revised in the classical era and completed by Vişnugupta (200 ACE), *vide.*, Appendix I, The Date of the *Arthaśāstra*, 218–225. See also R. Thapar, *A History of India, op. cit.*; R. Thapar, *Early India: From the Origins to AD 1300*, Berkeley: University of California Press, 2002, 184–186.

23 Vişnugupta's final words are (*AS* 15.19.73): 'Thus ends the Chapter I, "Paragraphic divisions of the Treatise" in the fifteenth Book, "Plan of Treatise." This is the one hundred and fiftieth chapter from the first chapter of the entire work. The fifteenth book, "Plan of Treatise, of the Arthasástra of Kautilya is thus brought to a close." *Having seen discrepancies in many ways on the part of the writers of commentaries on the Sástras, Vishnu Gupta himself has made (this) Sútra and commentary'.

24 K.A.N. Sastri, "Mauryan Polity", in K.A.N. Sastri, ed., *Age of the Nandas and Mauryas, op. cit.,* 193.
25 Thomas R. Trautmann, *Kauṭilya and the Arthaśāstra,* Leiden, Netherlands: E.J. Brill, 1971.
26 On the *Manu Smṛiti,* see P. Olivelle, "Manu and the 'Arthaśāstra': A Study in Śāstric Intertextuality", in *Journal of Indian Philosophy, op. cit.*, 281–291; P. Olivelle, trans., ed., *Manu's Code of Law: A Critical Edition and Translation of the Mānava-Dharmáśāstra with the Editorial Assistance of Suman Olivelle, op. cit.*; P. Olivelle, *The Law Code of Manu: A New Translation Based on the Critical Edition, op. cit.* (pbk).
27 P. Olivelle, "Manu and the 'Arthaśāstra' ": A Study in Śāstric Intertextuality", in *Journal of Indian Philosophy, op. cit.*
28 P. Olivelle, *The Law Code of Manu: A New Translation Based on the Critical Edition, op. cit.*, 2009, xx; P. Olivelle, trans., ed., *Dharmasūtras: The Law Codes of Āpastamba, Gautama, Baudhāyana, and Vasiṣṭha, op. cit.,* xxv.
29 P. Olivelle and M. McClish, *Arthaśāstra: Selections from the Classic Indian Work on Statecraft, op. cit.*, xv–xx; and P. Olivelle, *King, Governance, and Law in Ancient India: Kautilya's Arthasastra: A New Annotated Translation, op. cit.*, 2013. Also see these further studies by Patrick Olivelle on the *Arthaśāstra* and *Manu Smṛiti*; P. Olivelle, "Manu and the 'Arthaśāstra': A Study in Sastric Intertexuality", in *Journal of Indian Philosophy, op. cit.*, 281–291; P. Olivelle, *The Law Code of Manu: A New Translation Based on the Critical Edition, op. cit.*; P. Olivelle, trans., ed., *Manu's Code of Law: A Critical Edition and Translation of the Mānava-Dharmáśāstra with the Editorial Assistance of Suman Olivelle, op. cit.*; P. Olivelle, *The Law Code of Manu: A New Translation Based on the Critical Edition, op. cit.*
30 My translations of these *Arthaśāstra* verses and their transliteration into English. The original Sanskrit text in PDF file is available at this site: Sanjeev Sabhlok, ed., "Chanakya (Kautalya)'s Arthashastra in Sanskrit", with R. Shamasastry's trans. (1915), Melbourne, Australia, 11 September 2012. Melbourne, Australia, at this website: www.sabhlokcity.com/2012/09/chanakya-Kautalya-arthashastra-chanakya-niti-chanakya-sutras-full-text-sanskrit-and-translations/.
31 Sanjeev Sabhlok, ed., *Chanakya (Kautalya)'s Arthashastra, op. cit.* My transliterations are: *AŚ* 1.3.13: '*Sarveṣām ahimsā satyam śaucham ansūya ānṛśamsyam kśhmā ca; AŚ* 1.3.14) *sarva dharmah svargāyānantyāya cha; AŚ* 1.3.15) *tasyātikramay lokah saṅkarādu uchchhdeta; AŚ* 1.3.16) *tasyāt sarva dharman bhūtānām rājā navyabhichāret; sarva dharma sandhāno hi pretyacha ihacha nandati;* 17) *vyavasthitārya maryādah krta varnārśramasthitih; tryyā abhirakshito lokah prasīdatī, na sīdati*'.
32 I have transliterated the *Arthaśāstra's* Sanskrit verses *(AŚ* 1.4.7–16): '1.4.7: *Na iti Kauṭilyah;* 8–9) *tīkśadaṇdo hi bhūtānām, mṛidudaṇdah paribhūyate;* 10) *yathā aharya daṇdah pūjyate;* 11) *suvijñyāta pranīto hi daṇdah prajā dharmārtha kāmair yojayati;* 12) *duṣpranītah kāmakrodhyābhyām avjñyādu vā vānaprastha parivrājkān api kopayati, kimaṇga punargṛihasthān;* 13) *apranītah tu mātsyanyāyam udbhāvayati;* 14) *balīyān abalam hi graste dandadharābhāve;* 15) *sa tena guptah prabhavati iti;* 16) *chaturvarnāśramo loko rājñā daṇdena pālitah; svadharma karmā bhirato vartete sveṣu vartamasu (iti)*'.
33 My translations of *Arthaśāstra* verses (*AŚ* 1.19.1–5), with these transliterations: *AŚ* 1.19.1: '*rājān utithan anūt tiṣṭhante bhṛthyāh*'; 2): '*pramādhayante anupramādhyanti;* 3):'*karmāṇi chāsya bhakśyanti*'; 4): *dviṣadbhiśchāti sandhīyate;* 5): '*tasmād uthhān ātmanah kurvīta*'.
34 The *Arthaśāstra's* last verses *(AS* 1.19. 33–36) with transliterations of each two-line *sloka: AS* 1.19. 33 a&b) '*Rājñyo hi vratam uthānam yagñyah*

kāryānuśāsanam; dakśiṇā vṛittisāmyam tu dīkśā tasyābhiṣechanam'; 1.19.34 a&b) *'prajāsukhe sukham rājñyah prajānām cha tu hite hitam; nātmapriyam hitam rājñyah prajānām tu priyam hitam'*; 1.19.35 a&b) *'tasmān nitya uthito rājā kuryādu arthānuśāsanam; arthasya mulam uthānam anarthasya viparyayah'*; 1.19.36 a&b) *'anuthāne dhruvo nāśah prāptasyānā gatasya cha; prāpyate phalam uthānāllabhate chārtha sampadam'*. See also R. Shamasastry, trans., ed., *Arthaśāstra, op. cit.*, 38–39.

35 R. Shamasastry's translation of *AŚ* 6.1.15–18, *ibid.*, 364–365. Transliterated 2 line verses are: *AŚ* 6.1.15a-b:*'arivarjāha prakṛtayah sapta ekatah svaguna udayāh'*; 15c–d: *'uktaha pratyagna bhutaha tāha prakṛtān rāja sampadaha'*; 6.1.16a–b: *'sampādityatya sampannaha prakṛtīrātma vānnṛipaha'*;16c–d: *'vivṛiddhāśchā nuraktāścha prakṛitīr hantyanātmavān'*; 6.1.17a–b: *'tatah sa duṣta prakṛitīśchā turanto āpyanātmavān'*; 17c–d: *'hantye vā prakṛitībhiryāti vā dviṣatām vaśam'*; 6.1.18a–b: *'ātmavānah tvalpadeśo api yuktah prakṛiti sampadā'*; c–d: *'na yajñāha pṛithivīm kṛitastrām jayatyeva na dīyate (iti)'*.

36 Transliterations of these Sanskrit verses of *Arthaśāstra* (*AS* 1.20.14–17) read: *AŚ* 1.20.14*) antara gṛihagatah sthavira strī pariśūddhān devīn paśyet;* 15) *devī gṛihe līno hi bhrātā bhadrasenam jaghān; mātuha śayyāh antargataścha putrah kāruṣam;* 16) *'lājān madhuna itiviṣeṇa paryasya devī Kāśirājān; viṣdigdhena nūpreṇa vairantyam, mekhalāmāṇinā sauvīram, jālūtham ādarshena vayṇyām gūdham śāstram kritvā devī vidūratham jaghān;* 17) *'tasmād aitānyāsapadāni pariharet'*.

37 Strabo's quotation from Megasthenes, *Fragment* XXVI, cited by K.A.N. Sastri, "India in Early Greek and Latin Literature", in K.A.N. Sastri, ed., *Age of the Nandas and Mauryas, op. cit.*, 119.

38 My transliteration of *Arthaśāstra* verses (*AŚ* 2.27.7–8) read: 2.27.7: *'Ashta varshaat prabhriti rajñyah kushila vakarma kuryāt;* 2.27.8: *'gaṇikādāsi bhagnabhogā koshthagāre mahānse vā karma kuryāt '*.

39 The transliteration of *Arthaśāstra* (*AŚ* 1.17.51) reads: *'na cha ekaputran avinītam sthāpayet'*.

40 My translations of *Arthaśāstra* (*AŚ* 1.10.7–8), with these transliterations:
1.10.7: *'Parivrājikā labdha viśvāsāntah purai kṛitasatkārā mahāmātram ekaikan upajapet – 'rājamahīṣī tvām kāmayate kritasamāgam upāyā, mahān arthaśracha te bhaviśyati iti'*.1.10.8 *'pratyākyāne śuchih; iti kāma upadhā*

41 Stephanie W. Jamison, "Women 'Between Empires' and Between Lines", in P. Olivelle, ed., *Between the Empires, op. cit.*, 207–209.

42 My translation of the *Arthaśāstra* (*AŚ* 1.12.4–5).

43 Dilip K. Chakrabarti, *India: An Archaeological History, op. cit.*, 295–300.

44 R. Shamasastry, trans., ed., *Arthaśāstra, op. cit.*, 543–544, selections.

45 *Arthashastra* (*AS* 1.19).

46 *Arthaśāstra* (*AŚ* 3.2.14–18); the transliterated verses read:
3.2.14: *'vṛittirābandhyam vā stṛīdhanam'*; 3.2.15*: 'paradvisāhastra sthyāpyā vṛittih ābandhyā niyamah'*; 3.2.16: *'tadu ātmaputrasnuṣābharṇi pravāsā prati vidhāne cha bhāryāyā bhoktum adoṣah'*; *'pratirodhaka vyādhi durbhikśa bhaya pratīkāre dharmakārye cha patyuh, sambhūya vā dampatyor mithunam prajātayoh'*; 3.2.17: *'trivarśa upabhuktam cha dharmiṣtheṣu vivāheṣu nānuyuñjīta'*; 3.2.18: *'gāndharvāsura upabhuktam savṛiddhikam ubhayam dāpyeta, rākśa paiśācha upabhuktam steyam dadhyāta'*.

47 My translation of these *Arthaśāstra slokas* (*AŚ* 3.2.36–37) with transliterations below:
AŚ 3.2.36: *'Jīvati bhartari mṛitāyāh putrā duhitarśscha strīdhanam vibhajerana, aputrāyā duhitarah, tadu abhāve bhartā'*; 3.2.37: *'Śulkam anvādheyam anyadu vā bandhu bhirdattam bāndhvā hareyuh iti strīdhana kalpah'*.

48 My translations of these *Arthaśāstra* verses (*AŚ* 3.2. 19–23), with transliterations below:

AŚ 3.2.19: *'Mṛite bhartari tadānṛm egha sthyāpyā bharanam śuklaśeṣam cha labhate';*

3.2.20: *'Labdhbāvā bindamānā sa vṛiddhikam ubhayam dāpyete';* 3.2.21: *'Kutumbakāmā tu śvaśurapatidattam niveśakāle labhate';*3.2.22: *'Niveśakālam hi dīrghapravāse vyākhyāsyāmah';* 3.2.23: *'Śvaśura pratilomyena vā niviṣtā śvaśurapatidattan jīyeta'.*

49 My translations of these *Arthaśāstra* verses (3.5.7–10) with transliterations in brackets:

AŚ 3.5.9–10: 'If a man has no sons, his brothers living with him (*sahajīvino*) can take his moveable property (*dravyam*), and his daughters born of lower forms of marriage (other than the four highest) can have his immovable property (*riktham*). If he has sons, they will get the property; but if he has only daughters from the four highest forms of marriage, they will get the property' (*'Dravyam aputrasya sodaryā brārtarah sahajīvino vā hareyuh kanyāścha; 'Riktham putravatah putrā duhitaro vā vivāheṣu jātāh*').

50 I have translated verse *AŚ* 3.5.21 as: 'Unmarried daughters are also entitled to a dowry to be given to them upon marriage' (*i.e.*, '*kanyā bhyaścha prādānikam*')'.

51 See Stephanie W. Jamison's insightful, "'Between the Empires' and Between the Lines", in P. Olivelle, ed., *Between the Empires: Society in India 300 BCE to 400 CE, op. cit.*, 191–214, vide 207–208.

52 The transliterated verses read: '*AŚ* 3.4. 42 a–b: '*Ethān utkramya dāyādān vedane jārakarmaṇi; jāra stṛī dātri vetāttārah samprāptāh sangrahātyam'.*

53 R. Shamasastry, translation, *Arthaśāstra* (8th ed., 1967), *op. cit.* I have synopsized, revised his translations, and transliterated these verses: (*AŚ* 4.13.30–31–32).

AŚ 4.13.30–31: 'Any man who uses witchcraft to have sex with the sister of his father or mother, or his maternal uncle's wife, or the wife of his teacher, or his daughter-in-law, or his sister will have his limbs cut off and then put to death. If the woman succumbs to him, she too will have the same punishment; and a woman who accepts the advances of a slave (*dāsa)* or laborer will be similarly punished. (*Mātāpitrorbhaginīm mātulānīm āchāryāṇīm stṛīṣām duhitaram bhaginīm vyāhādhicharatah trilangachachedanam vaghascha'; 'sakāma tadu eva labhate, dāsa parichārakahit kabhuktācha';*

AŚ 4.113.32: 'A *kśatṛiya* who commits adultery with an unsuspecting *brāhman* woman will pay the highest fines as penalty, the *vaiśya* who does this will forfeit all his property, and the *śudra* will be burnt alive with wooden faggots.' ('*Brāhmanyām aguptāyām kśatriyasya uttamah, sarvasyam vaiṣyasya, śudrah kathāgninnā dehyet*').

7

EARLY CLASSICAL ERA

I. Historical review (600–200 BCE)

This chapter examines each law code through the lens of political and social history, with a primary focus on women's marriage and property, the royal state, and the *varna* hierarchy. We begin with a review of the later Vedic era and its *Dharma Śūtra* codes and the Mauryan codes (ca. 600–180 BCE); followed by a preview of the classical era and its codes (180 BCE–570 ACE).

Upon entering the subcontinent, early Sanskritic clans (ca. 2500 BCE) had three occupational classes (*varnas*), that is, *brāhman* priests, *kṣatṛiya* chiefs (*rājans*) and soldiers, and *vaiśya* farmers-merchants, who were later called *dvījas* ('twice-born') and entitled to learn the *Vedas* (1800–600 BCE). As the initial clans were predominantly male, they soon married local women, and their progeny were often included in their ranks. They also often inducted their extended families from local communities into the *varna* order as *śudra* workers. By 1000 BCE, the clans had reached the Yamuna-Ganges Doab and acquired vast territories, which crystallized into the first states (*janapadas*). Around 800 BCE, the *janapadas* comprised sixteen kingdoms (*rāṣtras/rājyas*) and oligarchic confederacies (*gana sanghas*). The leaders were *kṣatṛiya rājans* and *brāhmans*, while subjects included clan members, as well as indigenous communities. There now ensued an elite male *dvījā* pact in which *brāhmans* ritually consecrated *kṣatṛiya* kings, who appointed *brāhmans* as advisors. While kingdoms became dominant (ca. 500 BCE), some powerful oligarchies remained until the classical centuries. These included the martial Mālavās of Mālwa and the wealthy Vṛijji *gana sangha* near Nepal.

Recognizing the need for formal legal treatises (*śāstras*) to govern their states and to ensure that legitimate sons inherited property, including the throne and its lands, erudite male *brāhmans* composed the *Dharma Sūtras*. As the codes instructed kings on their royal (*rāja*) *dharmas* to defend, govern righteously, and mete out justice, the term '*dharma*' took on an expanded meaning. Originally signifying the sacred duties of *dvījas* and *śudras*, *dharma* now also connoted righteous temporal laws of the state. As the first codes, the *Dharma Sūtras* were skimpy on legal procedures (*vyavahāra*), such as witnesses and evidence, but they set the pattern for male authorship for subsequent codes. They had a seminal impact on gender norms, as the laws were defined by benign paternalists, stern patriarchs, or misogynists.

Women's rights diminished in the patrilineal/patrimonial *janapadas* of the later Vedic era as these states spread across the northern subcontinent. Once entitled to learn the *Vedās* and address gatherings, women were often restricted to domestic pursuits, although even the household was dominated by men. The gender restrictions were ostensibly to protect females, but fewer girls now attended Vedic schools or spoke at public assemblies. The *Dharma Sūtra* authors lauded female chastity, but only Āpastamba, a southerner familiar with matriarchy, honored married couples and gave widows a share of spousal property. The *Rig Veda* described female property (*stṛīdhana*) as a bride's dowry, and various gifts given to her at her marriage by her family, and any subsequent gifts, all constituted matrilineal property. The *Dharma Sūtras* of Gautama, Baudhāyana, and Vasiṣṭha restricted *stṛīdhana* to moveable objects like jewelry, thus effectively preventing women from inheriting the throne and its domains. It also transpired that dowry lands given to a princess were often controlled by the royal husband.

Āpastamba, Gautama, Baudhāyana, and Vasiṣtha validated filial inheritance and patrilineal succession to the throne. As they did not advocate primogeniture, a king's death often led to a protracted princely struggle. Āpastamba honored the married couple, and he gave widows inheritance rights. In contrast, Gautama, Baudhāyana, and Vasiṣtha sanctioned polygamy for *dvīja* men across *varna* lines, thus ensuring them several sons, although sons' rights were based on the mother's *varna*. This law helped to create a society with numerous sub-castes while keeping alive the myth of *dvīja* purity. These three *Dharma Sutrā* authors expressed their anxiety over the influx of casteless foreigners (*mlecchas*), a trickle that became a river after Alexander's departure, when a Graeco-Bactrian state formed in the northwest (326 BCE). Xenophobia accompanied misogyny, as these authors validated early puberty marriages and suspected women of sex with *śudras* and *mlecchas* and of foisting illegitimate sons off as heirs of the husband. While *dvīja* men could marry *śudra* wives, *śudra* men who had sex with *dvīja* women were castrated and forfeited property.

Sanskrit terms like '*dharma*', '*artha*', and '*kṣaṭriya*' now assumed broader meanings in the political context of the growing state. *Dharma* originally meant the moral order supporting society, in which each *varna* performed its sacred duties. In the *Dharma Sūtras, dharma* took on a fresh connotation, as it now also signified temporal laws of the state, which depended on the king's righteous duties (*rāja dharma*). Buddhist and Jaina texts in Pāli and Prakrit used the equivalent '*dhamma*' to signify morality, as well as sacred duties and laws. In a similar manner, the term '*artha*', or material wealth, was modified when the royal state burgeoned into the Mauryan Empire (321–184 BCE). In the *Arthaśāstra*, the first major code on statecraft, *artha* signified the bureaucratic and military wealth of the state. As the author Kauṭilya was a *brāhman* who advised emperor Chandragupta Maurya, his *Arthaśāstra* validated male polygamy and patrilineal inheritance, especially for the throne. At the same time, Kauṭilya praised women as the king's loyal servants, protected women's *strīdhana* from male control, and gave widows indirect rights to spousal property through a son. In another example of new connotations, the word '*kṣaṭriya*' originally specified the martial *varna* of soldiers and kings, but this was now applied to the non-*dvīja* military strategist, Jaina emperor Chandragupta, who inspired Kauṭilya's ideal of kingship. Due to a strategic Mauryan-Bactrian pact, Kauṭilya did not denigrate other ethnicities, castes, or sects. Later, the Buddhist emperor Āśoka Maurya equated *dhamma* with compassionate tolerance, which he described in his edicts as the 'essence' of all sects and the duty of kings and subjects.[1]

II. Preview: classical kingdoms and codes

The classical centuries comprised two chronological periods, that is, the early classical era (180 BCE–200 ACE), and the later classical era (200–570 ACE). Chapters 8–9 examine the early classical era's key political events, royal ideals, society, and two major law codes, that is, 1) the Mauryan *Arthaśāstra*, now expanded by eponyms and completed by Viṣnugupta (ca. 150 ACE), and 2) the first *Dharma Śāstra,* that is, the *Mānava Dharma Śāstra/Manu Smṛiti* (ca. 100 BCE–150 ACE). Chapters 10–11 are on the later classical centuries' kingdoms and social changes and the next two *Dharma Śāstras*, that is, *Yājnyavalkya Smṛitī* (200 ACE) and *Nārada Smṛitī* (400 ACE). The orthodox early classical *Manu Smṛiti* incorporated the legal features of the *Arthaśāstra* but glorified *kṣatṛiya* kings, praised *dvījās,* vilified heterodoxy, and constrained women.[2]

The later classical era's more stable pre-Guptan kingdoms and the Guptan Empire monarchs recognized the economic and social benefits of sectarian/caste/ethnic tolerance. As ideals of kingly *dharma* were now well established, Yajñyavalkya and Nārada did not restate well-established kingly ideals but focused on details of legal procedures (*vyavahāra*). The *Yajñyavalkya Smṛiti* possibly served liberal Hindu dynasties, like the Andhra Ikṣvākus, whose wives donated to the Buddhist Sangha (ca. 250 ACE), while the imperial Guptans (319–520 ACE) relied on the *Yajñyavalkya Smṛiti* and the *Nārada Smṛiti* to govern their vast domains.

III. Early classical era (200 BCE–200 ACE)

A. New kingdoms and empires

After Alexander's brief invasion and departure from Punjāb (326 BCE), an Indo-Greek kingdom had been established under subsidiaries in Bactria

(Afghanistan). In 304 BCE, its ruler Seleucus Nikator attempted to reconquer Punjāb, but when defeated by Chandragupta Maurya, Seleucus ceded Kabul and Gāndhāra. The two monarchs signed a successful peace treaty that promoted cultural and trade contacts for over 120 years. Mauryan imperial collapse ended the treaty (184 BCE) and triggered waves of invasions from the northwest. Demetrius the Indo-Greek reconquered Punjāb and Gāndhāra (165 BCE), and his successors' domain later included Mathura, Malwa, and Gujarat. Indian texts collectively referred to westerners as 'Yāvanā' (*i.e.*, Ionian), including Persian Pahlavas of Parthia, who later seized Taxila, Gāndhāra (90 BCE), from the Indo-Greeks. Art and literature indicate that Yāvanā kings fostered a mix of Hindu-Buddhist-Zoroastrian traditions. The Indo-Greek king Menander (Milinda; ca. 150 BCE) thus became a Buddhist after a philosophical discussion with the monk Nāgasenā. Their question-answer sessions in the Pāli *Milindapañho* text resemble teacher-student discourses in the *Upaniṣads*, with an echo from Plato's dialogues.[3] In 80 BCE, the Indo-Greek Atialkidas sent one Heliodorus as his ambassador to the Śunga court of king Odraka. Heliodorous's famous Besnagar pillar describes him as a Bhāgavatā, or devotee of Kṛiṣna.[4] Sculptures of Greek deities gave way to Hindu-Buddhist nature goddesses (*yakṣīs*), while Kṛiṣna legends merged with Greek myths of Herakles. In his *Indika* (ca. 300 BCE), Megasthenes wrote that 'The Pandaean nation is governed by females, and their first queen is said to be a daughter of Herakles. . . . who begat a daughter in India whom he called Pandaia'. Herakles was suggesting that the first queen of the matrilineal Tamil Pāndyas was possibly Greek. He may have believed this after observing popular reverence for goddess Uma-Pārvati, whom Indian myths portray as Kṛiṣna's sister.[5]

The fall of the Mauryan Empire (184 BCE) created a power vacuum that led to a series of invasions from the northwest. In these invasions and subsequent battles for territorial domains, new kingdoms were established, while the influx of numerous immigrants dynamically changed society and culture. At this time, rulers became cognizant of new land and sea routes, which led to greater trade and social interactions. Diverse ethnic groups now entered the subcontinent, and their presence genetically altered South Asian societies and cultures. Immigrant and local kings fostered an eclectic mix of Buddhist, Hindu, and Jaina cultural traditions (200 BCE–300 ACE) and reshaped ideals on kingship and governance. In contrast to the centralized Mauryan administration, early classical kingdoms had decentralized governance, and there ensued two concurrent legal systems, which were a notable concession to social and ethnic diversity. The king meted out court justice with a formal law code (*śāstra*), but he also allowed local communal laws on marriage and property. Yet, since the Sanskrit code was the final royal court of appeal, patriarchal norms had either a strong or subtle imprint on gender relations in many local communities. Eponymous scholars now added to the *Arthaśāstra*, which may have served heterodox states like the Kuşāna Empire, whose most eminent emperor, Kanişka, was a Buddhist. Early scholars dated Kanişka's rule to have occurred between 78 and 144 ACE, but recent scholars date his accession to 127 ACE.[6]

In the post-Mauryan centuries, Magadha was ruled by two dynasties who favored Vedic rites and norms for nearly 150 years (184–28 BCE). The first hundred years were under the Śungas, a dynasty founded by the martial *brāhman* Puşhyamitra. Despite their preference for *brāhmans*, they also endorsed additions to the important Buddhist burial monument (*stupa*) at Sānchi (Madhya Pradesh). The Kanvas usurped power, and they are known chiefly for supporting *brāhmans* and for resisting the formidable Jaina king Khāravela (ca. 50 BCE) of Kalinga (Orissa), a mineral-rich region with a large indigenous tribal population.[7] Khāravela's martial as well as benevolent exploits appear in the Hāthīgumpha inscription in the Udayagiri Hill caves near Puri. This document on the cave walls speaks of him as the conqueror of 'Bharatvarśa', a king who invaded Magadha, drove Demetrius the Indo-Greek from the Ganges, defeated the Bhoja ruler, and crossed the Krishna river to fight the Andhra Śātavāhanās and the Tamil confederacy led by the Pāndyas. At the same time, it lauds Khāravela as an 'illustrious' king who remitted taxes for all subjects, including *brāhmans*, a ruler who rebuilt an ancient irrigation canal, employed builders, fostered trade, supported Jaina monks, and hosted a Jaina canonical conference.[8] The Hāthīgumpha edict echoes Aśoka's 7th Pillar Edict (Lauriya-Nandangarh), in which the Mauryan emperor stated that he had dug wells and planted mango groves and 'banyan trees to give shade to man and beast'.[9]

Upon the heels of the Indo-Greeks arrived the Śakas of Central Asia. The first leader, Maues (ca. 80 BCE), wrested Punjab, Gāndhāra, Ujjain (Mālwa), and Mathura from the Indo-Greeks, while his son Azes I (58 BCE) ruled over an empire that included parts of Saurashtra and Maharashtra. However, the Śakas eventually lost Punjāb to the Pahlava king Gondophernes (ca. 50 BCE). Śaka kings gave considerable autonomy to sons as regional kings or governors (*kşatrapas*). Titles such as *kşatrapāvan*, the shortened *şatrap*, and 'Shahin-Shah' (King of Kings) originated in Achaemenid ideals of kingship after Cyrus of Persia (530 BCE) conquered the Indus region, Gandhara, and Kambhoja. Yet royal ideals were reshaped after immigrants formed new kingdoms on the subcontinent in the early classical era. They borrowed the ideals of the martial *kşatṛiya* king from local *rājās*, used the *Arthaśāstra*'s guidelines on statecraft, and were perhaps inspired by lingering Mauryan Aśokan ruins. Immigrants battled local *rājās*, but as they also signed peace treaties with marital clauses, inevitably, Persian royal honorifics were absorbed into the Sanskrit and Prakrit lexicons. This is seen in the dynastic name of *Mahā-Kşatrapa* (Great King), coined by merging *şatrapa* with *kṣatṛiya* and *mahā*. Other grandiose titles were *Rājā-ti-Rājā* (King of Kings) and *Mahārāja* (Great King), used also by Dravidian rulers.[10]

Coins and inscriptions provide information on early classical society and economy and the political interactions between the Deccan Śātavahanas and Śakas and the Tamil dynasties.[11] The Śātavahana Empire extended from Andhra to Maharashtra and Saurashtra (ca. 50 BCE–250 ACE). Around 100 ACE, Bhumaka, the Śaka king, seized Saurashtra from the Śātavahanas and issued coins in Prakrit. His successor, Nāhapana, also issued silver coins lauding him in Prakrit as 'Rano Kshaharata Nahapanasa', using the Brahmi and Persian Kharoshti scripts (ca. 120 ACE).[12] Nāhapana's Nāsik cave edict describes him as the powerful overlord of the west whose territories stretched from Broach to Konkan. Roman vessels docked at seaports with Greek, Bactrian, Persian, Jewish, Egyptian, and Abyssinian sailors and merchants, who paid gold or silver in their dealings with Hindu, Buddhist, and Jaina local traders.[13] Another inscription describes the marriage of Nāhapana's daughter Dakṣāmitra, who was probably a Hindu, to his Śaka general Uṣavadāta, who undertook a religious pilgrimage after a victorious battle.[14] Nāhapana's power is independently affirmed by the *Periplus of the Erythraean Sea* (Chapter 41; ca. 68–100 ACE), the nautical log of an Egyptian-Greek captain who refers to Nāhapana as 'Mambanus', overlord of a fertile region whose products were rice, wheat, sesame oil, and fine cotton cloth.[15]

Although gold beads occur in the Indus civilization's site at Lothal (ca. 1800 BCE), and the Mauryans were aware of mines in Mysore and Chota Nagpur, gold was too expensive to issue as coins. Indian kings generally minted copper, silver, and tin coins and sometimes those of even cheaper metal. The opening of the northwest to Indo-Greeks, Parthians, and Central Asians in this early era stimulated overland trade to Asia and the outskirts of Europe. Imperial Rome now sent ships with gold and silver to buy valuable Indian goods, such as pepper, cardamom, ginger, malabathrum oil, pearls, beryl, rubies, and more than thirty varieties of fine cotton cloth.[16] The vessels arrived at the Śaka port of Broach; at Śātavāhanā ports on both coasts of the Deccan; and at the southern Cherā, Pāndya, and Chola ports like Muciri, Cochi, and Puhār (Kaverippumpaṭṭinam). Sources include the anonymous Greek-Egyptian captain's log, *Periplus of the Erythraean Sea*,[17] and classical Sangam Tamil texts, like the epic *Silappadikkāram* (3rd c. ACE). Thousands of Roman gold coins have been discovered in the southern regions ruled by Dravidian Pāndyas and Cheras, whose first coins were made of copper (ca. 3rd c. BCE).[18] Gold and silver stimulated industries that produced textiles of cotton and later of silk after silkworms were smuggled in from China, possibly in the robes of itinerant monks. Among those who grew wealthy were heterodox and high-caste merchants, as well as male and female *śudra* artisans, all of whom donated sums to religious charities. The demand for Indian silk ended when Rome declined and the art of silk weaving was learned by artisans in the Byzantine Empire (3rd c. ACE).

The Śakas were followed by the Central Asian tribe of the Kuşānas, called Chīnas in some contemporary texts. King Kajula Kadiphises founded the Kuşāna Empire (100 BCE–100 ACE), which later included sections of Central Asia, notably in Bactria, Parthia, Kashmir, and parts of Rajasthan to the Doab.[19] An important source for the Kuşāna Empire are numerous coins in copper and silver issued by kings, while the first gold coins of the subcontinent were issued by the Kuşāna Vīma Kadiphises. These coins were engraved in the language and script best understood in the local regions of this vast empire. The coins were thus either in Sanskrit/Prakrit written in the Brahmi script or Greek and Bactrian in the Kharoshthi script. The ruler was often given a grandiose title, for example, King of Kings in Sanskrit (*mahārājātirājā*), in Greek (*basileo basilei*), and in Latin as Caesar (*kaisara*).[20] Like the Śakas, the Kuşānas fostered an intriguing mix of Hindu, Buddhist, Jaina, Zoroastrian, and Chinese religious beliefs. Some coins are carved with images of the Hindu god Śiva, while king Vāsudeva (ca. 67 ACE) declared himself a devotee of Vişnu. The most notable emperor was Kanişka (78 or 127 ACE–144 ACE), who hosted a grand, international Buddhist canonical conference.[21] As this vast empire controlled overland trade routes, Mahāyāna Buddhism spread to Central and East Asia, while the older Hinayāna sect became highly popular in the east and south, spreading coastally to southeast Asia.

Invasions overthrew existing dynasties and triggered dynamic mass migrations in which newcomers displaced locals and recent settlers, who then moved elsewhere, uprooting others. Among these who left the northwest were oligarchic clans (*gana sanghas*), whose leaders lived like *kşatŗiya* kings. Pāňini's important Sanskrit grammar (ca. 150 BCE) mentions the Ābhīras, who relocated to Gujarat where they fought, but also merged with Śāka inhabitants. Some Ābhīras moved into the Deccan, where they fought the Śātavāhanas.

Another politically significant group that migrated was the Mālava clan. Roman historian Curtiss described the Mālavas (Malloi) as a 'warlike' tribe that resisted Alexander, then migrated to Rājasthān's Mālwa plateau. Some historians believe that the Mālavas were ancestors of the Western Kşatrapas, who were former *şatraps* of the Śakas; others believe they were remnants of an early *gana sangha*.[22] The Hindu Śaka calendar era began with the accession of the first Kşatrapa king, Chaşţana (ca. 78 ACE), who took the title of Maha-kşatrapa. The dynasty's most famous ruler was his grandson, Rudradāman I (130–150 ACE), whose copper coins inscribed with Prakrit words in the Brahmi script praise him as 'Rajno Mahakşatrapa'. Although a non-*dvīja* son of Śaka immigrants, Rudradāman is known for his Sanskrit inscription on a rock in Junagarh, Kathiawar, which also bears Aśoka

Maurya's Prakrit edict. Even heterodox kings now increasingly used Sanskrit instead of Prakrit, a cultural change evident also in Mahāyānā Buddhist scriptures. Rudradāman may have chosen Sanskrit as he wished to be associated with *kṣatṛiya* ideals or with modified Vedic rites. The edict makes a reference to his restoration of the vast Sudarśana lake and to his victories over the Śātavāhanas, so that his empire stretched from Sindh, Punjab, Mālwa, Kutch, and Gujarat to the Konkan.[23]

Archaeology and literature reveal that an ancient Dravidian civilization (ca. 300 BCE) thrived in southern India. Sanskritic culture had penetrated the Deccan and peninsula during the later Vedic era, and this process accelerated as Buddhism and Jainism spread under the Mauryans. Dravidian kings adopted *kṣatṛiya* honorifics like *rājā* and *mahārājā*, while women of the Śātavāhana, Pāṇḍyā, Chola, and Chera royal families had some leadership roles, and some kings were known by their matronymics. Some Dravidian communities proudly retained their ancient matrilineal customs, and others retained some matrilineal norms but also adopted Sanskritic practices, while *brāhman* settlers selectively absorbed Dravidian matriliny and languages.

The Śātavahana Empire (ca. 80 BCE–250 ACE), founded by the Andhra *brāhman* Simuka, later extended over parts of Gujarat, Saurashtra, and Maharashtra. The distinguished founder was Gautamiputra Śatakarni (ca. 50 BCE), whose staunch rival was Khāravela of Kalinga. The Śātavāhana Empire benefited from its central location, which fostered overland trade, while checking the ambitions of northern and southern kings. Its seaports on the Arabian Sea and Bay of Bengal were visited by foreign ships to conduct trade with Buddhist, Jaina, and Hindu merchants. Contacts with imperial Rome are attested by Roman coins excavated in the Deccan and by references to Yāvanās in classical Tamil texts. Śātavāhana kings called themselves *brāhmans*, yet they bore a matronymic, which indicates that they followed Dravidian matrilineal customs. An early Śātavāhana queen named Nāganikā, who was the daughter of a Deccan king, served as regent for her two minor sons after her husband's death. Dowager queen Gautami Balaśri commissioned the Nāsik inscription to commemorate her son Gautamiputra Śatakarni, whom she praised as a unique *brāhman* who quelled arrogant *kṣaṭriyas* with the sword. She compared him to the legendary southern *brāhman* Paraśurāma, Viṣnu's incarnation (*avatāra*) before Rāmā.[24] The Śātavahana Empire declined (ca. 250 ACE) after it lost territories to the Vakatākas of Berar, Ābhīras of north Deccan, Kadambas of Karnataka-Maharashtra, and Ikṣvākus of Andhra.[25] The Śātavahanas, Kadambas, and Ikṣvākus bore matronymics, indicating their Dravidian origins.

The earliest Tamil dynasties were the Pāṇdyas of Madurai, the Cholas on the eastern coast and Kāveri delta, and the Cheras on the western coast. Their proximity naturally led to intricate cultural exchanges, some ensuing from competition, while others stemmed from trade interactions, which continue to this day. Recent excavations at Keezhadi and 293 other sites along the Vaigai River near Madurai have unearthed some 5300 artifacts from a planned urban civilization (200 BCE) that traded with Rome.[26] These corroborate Tamil epigraphical evidence (200 BCE), while discoveries of gold coins indicate a vibrant trade with ancient Rome. A third valuable source is the magnificent corpus of Tamil literature composed for literary conferences (Sangams) hosted by the Pāndyas at Madurai. Sangam texts include the *Tolkāppiyam*, relating the legend of god Murugan who taught Tamil to sage Agastya; the *Tirukkural* by the Jaina saint Tiruvalluvar, whose aphorisms still guide Tamils; the poetic anthologies *Puranānūru, Ahanānūru,* and *Ainkurunūru* describing valiant kings and mothers, Murugan, and goddess Koṟṟavai, who became Hindu deities; and the epics *Śilappadikāram* and *Manimekhalai* (300–400 ACE), which describe powerful chaste women and nuns, Jainism and Buddhism, and Roman Yāvana presence in south India.[27] The earliest non-Tamil source is Megasthenes's exotic *Indika*. Aśoka's edicts speak with some awe of the 'Choḷas, Pāṇdyas, Sātyaputras, Keralaputras' who ruled 'as far as Ceylon' (Rock Edict 2) and with paternal pride of the Andhras, Choḷas, and Pāṇdyas as 'his people' (*antas*; Rock Edicts 13).[28] The *Arthaśāstra* of Kauṭilya and his eponyms refer to this region's pepper, pearls, and beryl stones (*AŚ* 5.2); the Periyār river (*Churni*); casteless foreigners (*mlecchas*; *AŚ* 7.10); and the Chera family clan (*kula sangha*) of Kerala, whose kings inherited the throne from a maternal uncle.[29] Khāravela's edict in Orissa (50 BCE) refers to pearls from the south, while the anonymous foreign author of *Periplus of the Erythraean Sea* listed the ports and products of Muchirī (Cochin) and Kāveripūnpattinam (near Thanjavur).[30]

The sacred Sanskrit epic *Rāmāyana* (ca. 500 BCE) indicates that Indo-Āryan cultural norms reached the south and Sri Lanka in the later Vedic era. Āśoka Maurya's edicts indicate that his empire had Tamil dynastic allies, while references in the *Arthaśāstra* to Kerala's matriliny and products suggest that Kauṭilya or an eponym was from the south. Cultural interactions increased between north and south in the classical era, as seen in some similarities between the *Rāmāyana* and the Sangam Tamil epic *Śilappadikāram* (ca. 300 ACE). The *Rāmāyana* lauds chaste mothers and wives and the Vedic fire god Agni as the ultimate sacrificial medium. The heroine Sītā of Mithila (Bihar) jumps into the fire to prove her purity to a male audience led by Rāma of Ayodhya, but she emerges unscathed. These ideas were refashioned in the *Śilappadikāram* to suit a matriarchal culture, as the Tamil epic exalts powerful mothers, chaste wives, and noble Jaina nuns, who remain heroic under duress. While respecting fire as a natural element capable of wreaking havoc, its heroine Kaṇṇagi wreaks powerful revenge on her husband's murderers by razing their town to ashes. This is in sharp contrast to the patriarchal biases in contemporary Sanskrit texts, such as the later volumes of the *Arthaśāstra* and *Manu Smṛiti*, both composed in the north.

B. Governance, varna, *and laws*

While local and immigrant kings battled over domains, they valued the profit from growing trade across borders, and they promoted sectarian and cultural innovations. Trade routes crisscrossed the peninsula into Asia, while ships crossed the seas to Africa and Europe. Wealth now accrued to merchants, bankers, and landlords of various sects and sub-castes (*jātīs*), as well as to *śudra* and *vaiśya* farmers and artisans. The Buddhist text *Milindapanho* refers to numerous occupational guilds (*śrenī*) producing artisanal goods in the northern towns of Taxila and Mathura, while similar guilds operated in the Deccan and southern peninsula. The *śrenīs* of metal workers manufactured gold, silver, copper, brass, tin, and lead products, some embedded with jewels. There were also *śrenīs* for cotton weavers and those who made textiles of five different materials, including silk, an art learned after silkworms were smuggled in by Chinese monks, and *śrenīs* for leather workers, who were often Dalits and *śudras.*[31] Inscriptions indicate that the elite and the common folk became wealthy enough to make donations (*dāna*) of gold, silver, and land to shrines and monastic groups. A Śātavahana inscription states that king Gautamiputra Satakarni (ca. 150 BCE) donated village lands (*grāmā*) with administrative duties to *brāhmans* who conducted Vedic rites. Another text states that some *brāhmans* accepted *dāna* from *śudras.*[32]

Unlike the tightly knit Mauryan administrative model, decentralized governance was a feature of most subsequent kingdoms. The practice probably arose due to frequent territorial battles and exchanges in the early classical era, and the subjects of these regions were of numerous ethnic, caste, and sectarian communities. Victors often returned local autonomy to the vanquished foe in exchange for a seasonal tribute. This subsidiary system was practiced even after 100 ACE by pre-Guptan dynasties, such as the western Śakas (Kşatrapas) of Mālwā, the Vakatakas of Berar (200–319 ACE), and the Ikşvākus of Andhra. It was also a feature of the vast Guptan Empire (319–ca. 520 ACE), which gave grants of land with magisterial duties to favored individuals. Some classical-era kingdoms did not maintain an expensive standing army but instead recruited soldiers and sought the help of allied subsidiaries to fight a common enemy.

Kings of the classical era also implemented two concurrent sets of laws, the first used in the royal court, the other consisting of local customs. Kings thus meted out court justice with a temporal law code (*śāstra*), as this constituted a primary royal duty (*rāja dharma*). At the same time, they allowed diverse subjects to practice their own patrilineal or matrilineal laws on marriage and inheritance. This dual system remained in vogue even after the Indian constitution, a fact seen in the lingering of local customs in geographical pockets. Those groups that followed patriarchal Sanskritic norms recognized the *varna* hierarchy, while many tribal and Dravidian groups retained ancient matrilineal customs but selectively absorbed Sanskritic rules. This explains why Chera kings inherited the throne from a maternal uncle until 1947 and why some tribal and southern women still enjoy inheritance rights today. Meanwhile, social morality was regulated by local sectarian groups, either through benefactions, public atonement, or ostracism. *Brāhmans* supervised ritual penances (*prāyasçitta*), tribal and Dravidian groups performed rites to their deities, and Buddhist and Jaina monastics advised retributive acts as *dhamma*.[33]

As the authors of the Vedic *Dharma Sūtras* lived in a patriarchal society based on *varna* ranks, they legally validated patrilineal succession, including to the throne. In the Mauryan Empire, the *Arthaśāstra* reaffirmed male succession, but it was less orthodox on *varna*, a feature that probably appealed to heterodox and immigrant rulers in the early classical era, when the code was expanded by eponyms. Meanwhile, orthodox kings probably chose to mete out justice with the first *Dharma Śāstra* or *Manu Smṛiti*, which lauded *kṣaṭriya* kings and *dvīja* men. In the more stable later classical era, the *Yājñavalkya Smṛiti* and Guptan *Nārada Smṛiti* did not negate gender and class hierarchies but worked around these social parameters to require the king to serve justice more equitably. While under decentralized administration, local communities followed their own laws on marriage and inheritance, all disputes were resolved by the king in court, and by the Guptan Empire, the monarch's chief function became juridical, and he had to mete out justice with some ethical guidelines. *Dharma* now meant the king's chief duty or *rāja dharma*, law, and justice. The *Dharma Śāstras* of Manu, Yājñavalkya, and Nārada are quite distinct in format and length, and each represents the author's historical milieu and his specific social biases.

Unlike early philosophical texts and traditions that continue to inspire us today, these law codes had a worldly, social, and political purpose in early Indian history. As their laws are no longer valid in a democratic nation in the twenty-first century, we must now view them rationally as historical documents rather than as semi-sacred texts. Each code reflects a specific historical context, and eponymous sections were added to suit later conditions. In the Vedic-classical millennium of dynamic interactions among Sanskritic, Dravidian, tribal, and immigrant groups, the royal state led by elite male *dvījas* became the vanguard of a movement that spread Sanskritic religio-cultural-social norms across the subcontinent. Elite men ruled, and women followed two paces behind, while *śudras*, sub-castes, and *mlecchas* each had a pecking order. When local and foreign non-*dvījas* became kings, they adopted *kṣatṛiya* titles of *rājā* and *mahārājā*, and if they appointed *brāhman* ministers, local groups became lesser castes, sometimes excluded from public authority. In Dravidian kingdoms, which retained aspects of matriarchy, queens served as regents for minor sons, but the throne ultimately belonged to kings. These matrilineal rules remained social customary practices even after the introduction of the Indian constitution.

Notes

1 Georg Buhler, trans., "Aśoka's Twelfth Rock Edict", in James Burgess, Eugene J.T. Hultzsch, and A. Fuhrer, eds., *Epigraphica Indica: A Supplementary to the Corpus Inscriptionum Indicarum,* Vol. 1 (1892), Calcutta: Archaeological Survey of India (revised ed. 1981), 16–20. In this important edict, Aśoka declared that *dharma* was righteousness, the 'essential' doctrine transcending worldly gifts, honors, and sectarian differences, as seen in line 2. (Line #2): '*Devanam priyo mañyati yatha kiti/salavadhi siya sarva praśandanam salavadhi tu bahuvidha/tasa tu iyo mulayam vachagati*'.

In the last two lines (9–10) Aśoka declared that he had sent various officials, including women, to promote righteous 'essentials', which added glory to sect and *dhamma:*

(Line #9): '*Vapata dhrama mahāmatra (dharma mahāmatra) yaccha maha-bamatra vach bhumikañye cha nikaya/imamcha yetisa phalam yam ataprașadha vadhi;*

(Line #10): *dhamma sacha dipanā*'.

Also see Georg Buhler, trans., "The Siddapura Edicts of Aśoka", in Eugene J.T. Hultzsch, eds., *Epigraphica Indica, op. cit.* In the second of these two edicts from the Deccan, Aśoka asks us to follow *dhamma* by respecting parents, teachers, and 'all living creatures'. A detailed study with fresh translations is by R. Thapar, *Aśoka and the Decline of the Mauryas, op. cit.*, 228–270, 254–255, Appendix III (12th Rock Edict).

2 P. Olivelle, "Manu and the 'Arthaśāstra': A Study in Śāstric Intertexuality", in *Journal of Indian Philosophy, op. cit.*

3 T.W. Rhys Davids, trans., *The Questions of Milinda,* from *The Sacred Books of the East,* Vol. 35, 36, Oxford: Clarendon Press, 1890 and 1894. These volumes are available at this website: www.sacred-texts.com/bud/milinda.htm.

4 Ramashankar Tripathi, *History of Ancient India,* Delhi: Motilal Banarsidass, 1999 (9th ed.; 1st ed., 1942), 188, 201–207, 214.

5 Megasthenes's *Indika* was cited by J.W. McCrindle, *Ancient India as Described by Megasthenes and Arrian,* Calcutta: Ker and Spink, 1877, 156, 158–159, *vide.,* at this site: https://archive.org/details/AncientIndiaAsDescribedByMegasthenes AndArrianByMccrindleJ.W/page/n139/mode/2up. McCrindle was quoted by K.A. Nilkanta Sastri, ed., *Foreign Notices of South India: From Megasthenes to Mahuan*, Chennai: University of Madras, 2001 (3rd ed.; 1st ed., 1939), 41–43.

6 Many scholars view Kanișka's reign as the beginning of the Śaka-Kușāna era in Indian history, although this ruler was a Kușāna and not a Śaka. Eminent scholar A.L. Basham dated his reign from 78 ACE to 144 ACE, *vide.,* A.L. Basham, *The Wonder That Was India,* New York: Macmillan, 1954, p. 51. More recently, German Indologist Harry Falk has dated his reign to 127 ACE, *vide.,* Harry Falk, "The Kanișka Era in Gupta Records", in *Silk Road Art and Archaeology,* Vol. X, 2004, Kamakura, Japan: Institute of Silk Road Studies, 167–176; and Harry Falk, "The Tidal Waves of Indian History", in Patrick Olivelle, ed., *Between the Empires*, New York: Oxford University Press, 2006, 145–168.

7 For the Śungas and Kanvas, Śātavāhanas, and Khāravela, see Ramashankar Tripathi, *History of Ancient India*, Delhi: Motilal Banarsidass, 1999 (9th ed.; 1st ed., 1942), 183–190–201; R. Thapar, *Early India: From the Origins to AD 1300, op. cit., vide,* 209–213, 225–228, 229–234. For the Śātavahanas and Śakas, and an interesting Marxist perspective, see D.N. Jha, *Ancient India in Historical Outline,* Delhi: Manohar, 1998, 119–122; 149–173.

8 Thapar, *Early India: From the Origins to AD 1300,* op. cit., 211–213. Thapar cites a long section from the epigraphical report of Professors K.P. Jayaswal and R.D.

Banerji, "The Hāthīgumphā Inscription of Kharavela", in Hirananda Sastri, ed. *Epigraphica Indica,* Vol. 20 (1929–30), Delhi: Government of India, 1933, 71–89.

9 Ainslie T. Embree, ed., *Sources of Indian Tradition, Volume 1: From the Beginning to 1800, op. cit.*, 148–149. See also R. Thapar, *Aśoka and the Decline of the Mauryas, op. cit.* (pbk), 232–233.

10 R. Thapar, *Early India: From the Origins to AD 1300, op. cit.*, 2002, 213–225 (Yavanas, Śakas, Kuṣānas).

11 On settlements, inscriptions, coins see Dilip K. Chakrabarti, *India: An Archaeological History, op. cit.*, 289–300.

12 Chakrabarti, *ibid.*, 295–300, in which he cites K. Rajan, "Early Historic Archaeology of Tamil Nadu", in *Archaeological Gazetteer of Tamil Nadu*, Thanjavur, Tamil Nadu: Mano Pathippakam, 1997. Also see Shailendra Bhandare's "Numismatics and History: The Maurya-Gupta Interlude in the Gangetic Plain", in Patrick Olivelle, ed., *Between the Empires: Society in India 300 BCE- 400 CE, op. cit.*, 67–112, *vide.*, 69.

13 For south India's trade with Rome, see R. Champakalakshmi, *Trade, Ideology and Urbanization: South India 300 BC to AD 1300*, New Delhi: Oxford University Press, 1996, 175–202. Champakalakshmi cites early Roman historian Pliny, who mentioned Muziris and Nelcynda (Kottayam), whose prosperity stemmed from selling pepper. This resonates in the Sangam Tamil text *Paṭṭinappālai*, which describes sacks of pepper, *vide,* R. Champakalakshmi, *Trade, Ideology and Urbanization, op. cit.*, 186–187. Also see Rajan Gurukkal, "The Beginnings of the Historic Period: The Tamil South (Up to the End of the Fifth Century AD)", in R. Thapar, ed., *Recent Perspectives of Early Indian History, op. cit.*, 237–265, *vide.*, 246–251.

14 Ramashankar Tripathi, *History of Ancient India, op. cit.*, 216–217.

15 K.A.N. Sastri and G. Srinivasachari, *Advanced History of India,* Bombay: Allied Publishers, 1971, 162–165.

16 R. Champakalakshmi, *Trade, Ideology and Urbanization: South India 300 BC to AD 1300, op. cit.*, 179–187.

17 *Periplus of the Erythraean Sea,* 54–60, reproduced by K.A.N. Sastri, in *Foreign Notices of South India: From Megasthenes to Mahuan, op. cit.*, describing ports in Kerala and Tamil Nadu, chapter 5, pp. 54–60.

18 Dilip K. Chakrabarti, *India: An Archaeological History, op. cit.*, 289; D.N. Jha, *Ancient India in Historical Outline, op. cit.* (2nd ed.; 1st ed. 1977), 35, 100, 118, 126.

19 R. Thapar, *Early India: From the Origins to AD 1300, op. cit.*, 146–147, 209–213, 225–228, 229–234 (regional dynasties).

20 R. Thapar, *Early India from the Origins to AD 1300, ibid.*, 210–11, 221–224.

21 As stated in Part I, Kaniṣka's rule was regarded by scholars as the start of the Śaka-Kuṣāna era, although he was not a Śaka but a Kuṣāna. A.L. Basham stipulated that he ruled from 78 ACE to 144 ACE, *vide.*, A.L. Basham, *The Wonder That Was India, op. cit.* Recently, scholar Harry Falk has revised the date of Kaniṣka's accession to 127 ACE, *vide.*, Harry Falk, "The Kaniṣka Era in Gupta Records", in *Silk Road Art and Archaeology*, Vol. X (2004), Kamakura, Japan: Institute of Silk Road Studies, 167–176.

22 R. Tripathi, *History of Ancient India, op. cit.*, 136–137, 244. D.N. Jha, *Ancient India: In Historical Outline, op. cit.*, 111–149.

23 R. Tripathi, *ibid.*, 217–219.

24 R. Tripathi, *ibid.*, 193–194.

25 D.N. Jha, *Ancient India in Historical Outline, op. cit.*, 118–119.

26 See these news articles by S. Annamalai, B. Kolappan, Pon Vasantha Arunachalam, and Special Correspondents, "Keezhadi Excavation Leads to Ancient

Civilisation on the Banks of Vaigai", in *The Hindu,* June 18, 2015–May 16, 2017 at this updated website: www.thehindu.com/news/national/tamil-nadu/keezhadi-excavation-the-story-till-now/article18464920.ece?homepage=true.

27 For Sangam Tamil texts with English translations, see: P.V. Somasundaram, trans., ed., *Aiṅkuṟunūru,* Chennai: Saiva Siddhanta Society, 1972; P.V. Somasundaram, trans., ed., *Akanānūru* (2 vols.), Chennai: Saiva Siddhanta Society, 1970; P.V. Somasundaram, trans., ed., *Ilankōvatikāl Iyaṟṟaruḷiya Cilappatikāram,* Chennai: Saiva Siddhanta Society, 1969; W.H. Drew and John Lazarus, *Thirukkural* (W.H. Allen, 1886), Madras: Asian Educational Services, 1989 (rpt.); A.K. Ramanujan, trans., *Poems of Love and War: From the Eight Anthologies and the Ten Long Poems of Classical Tamil,* New York: Columbia University Press, 1985; P.V. Sundaram, trans., *Tiruvalluvar: The Kural,* Madras: Vijayalakshmi Graphics, 1987. For studies on the Tamils, see: Kamil V. Zvelebil, *The Smile of Murugan: On Tamil Literature of South India,* Leiden: E.J. Brill, 1973; Kamil V. Zvelebil, *Tamil Traditions on Subrāhman ya-Murugan,* Madras: Institute of Asian Studies, 1991; George L. Hart III, *The Poems of the Ancient Tamil: Their Milieu and their Sanskrit Counterparts,* Berkeley: University of California Press, 1975; David Dean Shulman, *Tamil Temple Myths: Sacrifice and Divine Marriage in the South Indian Saiva Tradition,* Princeton: Princeton University Press, 1980; Sita Anantha Raman, "Popular Pujas in Public Places: Lay Rituals in South Indian Temples", in *International Journal of Hindu Studies,* Vol. 5, No. 2, August 2001, 165–198.

28 R. Thapar, *Aśoka and the Decline of the Mauryas, op. cit.,* 251, 255–256.

29 Also see Hermann Kulke and Deitmar Rothermund, *A History of India, op. cit.,* 67–81, 91–102 on the early dynasties.

30 On Tamil Brahmi inscriptions, trade relations with Rome, and the *Periplus of the Erythraean Sea,* see this excellent study by R. Champakalakshmi, *Trade, Ideology and Urbanization: South India 300 BCE to AD 1300, op. cit., vide.,* 102–117.

31 D.N. Jha, *Ancient India in Historical Outline, op. cit.,* 128–130.

32 Jha, *ibid.,* 119–124.

33 Bina Agarwal traces tribal and Dravidian matrilineal rights and their modern erosion in her pioneering work, *A Field of Ones Own: Gender and Land Rights in South Asia,* Cambridge: Cambridge University Press, 1994, *vide.,* 82–120, 154–180. The following works on modern India shed light on the historical separation of public/state and communal/religious legal domains: Janaki Nair, *Women and Law in Colonial India: A Social History,* Delhi: Kali for Women, 1996; Pratap Bhanu Mehta, "Authority, Religion, and the Indian State", in Indira Jaising, ed., *Men's Laws, Women's Lives: A Constitutional Perspective on Religion, Common Law and Culture in South Asia,* New Delhi: Women Unlimited & Kali for Women, 2005, 56–86; Archana Parashar, "Just Family Law: Basic to all Indian Women", in Indira Jaising, ed., *Men's Laws, Women's Lives, op. cit.,* 286–322.

8

ARTHAŚĀSTRA AND *MANU SMṚITI*

I. Sanskritic lineage, women, and *varna*

Class and gender hierarchies are common in many global cultures, including Indian civilization, and they resonate even today, despite more equitable legal systems. As the first Indo-Āryan clans on the subcontinent were predominantly male, these men soon married local women and produced mixed offspring. *Kşaṭriyas, brāhmans,* and *vaiśyas* bequeathed their genes and Sanskritic culture to their children, but local matriarchal customs also permeated Sanskritic society. An example was the great respect given to maternal uncles, as recorded in the *Mahābhārata* and *Purāṇa* legends and the later classical *Yājñavalkya Smṛiti* (*YS* 1.87), a practice that continues among Hindus even today.

Sanskritic society attached great value to male 'ārya' lineage, patriarchy, and *varna* identity, as seen in the *Vedas* and epics (1000–300 BCE). The *Rig Veda*'s (2000–1000 BCE) final volume contains two significant cosmogonic hymns, both with a hint of primal incest recognizing the female's role in reproduction. The first hymn states that the earth goddess 'Āditi was born of Dakşa, and Aditi was Dakşa's Child' (*RV* 10.72.4.2).[1] The more famous hymn is the *Puruşa Sukta* (*RV* 10.90) describing the sacrifice of primal Man, from whom emerged the *varnas*, the *brāhman* from his mouth, *kşaṭriya* from his arms, *vaiśya* from his thighs, and *śudra* from his feet. The *Puruşa Sukta* also states that out of Puruşa came the female Virāj, but that out of Virāj came Puruşa, thus acknowledging that even men were born only to women. Indian civilization's exaltation of the Earth Mother certainly inspires awe, but less admirable is its prolonged emphasis on social ranks based on birth. The *Puruşa Sukta* indicates that by 1000 BCE, Sanskritic society valued caste identity, as it declared that the *brāhman* came from Puruşa's mouth, the *kşaṭriya* from his arms, the *vaiśya* from his thighs, and the *śudra* from his feet.[2]

Brāhmans, kşatṛiyas, and *vaiśyas* thus had an implicit belief that patriarchy was a divinely inspired, natural order This is apparent in the first Sanskrit codes composed by *brāhman* men, as they viewed these entrenched power structures in large territorial *janapadas*, which comprised sixteen large kingdoms and oligarchic states (ca. 600 BCE). The *Dharma Sūtra* legally validated customs on marriage and property. They often accepted marriages among *dvījas* but frowned upon or disliked marriages to *śudras* and other groups and sanctioned female *strīdhana* but increasingly rejected their right to male spousal property. As Sanskritic society spread from the north to the east, center, and south, *dvīja* men grew increasingly protective of their women by guarding their chastity in order to maintain the imagined purity of ancient male Sanskritic bloodlines. The link between patriarchy and *varna* could be subtle or overt, but as the royal state was led by *dvījas* or depended on these groups, kings promoted Sanskritic culture. Sanskritic culture had several aspects, some that exalted all humans and thus uniting individuals, while some were based on elitist caste norms. *Dvīja* women ranked higher than *śudras* and they could bask in the power of their family men, but also reminded of their subordinate female status from childhood to old age, and therefore constrained to domesticity. Sanskritic customs were adopted by local *śudras*, so that ancient matriarchal rules were modified to domesticate their women. Female subordination was exacerbated by poverty, but it reduced when women worked as farmers, vendors, and artisans, whose contributions to the family and royal economy were specifically acknowledged by Yājñavalkya and Nārada in the later classical era.

The Sanskrit codes legally validated patriarchy and *varna*, yet Mauryan-classical society was a product of interactions among *dvījas*, *śudras*, local groups, and immigrants (*mlecchas*). Driven by ethno-cultural anxiety, *dvīja* men lauded male Sanskritic lineages and decried female sexuality for casting a blot on their bloodlines. The *Dharma Sūtras* of Gautama and Vasiṣṭha lauded chaste women but allowed *dvīja* men to marry a second or third wife of another *varna*, including *śudrās* (*GDS* 4.18–26; *VDS* 17.47–50). Yet despite their disapproval, *dvījas* often married local women and adopted their matriarchal customs. During this millennium, many communities and clans migrated across the peninsula, living among, borrowing, and accepting customs and ideas from local cultures. Widespread interactions laid the foundation for the genetically diverse, culturally rich phenomenon that is Indian civilization.

The eight codes examined in this study reflect the *brāhman* authors' *dvīja* anxieties, escalating in the historical context of political and social change. The authors included the paternalist yet orthodox Āpastamba; the unorthodox Kauṭilya, who worked for heterodox Mauryans; stern and orthodox patriarchs like Gautama, Baudhāyana, and Vasiṣṭha; Manu the avowed misogynist; the benign yet orthodox Yājñavalkya; and the humanist Nārada, who sternly enforced justice (*nyāya*). Even the southerner Āpastamba declared in his *Dharma Sūtra* that an '*ārya*' woman who slept with a *śudra* was deeply 'tainted' (*asūchi*; *ADS* 1.20.12–13) and that a *dvīja* was polluted by touching a *śudra* and eating food from a *śudra* (*ADS* 1.16.22; 1.17.1), a social norm repeated centuries later in the classical *Yājñavalkya Smṛiti* (*YS* 1.21). Āpastamba also warned *dvījas* to 'diligently guard this progeny of yours, lest strangers sow their seed in your field' (*ADS* 2.13.5).

Gautama's *Dharma Sūtra* instructed *dvījas* to control women's actions and demeanor, to conduct a girl's marriage soon after her puberty (*GDS* 18.1–2, 20–22), and to castrate a *śudra* who had sex with a *dvīja* woman (*GDS* 12.2). The *Dharma Sūtras* of Baudhāyana (*BDS* 2.3.34) and Vasiṣṭha (*VDS* 17.9) harshly repeated the adage that woman was the field in which men sowed their seeds. Baudhāyana declared that a *dvīja* woman was outcaste if she had sex with a *śudrā* (*BDS* 2.7–8), described woman as a 'curd pot' that soured milk making it unfit for sacred rites (*BDS* 2.22), and recommended pre-puberty marriages to keep females chaste (*BDS* 2.7–8, 22, 33–35; 4.11–16). Vasiṣṭha's lenience on some issues and strictness on others strongly suggests that eponyms modified his *Dharma Sūtra*. Vasiṣṭha lauded post-puberty marriages (*VDS* 17.67–68), but directed the father to marry off his 'still naked' infant daughter (*VDS* 17.69–75). He repeated the adage that a woman must be kept dependent from infancy to old age (*VDS* 5.1–5), and he ruled that sex between a *dvīja* man or woman and a *śudra* produced *śudra* progeny (*VDS* 18.1–17). Yet he forgave a woman for having impure thoughts as long as she did not act upon them, because women were purified by menstrual flow, a gift from the Moon. He also sanctioned remarriage for a virgin widow younger than sixteen years, and the levirate marriage (*niyoga*) of a young widow to her brother-in-law so that she may have a son in her old age (*VDS* 17.55–66).

Brāhman authors allowed a *dvīja* to marry a *śudra* wife, but they outcaste *dvīja* women who had intercourse with a *śudra, chāṇḍāla,* or *mleccha* man who was severely fined, beaten, burnt, or castrated. Some authors even outcaste the *dvīja* man who married a woman from these lower ranks. Eager to protect Sanskritic male bloodlines, they warned *dvījas* to guard family women as 'the field' in which other men could potentially sow their seeds. At the same time, they were realists who recognized that their rules were being circumvented, as evident in the multiplicity of mixed caste, sub-caste, and outcaste birth *jātīs* in this era. These scholarly *dvījas* therefore carefully listed, and possibly legitimized these new *jātīs*. As patriarchy and *varna* were extolled in the long centuries between the later Vedic to later classical eras, so also did the writers of early India's law codes. Yet ironically, these ancient social norms resiliently challenge the modern nation's more equitable, constitutional democracy in the twenty-first century.

II. Early classical society and codes: *Arthaśāstra* and *Manu Smṛiti*

The early classical centuries reinvented Indic civilization through momentous genetic and social mergers, which unsettled some elite male *dvījas*.

Some *brāhmans* and *kṣaṭriyas* began to fear that immigrants without caste (*mlecchas*) and indigenous *śudras* would dismantle the *varna* order, that heterodox kings would dominate all temporal affairs, and that women would produce a large population of mixed ethnicity and caste. Viewing these as interrelated issues, elite authors composed laws that had a profoundly negative impact on women. Such *angst* first appeared in the *Dharma Sūtras* of Baudhāyana and Vasiṣṭha in the later Vedic era but not in Kauṭilya's early chapters of the *Arthaśāstra* (see Part I). As the Mauryans were heterodox non-*dvījas* with an ethnically diverse empire, they recognized the danger of xenophobic policies and thus promised to protect citizens of all castes and sects, including useful *dvījas*. A friendly pact and diplomatic relations with Bactria demarcated boundaries and allowed Indo-Greeks to reside in Magadha.

As Mauryan collapse opened the door for Yāvanā, Śaka, and Kuṣāna invasions in the next centuries, *brāhman* scholars responded with two types of legal treatises (*śāstras*). Ever since the later Vedic era, law codes have been classified as either *artha* or *dharma* texts. Although the Vedic *Dharma Sūtras* defined the sacred duties or *dharmas* of individuals, these *dharmas* were primarily social and familial rather than religious. Kauṭilya had composed the first volumes of the *Arthaśāstra* as temporal or *artha* laws to govern the Mauryan imperial state. The prefixes '*dharma*' and '*artha*' in the titles appear to suggest that the codes had different purposes, that they were either religious (*dharma)* or temporal (*artha)*. However, all these *dharma* code writers were motivated by social, rather than religious aims, as they viewed *dharma* as the ethical foundation of society. They therefore highlighted important temporal issues, such as marriage, progeny, inheritance, employment, and the king's earthly duty to mete justice and punish crimes. As kings had a sacred duty to govern with equity, the term *dharma* acquired the extended meaning of ethical temporal law.

The Sanskrit epics *Mahābhārata* and *Rāmāyana* had exalted legendary kings who governed with righteousness as *dharma*, but the first Sanskrit texts to define the laws for real-life kings were the *Dharma Sūtras*. The guidelines on royal governance in the *Dharma Sūtras* must have guided Kauṭilya when he composed the *Arthaśāstra* for the Mauryan Empire, as he gave specific importance to *dharmic* kingship and legal procedures (*vyavahāra*). These ideals were expanded by Āśoka in his *dhamma* edicts and by Kauṭilya's eponyms in the later sections of the *Arthaśāstra*. The ideal of *dharma* as both virtue and law became the foundation stone of early Indian polity, and it resonated in the later classical codes of Yājňavalkya and Nārada.

The classical centuries witnessed the spread of devotional Hinduism, Jainism, and Mahāyāna Buddhism and growing genetic and cultural heterogeneity on the subcontinent. Each religious sect had its own scriptures that guided individuals on ethical *dharma/dhamma*. Yet, there also emerged other regional customs, which were followed, irrespective of sect or ethnicity. Local practices now often influenced a group's customary laws on marriage and inheritance, so that people in the same region shared some common social traits, and they often spoke a regional dialect/language that united sects and communities. In contrast, some customs differed across regions, even within sects of Buddhists, Jainas, and Hindus. For example, Jainas and Hindus in Gujarat share some patriarchal rules on inheritance and marriage, and they all speak variants of the same language/dialect. The most acute differences were between patriarchal and matrilineal communities in a particular region, which soon had its brand of cultural features.

Sects and cultures each had customary laws on marriage, inheritance, and crimes like theft and rape of a minor girl. They largely resolved their differences within their own group and appealed to the king for justice only as a last resort. The early classical era witnessed the growing pattern of royal decentralized governance, and kings meted justice with their chosen temporal law codes, which were composed by *brāhmans*. As local communities were allowed to practice communal laws ethically, only serious crimes would have driven them to seek justice in the king's court. Yet, as kings styled themselves as *rājās*, they upheld the Sanskritic dictates of their chosen code, which enforced patriarchy and caste rules of *varnāśrama dharma*. Administrative decentralization explains the apparent lack of literary evidence that non-Hindus and/or tribal subjects objected to royal justice meted with a code written by a *brāhman*.

A. Arthaśāstra

In the early classical centuries, Kauṭilya's eponyms expanded the *Arthaśāstra*, which was completed by Viṣnugupta (ca. 150 ACE). As India was now ruled by numerous heterodox, immigrant, and less orthodox rulers who relied on the *Arthaśāstra* to mete out justice, Kauṭilya's eponyms emulated his avoidance of ethnic/caste/sectarian aspersions. This restraint satisfied some orthodox rulers, possibly like the *brāhman* Śātavāhanās, whose empire thrived from international trade mediated by merchants and bankers of diverse sects, who sold goods often produced by low-caste workers. Kauṭilya's eponyms also followed his guidelines on *vyavahāra*, as they carefully defined crime and punishment in the royal state.

Yet, the eponyms did not share Kauṭilya's paternal view of women, as their volumes of the *Arthaśāstra* are replete with misogynist verses. Kauṭilya had described female guards and spies for the Mauryan emperor but cautioned that even queens could harbor traitors in palaces. His eponyms stoked such fears by warning the king that seductive women could foist illegitimate sons upon the throne. They lauded stay-at-home wives and suspected women in public places of being prostitutes and spies, ready to entice men to commit treason (*AŚ* 3.3, 5.1, 8.2, 11.1).

Olivelle's analysis sheds light on the importance of *vyavahāra* in all law codes after the *Arthaśāstra*. The first *Dharma Sūtras* were skimpy on *vyavahāra*, yet it forms one-third of the *Manu Smṛiti* (*MS* 2–5, 7–9). In the later classical codes, *vyavahāra* comprises two-thirds of the *Yājñavalkya Smṛiti*, which has a separate 'Vyavahārapada' section, and it forms almost the entire text of the *Nārada Smṛiti*.[3] The views of the orthodox author of the *Manu Smṛiti* differed strongly from Kauṭilya and his eponyms, yet as Manu freely borrowed the *Arthaśāstra*'s legal terms on *vyavahāra*, the *Manu Smṛiti* was clearly the later composition.

B. Manu Smṛiti

Date and author

Shortly thereafter, the first orthodox *Dharma Śāstra*, that is, *Manu Smṛiti*, made its appearance (100 BCE–150 ACE). There were some early scholarly misconceptions on the date and the author's main purpose in writing the *Manu Smṛiti/Mānava Dharma Śāstra*. This title, and Manu's praise for *varna* and Vedic orthodoxy, led some scholars to theorize that it was primarily a Hindu code written in response to the end of Śunga-Kanva (184–28 BCE) support for *brāhmans*. This thesis has now been questioned, as the *Manu Smṛiti* made its appearance (ca. 100 BCE–100 ACE) almost a century after these dynasties had declined. Moreover, unlike the modern separation of religion and state, early Indians viewed sacred and temporal laws as twin pillars of righteousness (*dharma*) upholding society. While the *Manu Smṛiti* begins with sacred guidelines for male *dvījās*, it primarily consists of temporal state laws for *kṣatṛiya* kings. This indicates that the author's main purpose was political rather than religious.

Olivelle's literary analysis has shed a welcome light on many early Indian codes. He points out that the *Dharma Sūtras* are in prose, but that the *Manu Smṛiti* is in the later genre of metrical verses (*śloka*). Moreover, while the *Sūtras* are skimpy on legal procedures (*vyavahāra*), this was an important aspect of the *Arthaśāstra*. The author of the *Manu Smṛiti* was familiar with the *Arthaśāstra*, as he freely borrowed its terms on *vyavahāra* and its ideals on royal governance. Moreover, the *Dharma Sūtras* of Gautama and Baudhāyana mention a contemporary or earlier Vedic era sage called Manu. Gautama endorsed this Manu's opinion on three extreme sins, that is, killing a *brāhman*, imbibing liquor, and having sex with an elder's wife (*GDS* 21.7). Baudhāyana cited the earlier Manu's decree that a father became outcaste if he failed to have his daughter married three years after her puberty

(*BDS* 4.1.13). Olivelle thus points to the cohesive framework of the *Manu Smṛiti* to argue that in the classical centuries, a single author used the eponym of Manu to revamp a Vedic-era prose *Dharma Sūtra* into the first metrical *Dharma Śāstra*.[4] The author called himself by the anonymous name of 'Manu', or 'Man'.

Like the *Arthaśāstra*, the *Manu Smṛiti* consists primarily of temporal laws for the royal state, even though the title suggests a code of only religious laws. Early Indic society valued righteousness as a sacred goal found in both religious and social laws. Manu appears to have lost some of his righteous moorings, as he framed temporal laws that were unjust, motivated by a desire to reaffirm the authority of *kṣatṛiya* kings with *brāhman* advisors, as seen in his diatribes against heterodox, immigrant, and *śudra* rulers. Manu's xenophobia was also bolstered by misogyny, as he curtailed women's education and restricted them to the domestic sphere. Inevitably, women came to depend heavily on family men to manage female property as well as property inherited from the spouse. While the *Manu Smṛiti* may have initially appealed to *dvījas* like the Śātavāhanas, a dynasty founded by a martial *brāhman* (50 BCE–200 ACE), such kings would not have solely relied on a code that favored only *dvījas*. This was because kingdoms flourished from the expansion of internal and international trade, mediated by Hindu, Buddhist, and Jaina bankers and merchants, who sold the products of *śudra* artisans and farmers. While some orthodox castes used the *Manu Smṛiti*, it did not remain popular in ethnically diverse empires, whose rulers realized that social harmony benefitted the economy. In the new pattern of decentralized governance, kings sanctioned local, communal laws on marriage and property, including matrilineal inheritance rights. Most Buddhist, Jaina, tribal, and Dravidian cultures did not use the *Manu Smṛiti*. While southern kings invited *brāhman s* to conduct Vedic rites, thus spreading Sanskritic norms, many local groups did not adopt the *Manu Smṛiti*, as ancient Dravidian practices are prevalent even today in south India.

Post-classical code writers like Bṛhaspati (ca. 650 ACE) lauded the *Manu Smṛiti* as the first *Dharma Śāstra*, although it was preceded by the sacred *Dharma Sūtras* and the monarchical *Arthaśāstra*. Moreover, the next *Dharma Śāstras*, that is, *Yājňavalkya* and *Nārada Smṛitis*, had a more profound impact, as they influenced Vijňānesvara's and Jīmutavāhana's medieval commentaries (*prabandhas*), which prevailed as regional laws until the colonial era.[5] Ironically, when British jurists consulted orthodox *brāhmans* on ancient Hindu codes, *brāhmans* cited the *Manu Smṛiti*, which formed the basis of colonial Hindu law. The *Manu Smṛiti* had a lingering effect on modern jurisprudence, despite a more equitable Indian constitution.[6] It is imperative to examine the *Manu Smṛiti* as an archaic document reflecting ideas and biases of its own era.

Kings and varna

Despite his personal orthodoxy, Manu's chief aim was to frame temporal laws for the state, not theological rules in the *Manu Smṛiti*. Manu exalted *kşatṛiya* kings and the role of *brāhmans* as advisors rather than as priests for the royal state. He did not attack the Yāvana, Śāka, or Kuşāna kings for heterodox beliefs, but he denigrated them for not employing enough *brāhman* officials. As an orthodox *brāhman*, Manu probably knew that kings around him performed Vedic rites with less fanfare than in earlier times, but he must have noticed that Hinduism was not declining but being rejuvenated by powerful new scriptures like the *Bhagavad Gīta* and *Purāṇās* and by an upsurge of devotion (*bhakti*) for deities like Vişnu, Śiva, and Devi. Such *bhakti* also recharged the monastic sects of Buddhism and Jainism, and while Manu would not concede this, heterodox kings often fostered eclectic *bhakti* as a way to bridge their diverse subjects.

Manu's code may have initially attracted Hindu states, such as the Śātavāhana Empire, founded by a *brāhman*. Yet as economies thrived from an extensive land and sea trade, mediated by bankers and merchants of many sects and castes, kings became pragmatic and tolerant. After the Śātavāhanas captured parts of Bihar (ca. 100 BCE), they completed construction of Buddhist burial monuments (*stūpas*) at Sānchi begun by Aśoka Maurya and expanded later by the Hindu Śungas. These display carvings of the Buddha and his mother Māya Devī, the Hindu goddess Gaja Lakşhmi representing good fortune, and indigenous fertility nymphs or *yakşīs*.[7] On the other hand, Manu distrusted powerful non-Āryan, Dravidian dynasties, such as the Tamil Pāndyas, whose trade with Rome enabled them to host grand literary conferences (Sangams), and the Cheras, whose Kerala seaports invited foreign ships. Coastal states whose economies depended on ethnic-sectarian tolerance would have rejected the xenophobic *Manu Smṛiti*.

Manu feared that non-*dvīja* kings would diminish the stature of *kşatṛiya* rulers and that genetic mergers would reinvent the *varna* order. Yet he must have also known that non-*dvīja*, heterodox, immigrant kings adopted *kşatṛiya* norms and styled themselves as *kşatṛiya rajās*.[8] Manu acclaimed the return of *kşatṛiya* kings with *brāhman* advisors. He glorified *kşaṭriyas* as free of the 'taint of impurity', kings enthroned 'on the seat of Indra', 'forever one with *brāhman*' (*MS* 5.93). He did not praise martial *brāhmans* like the Śātavāhanas, but he did declare that *brāhman* scholars were the divine source of *kşatṛiya* authority (*MS* 1.87–108; 7.1–53; 9.321–324). Favoring *dvījas* over *śudras* and *brāhmans* above all, he decreed that if 'individuals of the three *varnas* give false testimony, a righteous king should first fine them and then execute them; but that a *brāhman*, on the other hand, he should send into exile' (*MS* 8.123).[9]

While later Vedic era *brāhmans* emphasized *varna* distinctions, they also listed numerous sub-castes created by sex crossing communal lines. Baudhāyana's *Dharma Sūtra* and Kauṭilya's *Artha Śāstra* endorsed cross-*varna* marriages, possibly as this ensured more sons for *dvījas*, and both decreed that the offspring of a *dvīja* and his *śudra* wife was also a *dvīja*.[10] Due to widespread ethnic/caste intermixing in the early classical era, or perhaps despite such upheavals, the orthodox *brāhman* Manu now declared that there were only four *varnas*, that is, *dvīja brāhmans, kṣatṛiyas, vaiśyas*, and low-ranking *śudras*, and all others were outcastes. He also decreed that *varna* was defined only by birth (*jāti*) to parents of the same *varna* (Skt. *savarna*), and that *dvīja* men could only marry *savarna* women (*MS* 10.4–6). Moreover, he warned of social chaos if *dvīja* men had sex with women of other *varnas* and if men took up a profession outside that decreed for their *varna* (*MS* 10.24). His code of twelve chapters is interspersed with long sections on *brāhman-kṣatṛiya* superiority and the inferiority of *śudras*, whose touch polluted *dvījas*, making inter-caste sex taboo (e.g., *MS* 1.87–101, 2.30–68, 4.205–225; 7.2–98; 8.20–22;9.122–125,149–157,179; 9.229–248; 10.1–130; 11.109–132; 12.54–60).[11] His first six chapters describe *varna, dvīja* duties, life stages (*āśramas*), and women's roles, and the second half concerns kingship, laws, crimes, and penalties, including those involving *şudras, vyavahāra* court rules borrowed from the *Arthaśāstra*. Manu fumed at powerful non-*dvījās* with incendiary *ślokas* (*MS* 8.20–22). His infamous prophecy warned the king never to hire *śudras* to interpret laws, as he would then watch 'helplessly' as his realm sank 'like a cow in mire':

> (*MS* 8.22): He should not live in a kingdom ruled by a Śudra, teeming with unrighteous people, overrun by people from heretical ascetic sects, or swamped by lowest-born people.[12]

He also urged the king to tax *śudra* artisans whose goods had enriched the royal treasury but who had incidentally become wealthy. He urged kings to demand free labor from *śudras*, advice taken seriously by later tyrants, especially during medieval economic slumps:

> (*MS* 1.91): The lord gave the *śudra* only one work, to serve the other *varnas* without complaint.
>
> (*MS* 7.137–138): The artisan, sculptor, self-employed *śudra* has to a day's labor each month to the king as his overlord.
>
> (*MS* 10.99–100): Only when a *śudra* is likely to lose his family and sons as he cannot find a job serving *dvījās*, should he then seek work as an artisan or a sculptor.[13]

He condemned *śudras* to eternal servitude (*MS* 9.334–336). His next chapter ends with an even more stringent verse, stating that: 'Even an able *śudra* must not be allowed to become rich, as the wealthy *śudra* would trouble even the *brāhman*' (*MS* 10.129: '*śaktaināpi hi şūdraina na kāryo dhanasamchaya; şūdro hi dhanamāsādhya brāhmaṇāneva bādhyate*'). Manu denounced kings who hired *śudra* officials and dismissed foreigners as casteless, unfit *mlecchas*, specifically spewing venom on Buddhist Indo-Greeks and Zoroastrian Pahlavas ('Yāvanas'), eclectic Śakās, and Kuśānas ('Chīnas'). He also targeted Tamil non-*dvījas* ('Dravidas'), diverse groups in the northwest ('Kāmbojas'), and Himalayan tribal leaders (Kīratas) as 'having the same traits as *śudras*', and being in fact only '*dāsyus*' (slaves). Yet, forced to concede their obvious valor, he suggested that they were once *kşaṭriyas* in a former life but now reborn as *śudras* for 'neglecting rites and failing to visit *brāhmans*' (*MS* 10.43–45).[14]

Yet Manu's fears of upheaval were largely unfounded, as social tolerance was later promoted by more progressive dynasties like the Vakatakās and Guptas. In his famous Allahabad edict, emperor Samudragupta (335–375 ACE) proclaimed that he had conducted a Vedic horse sacrifice (*aśvamedha*) after having subdued thirteen southern kings and fourteen regional and tribal tributaries, to which subsidiaries he had relegated local authority. Guptan emperors meted court justice with the *Yājñavalkya* and *Nārada Smṛitis*, but they also acknowledged local communal customs on marriage, property, and religion.[15] Decentralization may have eventually fragmented the Guptan Empire (ca. 570 ACE), but its policy of tolerance to Buddhists and Jainas, as seen in the spate of art from this empire, and true Hindu *bhakti* inspired future rulers. Manu was too shortsighted to predict this positive outcome.

The *Manu Smṛiti* was a code for *dvījas*, upheld by *dvīja* kings, unlikely to be used by southern Dravidian, tribes, heterodox sects, *śudras*, mixed caste *chāndālas*, and foreign *mlecchas*. Why then did the *Manu Smṛiti* so profoundly affect modern India? The answer lies in the colonial era, when British judges were bewildered by the array of Indian laws, customs, and languages. To facilitate legal control of their colony, they appointed *brāhman* scholars (*pandits*) to translate the *śāstras* and Muslim scholars (*maulvīs*) to clarify *Q'uranic* laws. The *pandits* offered *Manu Smṛiti* as the first *Dharma Śāstra*, brushing aside the first Hindu code, Āpastamba's *Dharma Sūtra*, possibly as it was unspecific on *vyavahāra*, and it gave women spousal property rights, not enjoyed even by British women until 1856. The *brāhmans* dismissed the *Arthaśāstra*, despite its rich details on *vyavahāra*, as the code of heterodox Mauryans rather than of Hindu *dharma*. The *Manu Smṛiti* became the basis of colonial Hindu law, and it has had a residual effect on modern jurisprudence, despite the more equitable Indian constitution.[16]

Women in the Manu Smṛiti

SANCTIFYING A TEMPORAL CODE

The code first introduces Manu as a contemplative sage, who is asked by lesser sages to relate the story of creation (*MS* 1.1–4). Manu then retold the *Puruṣa Sukta* hymn from the *Ṛig Veda* (*RV* 10.90) before recounting other creation myths, and he also declared that his main aim was to define laws for the four *varnas* of *brāhmans, kṣaṭriyas, vaiśyas,* and *śudras*. As many believe in the literal, rather than symbolic, meanings of myths, his version of legends sanctified an otherwise temporal *śāstra*. The *Puruṣa Sukta* describes the manifestation of a primal Male Being (Puruṣa) from the neuter Spirit ('Self-Existing Lord') encompassing the universe. Puruṣa focused his thoughts and poured semen upon his inner waters to create a 'Golden Egg' from which the cosmos emerged. Clearly, in this tale by a male bard, the primary female egg's biological role was superseded by the energizing sperm.[17] Manu then described the sacrifice (*śukta*) of Puruṣa's body to create the *varnas*, with *brāhmans* at the apex and women as the lesser sex in each rank (*MS* 1.5–31; 2.65). While some communities adhered to this semi-sacred code, many others ignored its inconvenient rules unless compelled by priests and kings.

It is significant that Manu chose only myths about male deities, although, as a *brāhman* scholar, he must have known that mother goddesses (*devīs*) were venerated by many sects. Manu must have known that Hinduism was far from declining but resurgent after the *Bhagavad Gīta* (ca. 300 BCE) validated folk devotional rites (*bhakti puja*; *BG* 9.26) to icons of abstract forces. Popular female deities included Vāk (Saraswati) (*RV* 10.71, 125) goddess of speech and wisdom from the *Ṛig Veda*; Umā Haimāvatī, the 'superbly beautiful' Himalayan *devī*, who instructed god Indra about Brāhman in the *Kena Upaniṣad* (*KU* 3.11–12, 4.1–3); and Gaja Laķṣmi, symbolizing good fortune, making her a favorite of kings, *vaiśyas*, and Buddhist merchants. Gaja Laķṣmi's oldest image shows her standing on a lotus beside two royal elephants, carved upon a stone railing (*vedika*) at the *stūpa* in Sānchi. Originally erected by Aśoka Maurya to house the remains of Buddha and his two close disciples, this *stūpa* was later enlarged by the Hindu Śungas who built *vedikas* (ca. 200 BCE), while the Hindu Śātavāhanas completed it with magnificent gateways (*toranas*) (ca. 100 ACE). The *toranas* display two more images of Gaja Laķṣmi seated on a lotus and showered by elephants beside fertility nymphs (*yakṣīs*) entwined around trees. Kings built monuments, but the donors included housewives and female ascetics who were literate and managed their property, despite the *Manu Smṛiti*.[18]

FEMALE EDUCATION

Nearly all twelve chapters of the *Manu Smṛiti* depict females as sexual beings whose subservience was necessary to maintain patriarchal order. By denying women personal rights once granted in early Vedic society, the author sought to curtail their public activities, such as sitting on a village council or upon a throne. Laws disempowered women by ending their education at puberty when marriage took place (*MS* Ch. 2), giving specific details on menstruation and marital sex to ensure more progeny for *dvījās*. The code also banned women's divorce and remarriage (Ch. 3; Ch. 4.40–44, 4.208; Ch. 5.66, 5.147–169) and limited their direct control over female property or *strīdhana* and their indirect rights to spousal property through sons (Ch. 8.27–29; Ch. 9.1–220). It was not only the king who closely watched women but husbands, fathers, uncles, brothers, and male cousins.

The *Manu Smṛiti* reaffirmed the duties (*dharmas*) of the four *varnas*, focusing on *dvījā* males in four life stages (*āśramas*), although these initially had applied to both genders. The *āśramas* were the life stage of a celibate student (*brahmachārin/brahmachārinī*), married householder (*gṛhastin/gṛhastinī*), forest hermit (*vānaprasthin/vānaprasthinī*), and recluse (*sannyasin/sannyasinī*). Although in the early Vedic era, *dvījā* boys as well as girls had been consecrated in a thread ceremony (*upanāyana*) before studying the *Vedas*, this changed in the later era, when few girls studied the *Vedas*. This is evident in Āpastamba's *Dharma Sūtra*, which describes the *āśramas* as pertaining to *dvījā* males (*ADS* 2.21.1–21). This deteriorated further in the classical centuries, when the author of *Manu Smṛiti* excluded girls from both *upanayana* and Vedic learning. He declared that a woman's chief rite was marriage; her main *āśrama* that of a *gṛhastinī*, and her main *dharma* to serve her husband, produce his children, and care for his family:

> *MS* 2.66–67: For females, on the other hand, this entire series should be performed at the proper time and in the proper sequence, but without reciting any vedic formula, for the purpose of consecrating their bodies. For females, tradition tells us, the marriage ceremony equals the rite of vedic consecration; serving the husband equals living with the teacher; and care of the house equals the tending of the sacred fire.[19]

The *Manu Smṛiti*'s second chapter describes the celibate *brahmachārin* as a male *dvīja*, most often as a *brāhman*, less frequently as a *kṣatṛiya* or *vaiśya*, but never as a *śudra* or as a woman. For example, his verses on chanting the Sāvitrī prayer (*mantra*) to the sun god Mitra (*MS* 2.81–87) play upon the words '*brāhman*' and cosmic Brāhman. If uttered softly but firmly, the verse would transform the *brāhman* into Brāhman, who was also the creator Prajāpati, and Mitra, the universal friend (*mitra*).[20] As this spiritual feat required sexual abstinence, the author warned that: 'It is in women's nature to seduce men; so, a wise man must be cautious in the presence of an attractive woman' (*MS* 2.213). The student had to honor his mother as goddess Earth, his father as progenitor, and teachers and other elders but to be on guard against teachers' wives. He had to 'assist them, but not to clasp their feet or take personal liberties' (*MS* 2.210–212), rules to follow even in the man's next *āśrama* as a married *gṛhastin*.[21]

Manu's rules stopped most girls from attending classes with boys held under a tree or on an open verandah (*pyal*). The small ray of light was his strictures were not always obeyed. Research on pre-modern Tamil *pyal* schools indicates that girls who were *dvījas* or from the class of musician-dancers (*devadāsīs, isai vellālas*) were taught non-Vedic scriptures (*śmṛitīs*), such as the epics and *Purāṇās* in inner rooms, often adjacent to the verandah where boys chanted the *Vedas*. This meant that many girls memorized Vedic verses, although they were forbidden from chanting them aloud.[22] Although many high-caste women circumvented such restrictions, illiteracy plagued most non-*dvīja* women farmers, merchants, and artisans. Denied an education, women and non-*dvījas* became less visible in the echelons of public authority.

MARRIAGE AND SEXUALITY

If illiteracy disempowered many women, their secondary status was reinforced by the laws on marriage and property. These two connected issues were explored in several sections of the *Manu Smṛiti*, beginning with the third chapter on the life of a married *dvīja* man (*gṛhastin*). As the author believed the chief purpose of marriage to be the birth of progeny, especially sons, he described marriage, intercourse, menstruation, and childbirth entirely from the male perspective (*MS* 3.55–70), even though these closely affected women. Some of the *Dharma Sūtra* authors advised the father to conduct his daughter's marriage before puberty, and if he did not do so within three years, she had the right to choose her own husband (*BDS* 4.1.11–14).

Manu reaffirmed eight traditional styles of marriage, male polygamy, and the inheritance rights of legitimate sons. He advised youths on how to choose a bride, who was to be a virgin (*kanyā*) from his *varna*, with healthy male relatives, as they showed that she could have healthy sons. He had to reject a woman with red hair or an extra limb and one who jabbered incessantly or had serious diseases like leprosy, dementia, or jaundice, which could impair her ability to bear children.[23] Disapproving of women who took on male roles, Manu warned against a bride without male relatives, as this would require her to act as a 'female-son' for her family, a custom among some Indo-Āryan clans (*MS* 3.4–11). *Dvījas* could marry several wives of any *varna*, but *brāhmans* were specifically prohibited from taking a *śudra* wife (*MS* 3.14–19).

Of the eight styles of marriage, Manu lauded those based on love, honor, and parental consent (*MS* 3.20–44). For *brāhmans*, he advised the ideal (*brahma*) and divine (*daiva*) weddings officiated by priests; the seer's wedding (*ārṣa*), in which the groom gifted a bull and cow to the bride's father; and the *prajāpatya* in which the couple jointly took vows, and he accepted the elopement of lovers (*gāndharva*). He frowned upon the *aśura* wedding, in which the girl's father accepted a bride-price from the groom out of greed, as an 'evil' custom in which relatives lived off the wealth earned from a woman, leading them on a downward, sinful path (*MS* 3.51–52). He expressly forbade *brāhmans* to engage in the 'fiendish' (*rākśasa*) marriage in which the man abducted a screaming woman, causing 'death and destruction'. He also denounced the ghoulish (*paiśāchaścha*) 'evil' rape of a sleeping, intoxicated woman (*MS* 3.33–34). Yet he allowed all eight styles for *kşatŗiya s*, and seven for *vaiśyas* and *śudras*, except for the *rākśasa* union.

In the later Vedic era, Vasiştha had praised menstruation as nature's way to cleanse women of sins (*VDS* 28.1–9). This view became outdated by the classical centuries, as the *Manu Smŗiti* endorsed orthodox rules on sex and ritual pollution during menstruation, miscarriage, and childbirth, which he described solely from the male perspective. The author declared that: 'a woman is defiled in thought by her menstrual flow' (*MS* 5.108), although he conceded that elderly women had the most knowledge about feminine issues (*MS* 3.45–50). The term for semen/male essence (*pumānpuṃso*) was modified to describe female sexual fluids (*pumānpuṃpstŗiyau*). Manu prohibited sex with a menstruating woman for three days, not only as conception was unlikely during this period but also due to a ritual taboo on blood. He gave his emphatic opinion that women were most fertile for sixteen days after menstruation, that sons were conceived on even-numbered days when male semen was most powerful, that girls were conceived on odd-numbered days when female fluids were stronger, and that twins and hermaphrodites were born when male and female fluids were equal in strength (*MS* 3.47–48).

In a patriarchal society that valued women for their ability to bear sons, Manu asked men to placate women by celebrating their festivals and showering them with gifts. These gentler verses suggest that they are remnants of a less turbulent Vedic-era *Dharma Sūtra*, as he declared that: 'Where women are revered, there the gods rejoice; but where they are not, no rite bears fruit' (*MS* 3.56).[24] At the same time, his self-serving logic appears in his argument that when a wife grieved, the family was troubled, but when she 'sparkled', she attracted her husband's sexual interest, which brought progeny (*MS* 3.61–62). Other verses clearly indicate that the classical Manu was a celibate *dvīja* sage who shunned sexual encounters. This later Manu warned men of ritual pollution if they had sex with a woman during her menstruation or after childbirth and miscarriage (*MS* 4.40–42, 57, 208–217; 5.66, 85, 108; 9.160, 175). Unlike Vasiştha, he warned that a woman was 'defiled in thought by her menstrual flow' (*MS* 5.108) and that by touching a menstruating woman, men were permanently depleted of their energy:

> (*MS* 4.41): when a man has sex with a woman besmirched with menstrual blood, his wisdom, energy, strength, sight, and life-force waste away.[25]

Taboos on menstruation, childbirth, and miscarriage occurred in several sections, but one set of verses was particularly virulent. The author warned men not to eat food cooked or served by women who were in their menstrual period, had had a child, or had miscarried or by promiscuous women or those 'without a husband'. He also denounced husbands who lived with an unfaithful wife and her lover and those who were henpecked (*MS* 4.208, 211–13, 216–217; 5.66, 85, 108).

MANU SMṚITI AND *DHARMA ŚŪTRAS*: CONUNDRUMS ON GENDER AND *VARNA*

The task of dating the *Manu Smṛiti* has been hampered by some chronological puzzles. While verses of the *Manu Smṛiti* resemble the Vedic *Dharma Sūtras* of Gautama and Baudhāyana, others suggest it was composed in the classical centuries as a *Dharma Śāstra*. We agree with Olivelle that sections that resemble the *Dharma Sūtras* but that it was revised in the classical era by eponyms who retained some early verses. A comparison of the *Manu Smṛiti*'s laws on women and *varna* with those in the *Dharma Sūtras* sheds some light on dating this code.

In the later Vedic era, *brāhmans* Gautama and Baudhāyana wrote *dharma* codes for *dvijā* men but with conflicted views on women and *śudras*. They were challenged by the presence of learned *śudras* but recognized the need for *śudra* artisans and workers. As celibate *brāhmans* in Vedic schools, they dreaded female sexuality and disliked the growing population of mixed caste/ethnic *varnas*, whom they identified by birth as sub-caste *jātis*, but as the writers of *dharma* codes on ethical behavior, they strongly denounced sexual crimes. Baudhāyana forbade men to molest or rape women, but he excluded *kṣatṛiyas* whose sacred duty was to use force, which thus became their 'dominant trait' (*BDS* 1.20.12). Gautama condemned the violent rape of a virgin, the 'fiendish' (*rāķṣasa*) abduction of a drunken woman, sex with a menstruating woman, adultery, incest, and abortion (*GDS* 23.34; 24.4–5,*10*; 15.16; 20.1). Manu also abhorred *śudras*, but he also decreed that men must respect all women (*MS* 3.55–59). The *Manu Smṛiti* declared that heinous crimes included sex with a woman during her menstruation (*MS* 4.40–42); with a woman who had just miscarried or given birth (*MS* 4.212; 5.66); the rape of a virgin (*MS* 3.34, 164, 8.364,367); adultery (*MS* 8.352,359, 371–385), especially with a teacher's wife (*MS* 2.210–212); and incest with sisters and cousins (*MS* 11.172).

The question arises as to whether male *dvijā* attitudes changed substantively between the later Vedic and classical centuries. In the Vedic era, the state was ruled by *kṣatṛiya* kings and *brāhman* advisors, and subjects represented diverse indigenous groups. After Alexander's invasion and Mauryan unification, there was a dramatic increase in ethnic diversity, so that immigrants sometimes displaced locals, who migrated elsewhere. Social interactions reshaped gene pools, and the proliferation of mixed castes petrified elite *dvījas* like celibate hermits like Gautama and Manu, who then chastised *dvīja* women for consorting with *śudras*, *chāndalās*, and *mlecchas*, while inflicting stringent punishments on the non-*dvijā* men. Gautama allowed a *dvīja* man to marry a *śudra* wife and gave their sons right to maintenance from paternal property (*GDS* 28.39), but he denied this to the son of a *dvījā* woman and a *śudra*, and he ranked such progeny as *śudras*. He even decreed that a *śudra* who had sex with an 'Ārya woman' be castrated and forfeit all his wealth (*GDS* 12.3).

Like Gautama, Manu decreed that only *dvijā* males had the right to learn the *Vedas* as celibate students (*brahmachārins*), that the son of a *dvīja* woman and a *śudra* was a *śudra* unentitled to study the *Vedas*, and that a *śudra*'s duty was to serve *dvijās* (*MS* 2.30–40–65,164–172). Manu further emphasized that the *śudra*'s name must reflect his low status and that a *śudra* would never grow wise in his old age. While Gautama's *Dharma Sūtra* was less severe on caste issues, the *Manu Smṛiti* has some conflicting verses. Those on caste reflect a deep fear of inter-class relationships, along with pragmatic awareness of new realities, that the artisanal skills of *śudras* enriched the kingdom. Manu ordered that: 'The artisan, sculptor, *śudra* working for himself must give a day's labor each month to the king as his overlord' (*MS* 7.138).[26]

The classical era's *Manu Smṛiti* is notably misogynist in tone, a fact that indicates that sections less offensive to women may be remnants of a Vedic *Dharma Sūtra*. This early classical code also spews hatred for powerful, heterodox immigrants, but one verse reveals that the author knew they were unlikely to depart. Like Gautama and other *dvījas*, Manu must have heard of legendary non-*dvījā* scholars, like the tribal Vālmiki who composed the *Rāmayanā*, and Ekalavya, who was the prize pupil of a *dvijā* sage in the *Mahābhārata*. Manu may even have met mixed-*varna* sages, like the real-life Mahidāsa Aitareya, whose *Arańyakā* and *Upaniṣad* (ca. 600 BCE) are included in the *Vedas*. Yet only a single verse in the *Manu Smṛiti* describes *śudras* with respect (*MS* 2.238):[27]

> (*MS* 2.238): A man with dedication (*śraddha*) should accept the highest Law even from a man of the lowest caste; and a splendid woman even from a bad family.[28]

After this gracious *śloka*, Manu drew the line on educating women. He compared respect for the non-*dvīja* sage to marriage with a 'jewel' of a woman despite her low birth ('*anyādapi param dharman stṛī ratnam duṣkulādapi*').[29] Manu clearly saw education as a male prerogative, allowed even for *śudras*, but not for women, for whom marriage was the primary occupation. His fear of *śudras* as the Other probably increased with the knowledge that among them were learned or powerful kings and that *śudra* artisans and farmers enriched the royal economy. Determined not to recognize their skills, he ordered that *śudras* give 'ungrudging service' to *dvījas* (*MS* 1.91) and unpaid labor to the king (*MS* 7.138). Manu clearly feared that learned *śudras* would usurp power and seduce *dvījā* women to produce more *śudras* (*MS* 3.14–19, 8.20–22). He warned that *śudra* advisors would be catastrophic to the royal state:

> (*MS* 3.15): When twice born men (*dvījas*) marry low caste (*śudra*) women out of foolish desire, the whole family and children sink to the rank of *śudras*.
>
> (*MS* 8.21): When the king uses a *śudra* to interpret *Dharma*, he will watch his kingdom sinking like a cow in mire.[30]

As society grew more complex, Gautama and Manu compiled specific laws for each *dvīja* rank, *śudras*, and mixed castes. Gautama's list is brief (*GDS* 4.16–21) compared to Manu's lengthy discussion (*MS* 10.1–73), indicating that their strictures were being ignored, that sex across communities was commonplace, and that new gene pools had infused the subcontinent by the classical era. Manu thus reaffirmed *dvīja* polygamy but warned *dvīja* men about seductive *śudra* women. Two chapters are devoted to *varna* occupations, sacred duties, sex, marriage, inheritance, inter-caste sex, inheritance and rank of mixed progeny, and sexual crimes (*MS* Chs.10–11). Manu's complex rules allowed *kşaţriyas* and *vaiśyas* to marry a second or third wife of any *dvīja* rank and sometimes even take a *śudra* wife. Yet he stipulated that *brāhmans* marry only *dvīja* women and forbade them to have sex with *śudra* and *chāndala* women. Like Gautama, Manu argued that 'women were created to bear children, and men to extend the line' through sons (*MS* 9.96). While he decreed that the married couple jointly perform sacred household rites, society grew more patriarchal and staunchly traced male *dvīja* bloodlines. In an era without DNA tests, Manu advised men to have sex with wives on specific days of her menstrual cycle, as he believed erroneously that boys were conceived on even-numbered days of the cycle, when male semen dominated female fluids (*MS* 3.45–50).

Strīdhana *and inheritance*

Early Vedic custom gave sons and daughters different rights to property. With the formation of territorial states in the later Vedic era, paternal property often comprised lands, including royal domains inherited only by sons. Female property or *strīdhana* given during a girl's marriage was guarded carefully and transferred to her offspring as matrilineal wealth. The *Dharma Sūtra* authors did not recognize primogeniture, in which the eldest son was the sole inheritor of the paternal estate. This often precipitated deadly princely succession struggles, as in the case of Āśoka Maurya, who is recorded as having imprisoned and killed his brothers. The *Manu Smṛti*'s author now espoused a form of primogeniture and thus deviated from the *Dharma Sūtra* practice of equal shares of paternal property. The *Manu Smṛiti* gave the eldest son the largest share of his father's property, as he now assumed his father's role in the family, while younger sons each received a lesser share (*MS* 9.104–119). This may have reduced the incidence of princely rivalry so that there was more dynastic stability in the later classical kingdoms.

If landed property was inherited entirely by sons, female property or *strīdhana* was intended to support women in times of financial need and to be 'joyfully' bequeathed to her offspring. *Strīdhana* consisted of gifts to a bride during her nuptials when she left to reside with her husband, gifts from siblings and parents, and any subsequent gifts, all of which she bequeathed to her children and not to her husband. The authors of the *Dharma Sūtras* directed kings to prevent the misappropriation of *strīdhana*. Āpastamba instructed a man to 'adorn his daughter with jewelry to the best of his ability' and to ensure that women could control their *strīdhana* as maternal property in 'perpetuity' (*ADS* 2.11.17, 2.14.9). As a scholar who knew about Dravidian matriliny, he also granted women spousal property rights, as this was owned jointly by the 'married pair'.[31] All the authors protected female property from male control, but the later authors differentiated between lands inherited solely by sons and *strīdhana* as largely moveable assets like bridal jewelry. Thus, these authors reaffirmed female subservience to men in terms of property. While Gautama decreed that: 'The wife's property goes to her daughters who are unmarried or indigent. A sister's dowry goes to her uterine brothers after her mother dies' (*GDS* 28.24–26), he also stipulated that: 'A wife cannot act independently' or 'against her husband' (*GDS* 18.1–2). Baudhāyana agreed that females were 'not fit to act independently' (*BDS* 2.3.45), although he also stipulated that: 'Daughters should take their mother's jewelry and anything else customarily given to her' (*BDS* 2.3.43).[32] Vaśiṣṭha dismissed *strīdhana* in a single line that said: 'The daughters should take their mother's wedding gifts' (*VDS* 17.46). These authors protected *strīdhana* but ensured that women could not aspire to lands or the throne.

The *Manu Smṛiti* reaffirmed these views on *strīdhana* in eight lengthy *ślokas* (*MS* 9.192–200), which sometimes conflicted. The author first stated that both sons and daughters inherited *strīdhana* or matrilineal property, some of which came from a grandmother, but he concluded that only daughters of daughters inherited the estate. His list of six types of *strīdhana* sometimes overlapped, that is, gifts to the bride during her wedding; those given when she left for her husband's home; gifts of love from relatives, parents, and siblings; and those given by the husband to be inherited by their children. He also stated that in a the '*brahma*', '*daiva*', '*arśa*', '*gāndharva*', and '*prajāpatya*' marriages, the property of a childless woman went to her husband, but that in a '*rākṣasa*' or other style of union, such property was inherited by her parents. A woman's jewelry could not be partitioned between her husband's heirs. Yet Manu also required a woman to have her husband's consent to spend her *strīdhana* and any wealth given by family. Manu's standard of six types of *strīdhana* was later adopted by Nārada and Kātyāna in their *Dharma Śāstras*.[33]

Manu protected *strīdhana* from misuse by family men, but he did not grant women complete control over their own *strīdhana*, and he gave them few rights to paternal property. Fewer women now sat with boys to study the *Vedas*, but many were taught to read and keep accounts in adjacent inner rooms or at home. Many women farmed, sold goods, and kept household and store accounts, but they were considered the weaker, less able sex, so few were in positions of authority, and many relied on sons to manage their own *stṛīdhana*. Manu reaffirmed Baudhāyana's dictum on women's subservience, which decreed that the rules on women applied to all the *varnas* ('*sarvavarnāṃ stṛīṇāṃ dharmānnibodhata': MS* 5.156b). His next verses (*MS* 5.147–150) declared that women must always depend on men:

> (*MS* 5.147): As a child, in youth, old age, a female must
> never work independently.
>
> (*MS* 5.148): As a child, she must be controlled by her father;
> as a young woman by her husband; as a widow by her sons.
> A woman must never be independent.
>
> (*MS* 5.149): She must never want to be separate from
> her father, husband, or sons; as separation will disgrace
> both families.
>
> (*MS* 5.150): She must always keep a cheerful face, be
> adept at housework, keep utensils clean, and never spend
> extravagantly.[34]

The *Manu Smṛiti* lauded a life of celibacy for widows and abandoned women. Manu compared this ideal with that of the noble male renunciant (*sādhu*), although their cases were entirely dissimilar. Male *sādhus* chose celibacy and were highly respected by lay society. In contrast, widows and abandoned wives did not choose their wretched condition, bore the stigma of inauspiciousness, and depended on the charity of family men. He declared that widow remarriage was a cardinal sin and that sons from the earlier marriage ranked low in the filial order, with few rights to paternal property, as seen in these verses (*MS* 9.160, 175):

> (*MS* 9.160): A son born to an unmarried woman, a son received with marriage, a purchased son, a son born to a remarried woman, a son given in adoption by himself, and a son by a *śudra* wife – these are six who are relatives but not heirs.

> (*MS* 9.175): When a woman who is abandoned by her husband, or is a widow who marries again and begets a son of her own will, he is called the *son of a remarried woman*.[35]

Yet Manu acknowledged the right of an unmarried daughter to share in her father's estate (9.118); in the absence of a son, the right of a daughter ('female-son') who could then bequeath such property to her son (*MS* 9.127–140); and the right of a mother to inherit property from her childless son (*MS* 9.217). At the same time, by denouncing levirate sex for barren wives and levirate remarriage for widows as a form of prostitution, he gave virtually few rights to the children of such unions (*MS* 9.143–148). He showed his dislike of *dvīja* men with non-*dvīja* wives by reducing the inheritance rights of their children, allotting 'no more than one-tenth to a son by a *śudra* wife' (*MS* 9.154).

The king's *dharma* was to rule wisely and protect weaker subjects, as seen in the *Manu Smṛiti*'s paternalistic laws against sexual predation and the protection of women's property. Despite these commendable principles, sometimes the phraseology disempowered women. The laws defined sexual assault (*MS* 8.352–367), lesbian assault (8.369–370), and adultery and inter-caste sex (8.352–385). Other laws advised the king to protect the property of women and minors (*MS* 8.27–29, 9.192–220) and to prevent the fraudulent sales of women, although the emphasis appears to be on 'fraudulent' rather than 'sales' of females (*MS* 8.204–205). Paternalism is evident in three consecutive verses (*MS* 8.27–29):

> (*MS* 8.27): The king should protect the estate of a minor until he returns home from studies or when he is no longer a minor.

> (*MS* 8.28): The same protection must be given to barren women, women without sons or a family, devoted wives, widows, and women without support.

> (*MS* 8.29): If their property is taken by their in-laws during their lifetime, a righteous king who rules on earth must punish this family as if they were thieves.[36]

Manu decreed constant supervision for females, girls by the father, the wife by her husband, the widow by her sons. Warning that women were addicted, tightly 'strung' to sensual pleasures (as if by a bowstring), it was a man's duty to guard his wife 'day and night' and to keep her busy with household chores (*MS* 9.1–31).[37] The father 'owned' his daughter until puberty, when he was duty-bound to conduct her marriage (*MS* 9.88–103).

Using the metaphor of earlier codes, he called woman 'the field' and man 'the seed', which owned the field and hence had first rights to the crop or progeny. In a convoluted argument drawn from nature, Manu warned men not to sow their seeds in another's field, except in a contractual agreement. This referred to a levirate union (*niyoga*), in which if the husband were impotent or dead, his brother or another man was ritually allowed to be his surrogate and thus produce a son to perform the married couple's last rites (*MS* 9.32–56). While Manu accepted *niyoga* for an impotent husband, as the 'line was about to die out' (*MS* 9.57–59), he did not allow *niyoga* for a widow without sons. Sons belonged to twelve ranks, each with a different inheritance right to paternal property. Manu sanctioned a lesser share to the son from a *niyoga* union (*MS* 9.143–148, 162–163), to a son born to a non-*dvīja* mother and *dvīja* father (*MS* 9.153–154), and the son born to woman who had remarried (*punarbhūtvā*) after her first husband had died or disappeared (*MS* 9.175). While widow remarriage was recognized in some later Hindu codes, Manu praised widows who remained celibate until they died. This ruling prevented many widows from remarrying, especially after the *Manu Smṛiti* became the basis of colonial Hindu laws. The final chapter of the *Manu Smṛiti* humanely protected females from sexual predation and punished men for crimes such as incest, deflowering a virgin, and intercourse with an elder's wife (*MS* 11.55–108). Although these laws gave justice to afflicted females, they did not obliterate numerous other laws on separate and unequal gender rights, which made the *Manu Smṛiti* a weighty, patriarchal burden for women across the centuries.

Notes

1 R.T.H. Griffith [1896], trans., *Rig Veda*, at: www.sacred-texts.com/hin/rigveda. The English translation and the Sanskrit verse is: *RV* 10.72.4: 'Earth Sprang from the Productive Power the regions from the Earth were Born; Dakṣa was Born of Aditi, and Aditi was Dakṣa's Child'.('*bhūrjajña uttānapado bhuva āśā ajāyanta; aditer dakṣoajāyata dakṣād vaditiḥ pari*'.

2 R.T.H. Griffith, trans., *op. cit*. The Sanskrit verses (*Rig Veda* 10.90.11–12) are: #11) '*yat puruṣaṃ vyadadhuḥ katidhā vyakalpayan; mukhaṃ kimasya kau bāhū kā ūrū pādā ucyete.* (12): *brāhmaṇo asya mukhamāsīd bāhū rājanyaḥ kṛtaḥ; ūrūtadasya yad vaiśyaḥ padbhyāṃ śūdro ajāyata*'. The English translations are: #11): 'When they divided Puruṣa how many portions did they make? What do they call his mouth, his arms? What do they call his thighs and feet? #12): The

Brahman was his mouth, of both his arms was the Rājanya made; His thighs became the Vaiśya, from his feet the Śudra was produced'.

3 According to Patrick Olivelle, only 6% of Āpasthambā's *Dharma Sūtra* concerns *vyavahāra*, but that increased to 12% of Gautama's code and 36% of Manu's code. P. Olivelle, *The Law Code of Manu: A New Translation Based on the Critical Edition, op. cit.* (pbk), xix. In an earlier study, P. Olivelle proposed that the *Manu Smṛitī* was written by a single author, *vide.*, P. Olivelle, trans., ed., *Manu's Code of Law: A Critical Edition and Translation of the Mānava-Dharmáśāstra with the Editorial Assistance of Suman Olivelle, op. cit.*, 18–23.

4 P. Olivelle, *The Law Code of Manu: A New Translation Based on the Critical Edition, op. cit.*, xviii–xxiii, xxxii–xxxiii, 37–41.

5 For medieval commentaries, see Lido Rocher, trans., ed., *Jīmutavāhanā's Dāyabhāga: The Hindu Law of Inheritance in Bengal, op. cit.*; Ashutosh Dayal Mathur, *Medieval Hindu Law: Historical Evolution and Enlightened Rebellion,* New Delhi: Oxford University Press, 2007; Werner Menski, *Hindu Law: Beyond Tradition and Modernity,* New Delhi: Oxford University Press, 2003.

6 Vijnānesvara's *Mitākśara,* based upon the *Yājñavalkya Smṛiti*, distinguishes between Hindu social and religious laws. The is work was followed widely across India, but not in Bengal and Assam, which followed Jimutavāhana's *Dāyabhāga*, which was a composite of all the *Dharma Śāstras,* including *Manu Smṛiti.* An informative analysis is by N.N. Bhattacharya, "Property Rights of Women in Ancient India", in L.K. Tripathi, ed., *Position and Status of Women in Ancient India,* Vol. I, Varanasi: Benares Hindu University, 1988, 62–71, *vide.*, 69–71. Also see Justice Markandey Katju, "The Importance of Mitakshara in the 21st Century", in *SCC (J)*, Vol. 7, 2005, 3, Lucknow: Eastern Book Company of India, available at their website: htttp://www.ebc-india.com/lawyer/articles/2005_7_ 3.htm.

7 Recent art historians have described Sanchi architecture, but the most significant are Benoy H. Behl's articles, "Harmony in Stone", in *Frontline Magazine,* 24, 18, September 8–21, 2007, at: www.frontline.in/static/html/fl2418/stories/20070921505506600.htm; B. Behl, "Sacred Stupas", in *Frontline Magazine,* 25, 23, November 8–21, 2008, at: www.frontline.in/static/html/fl2523/stories/20081121252306600.htm

8 R. Thapar, *Early India: From the Origins to AD 1300, op. cit.*, 209–225.

9 The Sanskrit *ślōka* reads: (*MS* 8.123): '*kauṭasākşyam tu kurvāṇāms trin varṇān dhārmiko nṛpah; pravāsayed daṇdayitvā brāhmaṇām tu vivāsayet*'. *Manu Smṛiti* websites are: http://hinduonline.com/Scriptures/Smriti/ManuSmriti.html. Also see P. Olivelle, annotated trans., *The Law Code of Manu: A New Translation Based on the Critical Edition, op. cit.*, 2009 (pbk), 132.

10 S. Chattopadhyaya, *Social Life in Ancient India (In the Background of the Yājñavalkyasmriti),* Calcutta: Academic Publishers, 1965, 11–29.

11 http://hinduonline.com/Scriptures/Smriti/ManuSmriti.html. Also see P. Olivelle, *The Law Code of Manu: A New Translation Based on the Critical Edition, op. cit.*

12 Sanskrit *ślōkas* (*MS* 8.20–22) are: '*na śūdrarājye nivasen nādhārmikajanāvṛte; nā pāşaṇdijanākrānte noppasṛşṭe 'ntyajair nṛbhih*'). For English translation, see P. Olivelle, *The Law Code of Manu: A New Translation Based on the Critical Edition, op. cit.*, 124; or P. Olivelle, trans., ed., *Manu's Code of Law: A Critical Edition and Translation of the Mānava-Dharmáśāstra with the Editorial Assistance of Suman Olivelle, op. cit.*, 40.

13 See earlier fn. #52 for *MS* 7.138.: '*Kārukān śhilpanaśaichaiva śūdrām śchātmopajīvanah; ekaikam kāryetkarma māsī māsī mahīpatih*'.

14 Sanskrit verses at: http://hinduonline.com/Scriptures/Smriti/ManuSmriti.html. See also P. Olivelle, *The Law Code of Manu: A New Translation Based on the Critical Edition, op. cit.*

15 Hermann Kulke and Dietmar Rothermund, *A History of India,* New York: Routledge Press, 1995 (2nd ed.), 85–87.

16 On colonial Hindu laws, see G.W. Forrest, ed., *Selections from the State Papers of the Governors-General of India, Vol. I – Introduction, & Vol. II – Warren Hastings Documents,* 295–296, Oxford: B.R. Blackwell, 1910. See Pratap Bhanu Mehta, "Authority, Religion, and the Indian State", in Indira Jaising, ed., *Men's Laws, Women's Lives, op. cit.,* 56–86; Archana Parashar, "Just Family Law: Basic to all Indian Women", in Indira Jaising, ed., *Men's Laws, Women's Lives, op. cit.,* 286–322.

17 Olivelle translations of *ślōkas* (MS 1.6–9). Transliterations of the Sanskrit are:
A.1.6.6: 'Then the Self-Existent Lord appeared – the Unmanifest manifesting this world beginning with the elements, projecting his might, and dispelling the darkness' *('Tatah svyambhur bhagavān vyakto vyañjyannidam; Mahā bhūtādi vṛittaujā pradurāsīttamonudah');*
1.1.7: 'That One – who is beyond the range of all senses; who cannot be grasped; who is subtle, unmanifest, and eternal; who contains all beings; and who transcends thought – it is he who shone forth on his own' (*Yoasāvatin indraya grāhyah saṇymoavyaktaha sanātana; Sarva bhutamayo achintyah sa eva svayambhubhadbhau');*
1.1.8: 'As he focused his thought with the desire of bringing forth diverse creatures from his own body, it was the waters that he first brought forth; and into them he poured forth his semen (*'Soabhidhyāya śarīrātsvātsi sṛiṇurvividhāh prajā; Apa eva sasarjādau tāsu vīryamavāsṛijat').*
1.1.9: 'That became a golden egg, as bright as the sun; and in it he himself took birth as Brāhma, who is the grandfather of all the worlds' (*'tadarṇñama bhava dhaimam; tasmiň jaňyai svayam Brāhma sarvalokāpitāmaha').*

18 On Sānchi, see: Vidya Dehejia, *Indian Art,* London: Phaidon, 2000 (3rd ed.), 50–76; Roy C. Craven, *Indian Art: A Concise History, op. cit.,* 60–73; J.C. Harle, *The Art and Architecture of the Indian Subcontinent, op. cit.,* (revised ed.), 30–38; Benjamin Rowland, *The Art and Architecture of India: Buddhist, Hindu, Jain,* Baltimore: Penguin, 1953, 50–60.

19 P. Olivelle's translation of *MS* 2.66–67 in *The Law Code of Manu: A New Translation Based on the Critical Edition, op. cit.,* 28. The Sanskrit verses read: '(2.66): *Amantrikā tu kāryeyam stṛīṇāmā vridaśeṣatah; samskārātham śarīrasy yathākālam yathākramam*'; '(2.67): *Vaivāhiko vidhih stṛīṇāmam samskāro vaidikah smṛtah; patisevā gurau vāsah gṛihārthoharagni parikṛiyā*'.

20 *Manu Smṛiti* is at this site: http://hinduonline.com/Scriptures/Smriti/ManuSm riti.html

21 The Sanskrit verse (*MS* 2.213) reads: '*Svabhāva eṣa nārīṇām nārāṇā miha duṣanam; pratoharthānna pramādhyanti pramadāsu vipaśchitah*'.

22 Sita Anantha Raman, *Getting Girls to School: Social Reform in the Tamil Districts, 1870–1930,* Kolkatta: Stree Publishers, 1996, xii, xvi. In the Tamil districts, girls studied secondary scriptures (*smṛitīs*) like the epics and *Purāṇās* in inner rooms adjacent to the verandah (*pyal*), where the boys learnt the *Vedas.*

23 The Sanskrit verse (*MS* 3.8) reads: '*Na dvaheta kapilām kanyā nādhikāngaṇī na rogiṇīm; nālomikām nātilomam na vāchātām na pingalām*'.

24 The Sanskrit verse *MS* 3.56 reads: '*Yatra nāryastu pūjyante ramante tatra devatāh; yatrai tāstu na pūjyante sarvāstatrā phalāh kṛiyāh*'. See P. Olivelle, *The*

Law Code of Manu: A New Translation Based on the Critical Edition, op. cit., 2009 (pbk), 47.

25 Sanskrit verses are: (*MS* 4.40): '*Nopagacchetapramatto hapi strīyamārta vadarśane, samāna śayane chaiva na śayīta tayā saha*; (*MS* 4.41): *rajasābhiplutām nārīṃ narasya hyupagacchatah, prajñya tejo balam chakśurāyu śraicha prahīyate*'; *vide*, http://hinduonline.com/Scriptures/Smriti/ManuSmriti.html, 376. I have retained the fine translation by P. Olivelle, *The Law Code of Manu: A New Translation Based on the Critical Edition, op. cit.*, 68.

26 *MS* 7.138 states: '*Kārukān śhilpanaśaichaiva śūdrām śchātmopajīvanah; ekaikam kāryetkarma māsī māsī mahīpatih*'. *Vide., Manu Smṛiti,* at this site: http:// hinduonline.com/Scriptures/Smriti/ManuSmriti.html.

27 Mahidāsa Aitareya's mother Itarā was a *śudra* who worshipped the goddess Earth. His *dvījā* father favored his other children born to high-caste mothers, but Aitareya was the most enlightened. See Swami Sarvānanda, trans., ed., *Aitareyopniṣad*, Chennai: Sri Ramakrishna Math, 2001, 3–4.

28 Translation by P. Olivelle, *The Law Code of Manu: A New Translation Based on the Critical Edition*, 41. The Sanskrit verse reads: (*MS* 2.238): '*Śradda dhānah śubhām vidhyāmādha dhītā varādapi, anyādapi param dharmam strīratnam duṣkulādapi*'. *Vide., Manu Smṛiti* at: http://hinduonline.com/Scriptures/Smriti/ ManuSmriti.html.

29 Translation by P. Olivelle, *The Law Code of Manu: A New Translation Based on the Critical Edition, op. cit.*, 41. The Sanskrit verse (*MS* 2.238) reads: '*Pradda dhānah śhubhām vidhyā mādadītā varādapi; anyādapi param dharman strī ratnam duṣkulādapi*'.

30 The Sanskrit verses are: (*MS* 3.15): '*Hīna jāti strīyam mohādudvahanto dvījātayah, kulānyeva nayantyāśu sasantānāni śūdradratāṃ*'. (*MS* 8.21): '*Yasya śūdrastu kurute rājñyo dharma vivechanaṃ, tasya sīdati tadrāṣtaṃ panke gauriva paṣyatah*'.

31 *Āpastamba Dharma Sūtra*, 2.29.11–12 states: '*Sāniṣṭaya vidyā strī śūdreṣucha śrāthar varnasya vedasya śeṣa ityupādhiśanti*' ('In conclusion, the knowledge among women and *śudras* are a lesser part of the *Vedas*'). The final line, 2.29.15, states: '*Strībhya sarva varnebhyascha dharmśeṣān pratīyādityeka ityeke*' ('It is said that one can learn the laws known to women and the other castes'). *op. cit.*, 72–73.

32 P. Olivelle, trans., *Dharma Sūtras: The Law Codes of Ancient India, op. cit.*, 110, 175.

33 Lido Rocher, trans., ed., *Jīmutavāhanā's Dāyabhāga: The Hindu Law of Inheritance in Bengal, op. cit.*, 104.

34 The *Manu Smṛiti's* Sanskrit verses in these transliterations: (*MS* 5.147: '*Bālayā vā yuvatyā vā vriddhyā vāpi yoṣitā; na svatantrayeṇa kartavyaṃ kiṃ chidkāryaṃ gṛiheṣvapi*'). (5.148: '*Bālye piturvaśai tiṣhthetpāṇi grāhasya yauvanai; putrāṇāṃ bhartari pretai na bhajetstrī svatantratāṃ*'). (5.149: *Pitrā bhartrā sutairvāpi necchaidvirah: mātmanah; eṣāṃ hi viraheṇa strī garhyo kuryādubhai kulai*'). (5.150: '*Sadā prahṛiṣtayā bhāvyaṃ gṛihakāryai chadaññyā; suṃsaskṛitopaskarayā vyayai chāmukta hastayā*').

35 Sanskrit verses are: (*MS* 9.160: '*Kānīnścha sahoḍhaścha krītah paunar bhvastathā svayamdattaścha śaudraścha ṣaṅadāyādabāndhavāh*'). (9.175: '*Yāpatyā vā parityaktā vidhvā vā svayecchayā utpāda yetpunarbhutvā sa paunarbhav uchyete*'), *vide.*, http://hinduonline.com/Scriptures/Smriti/ManuSmriti. html. 477–478. See also P. Olivelle, *The Law Code of Manu: A New Translation Based on the Critical Edition, op. cit.*, 166, 167.

36 My translation: (*MS* 8.27: '*Bāladāyādikkaṃ rikthaṃ tāvadrā jānupālayet, yāvatsa syātsamāvṛitto yāvacchātītśaiśavah*). (8.28: *vaśāputrāsu chaivaṃ syādrakśaṇaṃ niṣkulāsu cha, pativṛitāsu cha stṛīṣu vidhvāsvāturāsu cha*). (8.29: *jīvantīnāṃ tu tāsāṃ ye taddhareyuh svabāndhavāh, tānśiṣyācchaura daṇngena dhārmikah pṛithivīpatih*'). *Vide.,* http://hinduonline.com/Scriptures/Smriti/ManuSmriti.html. Also see P. Olivelle, *The Law Code of Manu: A New Translation Based on the Critical Edition, op. cit.,* 125.

37 My translations of the Sanskrit *ślokas*, which read: *MS* 9.2: 'Day and night, men must keep women from acting independently; as they are addicted to sensuality, they must be kept under control' ('*Asvatantrāh stṛiyah kāryāh puruṣaih svair divāniśaṃ; viṣyaiṣu cha sajjantyah saṃsthāpyā ātmanovaśai*'). (*MS* 9.3: 'The father must protect her as a child, the husband in her youth, her son must protect her after her husband dies, so that woman must never be independent' ('*Pitā rakśati kaumārai bhartā rakśati yauvanai, rakśanti sthavirai putrā na strī svātantraymarhati*').

Part IV

LATER CLASSICAL ERA

Yājñyavalkya Smṛiti and *Nārada Smṛiti*

9

PRE-GUPTAN AND GUPTAN MONARCHS

I. Later classical kingdoms and dynasties (200–570 ACE)

This chapter examines the main political dynastic changes and social features of the later classical centuries (200–570 ACE). This methodology sheds light on why later classical rulers used two later *Dharma Śāstras* that were more ethically just than the *Manu Smṛiti,* namely, the *Yājñavalkya* and *Nārada Smṛitis* to mete court justice.

The later classical era began with fewer foreign invasions, a respite that promoted royal dynastic stability. Kings still squabbled over domains, but they also valued the benefits of trade across boundaries across the peninsula. They also welcomed land trade with Asia and Europe on routes once traversed by invading armies and maritime trade with the Roman Empire, including Egypt. Inscriptions, texts, sculpture, and architecture reveal expanding ideals of royal *dharma.* Hindu and Buddhist rulers promoted tolerance amid diverse subjects and peaceful enterprises. As each had an economic role, coexistence was a necessity rather than an esoteric ideal. Kings granted regional authority to subsidiaries for a fee, avoided intruding into local affairs, and recognized communal laws on marriage and property. At the same time, kings meted out court justice with a liberal code, as they were the final arbiters on crimes and disputes.

By the Guptan era, Āśoka's ideal of royal *dhamma* had evolved from tolerance to legal justice. The righteous king's chief *dharma* was to provide legal justice without prejudice, as this protected all subjects. With this juridical confidence, the Guptans chose two *Dharma Śāstras* with a greater focus on temporal laws (*vivādā*) with more exact court procedures (*vyavahāra*) than on sacred rites. The earlier code, the *Yājñavalkya Smṛiti* contains more details on sacred duties than the later *Nārada Smṛiti*, which deals extensively with laws, crimes, and punishments. Without ignoring *varna* hierarchy, the *dvīja* authors emphasized ethical judgments by the king and magistrates. Pre-Guptans like the Vakatakās probably relied on the *Yājñavalkya Smṛiti*, while the Guptans governed their empire with the *Yājñavalkya Smṛiti* and the *Nārada Smṛiti.*

A. Pre-Guptan dynasties

Despite their grand titles, early classical dynasties, such as the Śaka, Kuśāna, and Śātavahana, could only control their domains by granting regional authority to governors and feudatories (*satraps*). By 100 ACE, these three empires began to weaken, and some powerful *satraps* and *gana sanghas* asserted their independence. These political changes directly affected trade along routes traversing the upper half of the subcontinent, with a secondary effect on the south.

The first to fall was the Kuśāna Empire under king Vāsudeva (ca. 100 ACE), as Persian Sassanids captured its important region of Taxila and its prosperous trade routes into Asia. Soon after this, the Śaka empire was challenged by its governors or *satraps*, namely the Western Kşatrapas of Mālwa and the indigenous Nāga dynasty. Carved on the Junagarh rock near Mt. Girnar is a 20-line Sanskrit prose proclamation (*praśasti*) by the Western Kşatrapa Rudradāman (ca. 150 ACE), who declared his own title as 'Mahāķśatrapa' ('*svayamadhigata mahāķśastrapa nāmana*'). Rudradāman declared that he had given his daughter in marriage to, but also twice 'vanquished Satakarni, lord of Dakshinapatha' and that he had 'conquered Kşatrapa domains' which included regions of Sind, Punjab, Rajasthan, as well as most of Saurashtra, Kutch, the Deccan, and Konkan. Yet, a century later, the Kşatrapas were in turn challenged by Īśvarasena (ca. 240 ACE) of the Abhira clan, possibly a branch of the Śakas.[1]

The Śātavahana empire was also dismembered by its subsidiaries in the Deccan, a region with numerous land and riverine routes and seaports on each coast. It was inevitable that new states would struggle to control these routes, which conveyed valuable goods, as well as migrations of diverse groups within the peninsula and abroad. The three most significant subsidiaries were the Ikşvākus of Andhra, whose queens patronized the Buddhist *sangha* in Nāgarjunākondā (ca. 250–350 ACE); the Kadambas (3rd–4th c. ACE) of Karnataka; and the powerful Vakatakās of Berar (3rd–5th c. ACE), whose inscriptions are found in the Ajanta caves in Mahārāshtra. The Vakatakās may have been *kşaţriyas*, as the founder's son Pravarasena performed four Vedic horse sacrifices (*aśvamedhas*) and assumed the Sanskrit title of '*Samrāt*' (emperor). Despite an initial threat to the Guptans over vital trade routes, they later became respected allies.

B. Guptan Empire

The Guptan Empire was founded by Chandragupta I (319–335 ACE) in Bihar. This ruler assumed the grandiose title of 'Mahārājādhirājā' after marrying Kumārādevī of the wealthy Lichchhavi clan, one of eight powerful Vrijji *gana sanghas* of Vaiśālī on the upper Ganges. His militaristic son Samudragupta (335–375 ACE) defeated the Vakatakā Rudrasena, who was pushed deeper south into the Deccan. Yet, a generation later under king Rudrasena II, the Vakatakā political state was powerful enough to seal a marriage alliance with the imperial Guptans through a mutually advantageous pact. Rudrasena II married Prabhāvatī, the daughter of Chandragupta II (375–415 ACE), and Kuberanāgā, a Nāgā princess from the Deccan. As Rudrasena died within a few years, Prabhāvati served as regent for their minor sons. She used the Vakatakā-Guptan alliance to successfully thwart the ambitions of the Kşatrapa Rudrasimha and prevented this dynasty from capturing trade routes from the Deccan. This story was immortalized by Bāna in his Sanskrit play *Harşacharitra* (7th c. ACE).[2]

As the apex of the later classical centuries, Guptan emperors combined political power with legal justice, social tolerance, and support for the arts. If Chandragupta I carved an empire with arms and diplomacy, his son Samudragupta (335–375 ACE) expanded it through military exploits. These appear in an elegant Sanskrit *praśasti*, a posthumous elegy possibly ordered by Samudragupta's son, Chandragupta II/Vikramāditya. The inscription appears on the Allahabad sandstone column, which bears an earlier Āśokan edict. The undated Guptan inscription lacks sectarian references but speaks of *dharma* as righteousness. It describes Samudragupta as Mahārājādhirājā: 'one whose happy mind was accustomed to associate with learned people, was the supporter of the real truth of the scriptures', who enjoyed 'the beauty of excellent poetry' (lines #1–5); who conquered those who did 'great wrongs' (#11); who 'bravely uprooted Achyuta and Nāgasena' (#13); who established the boundaries of *dharma* (#15); who marched south to Kānchipuram to liberate twelve kings in Andhra, Kerala, Tamil Nadu, and Sri Lanka (#19); who defeated many northern kings of 'Āryavarta' (#21); who compelled five frontier kings ('Samatata, Davāka, Kāmarupa, Nepāla, Kartripura') to pay tribute (#22); who exterminated foreign rulers like the Kuśāna ('Daivaputras'), 'Shāhis, Shāhānushāhis, Śakas' (#23); who embodied kindness, as he was engrossed with plans to help the 'miserable, poor, helpless, afflicted' (#26); and who was the illustrious son of Chandragupta and Kumaradevi, 'daughter's son of the Lichhavi' (#29), and a divine being on earth (#29–33).[3] References to conquest and tribute indicate that Samudragupta knew that this empire could not be governed directly but that he had a vision of an empire that commanded the subcontinent's numerous kingdoms, clans, and tribes.

Chandragupta II took the title of victor, or Vikramāditya. The fragments of a eulogistic Sanskrit play, *Devī-Chandragupta*, written two centuries later, describe his accession and his rescue of queen Dhrūvādevi, wife of his cowardly brother Rama, who sold her to his Śaka enemy. While this tale may be an exaggeration, what is clear is that Chandragupta II defeated the Śakas and shifted his capital to Ujjain to protect vital trade routes to Asia. He also sealed a strategic marriage alliance for Prabhāvati, his daughter through queen Kuberanāga of the Nāga dynasty, and the Vakatakā king Rudrasena

II. Prabhāvati's regency for twenty years ensured that the Guptan-Vakatakā allies prevented the Kṣatrapas from capturing trade routes in the Deccan.

Chandragupta II and his successors patronized art and Sanskrit literature, as seen in numerous compositions. The eminent playwright-poet Kālidāsa may have lived at the court of Chandragupta II or his son Kumāragupta (415–455 ACE). As Hindu emperors, the Guptans performed Vedic rites, and Kumāragupta even conducted the horse sacrifice. Yet they also practiced tolerance and built and endowed rest houses and temples with images of Viṣnu, Śiva, and the Buddha. The first invasions occurred during Kumāragupta's reign, spearheaded by the Puṣyamitra clan from the Narmada. There is no inscriptional evidence of a Guptan standing army, and its possible absence may have enticed Huna invasions. Repeated, debilitating onslaughts under Skandagupta (455–467 ACE) finally disintegrated this empire (ca. 520 ACE).

Guptan rule: an assessment

In the struggle for freedom from colonial domination, nationalist historians eulogized the Guptan Empire as the Golden Age. They lauded Samudragupta's 'unification' of the subcontinent and the cultural efflorescence promoted by his son Chandragupta II/Vikramāditya.[4] This hypothesis has been challenged by later scholars whose perspective is either based on Marxist economic theory or whose analysis is based on numerous factors. Jha thus argues that in the decentralized state, kings issued land grants with magisterial powers to the elite, whose oppression of low-caste peasants created a class of semi-serfs.[5] Thapar examines several historical factors with less theoretical constraints to conclude that the Guptan Empire was not an idyllic 'golden era' but 'threshold times' before medieval stagnation. The later classical centuries were neither unflawed nor static but experienced dynamic political, social, and economic changes, some resulting from events outside the subcontinent. For example, Roman imperial collapse staunched the flow of gold for Indian industries, and in this waning economy, women often worked with less or no pay, and some low castes became truly 'dāsa' slaves.[6]

More problematic is the view that under decentralization, the Guptans did not maintain a standing army, and they became vulnerable to Huna attacks. Our study presents counter-arguments that, despite decentralization, this vast empire thrived for nearly three centuries (320–520 ACE), and although inscriptions do not reveal a standing army, it formed an effective power bloc with subcontinental allies. This empire was thriving until Toramāna's Hunas occupied Mālwa and restricted the Guptans to Bihar and north Bengal. The Hunas certainly left carnage behind, but unlike previous invaders who merged into local society, they left just a meager genetic imprint on ancient India. The Guptan era may not have been 'golden', but the emperors' successful policies of royal *dharma* made their rule historically significant. In the Mauryan Empire, Āśoka's edicts had proclaimed *dhamma* as compassionate morality essential for kings and subjects.[7] In the early classical era, this ideal of royal *dhamma* was embraced by Kaniṣka the Kuśānā Buddhists who probably governed with the revised *Arthaśāstra* and by Rudradāman the Mahāķṣatrapa (72 ACE), who carved his Sanskrit inscription on the Junāgarh rock near Āśoka's edict. The Guptans expanded this ideal of royal *dharma*, and their policies became the yardstick for future kings.

One pragmatic policy was to recognize incontrovertible social complexity, which required decentralized governance. The first codes to list mixed-caste/ethnic groups were the later *Dharma Śutras*, and by the later classical era, there ensued numerous sub-castes. The Guptans realized that it was not feasible to govern this complex society with a centralized bureaucracy and a massive army, as once maintained by the Mauryans. Samudragupta's Allahabad inscription indicates that he wielded his sword to assert political authority but that he also granted local autonomy to subsidiaries, who could be allies during attacks. The Guptan Empire was decentralized and possibly without a standing army, but it formed a power bloc with its allies on the peninsula. The Guptans were Hindus who performed Vedic rites but not zealots who wished to foist a single cultural vision upon their diverse subjects. They recognized that tolerance was imperative, as this policy promoted social harmony and enriched the economy, whose farmers, artisans, traders, and bankers were from many communities.

Decentralization shaped the legal system, as kings allowed local customary laws, but they were the highest court of appeal for crimes and legal disputes, either directly or through appointed magistrates. The king's duty to mete out justice was first stipulated in the *Dharma Sūtras*, expanded in Kauṭilyā's *Arthaśāstra*, and reaffirmed in *Manu Smṛiti*. Guptan emperors apparently believed that their chief *rāja dharma* was to serve justice without prejudice to all subjects. This policy led them to reject the *Manu Smṛiti* with its tirades against women and non-*dvījās* in favor of the next two, more liberal, *Dharma Śāstras*, that is, the *Yājñavalkya* and *Nārada Smṛitis*. Yājñavalkya and Nārada were *brāhmans* who acknowledged Hindu social and religious traditions but focused on temporal laws (*vivāda*) and procedures (*vyavahāra*). The Guptan vision of royal *dharma* as righteous legal justice set a standard for later kings. The *Yājñavalkya* and *Nārada Smṛitis* gave women rights to spousal property, which were cited in medieval commentaries (*prabandhas*) that became regional laws. Benign royal *dharma* included welfare projects and patronage of the arts. Guptan rulers like Vikramāditya supported the poet Kalidāsa and numerous other writers of Sanskrit prose, drama, and non-fiction. Meanwhile, *śudra* artisans carved Hindu, Buddhist, and Jaina icons of stone, brass, and bronze, and their stone temples laid the foundation for Hindu architecture. Later kings emulated the Guptans by supporting writers and artisans.

After Huna invasions and a period of weak kings, north India was revitalized by the Buddhist emperor Harşāvardhana of Thāneśvar and Kanauj (ca. 605–648 ACE). Harşā reinforced the Guptan ideal of *rāja dharma* as equitable justice for all and patronage for artisans and writers. Harşā's court poet Bāna composed the Sanskrit drama *Devī-Chandragupta* eulogizing Chandragupta II, who rescued the wife of his wicked brother from the Śākas. In the next centuries, the Bengal Rāştrakutās and Pālās; the Deccan Chālukyas; and the southern Pallavās, Pāņdyas, and Cheras emulated the Guptans by promoting creative art, dispensing justice with a liberal code, and allowing local customs. Coastal kingdoms sold crops, fine textiles, and ironware to Arabia and Southeast Asia.[8] Guptan inscriptions that escaped destruction by Huns and Turks (10th c. ACE) inspired Muslim Mughals like Akbar (1542–1605), who founded the syncretic Dīn-ī-Ilāhī sect, and his son Jahangir (d. 1605) from the Rājput queen Harkabai/Jodhbai (d.1623) wrote his Persian words below Samudragupta's Sanskrit *praśasti* on the Allahabad pillar.[9]

Notes

1 Ramashankar Tripathi, *History of Ancient India,* Delhi: Motilal Banarsidass, 1999 (1999; 1st ed., 1942), 217–218. Tripathi quotes from Rudradāman's rock inscription at Junagarh in Sanskrit prose. This edict was deciphered by Lorenz Franz Kielhorn, and it is recorded by E. Hutlzsch, ed., *Epigraphica Indica,* Vol. VIII, Calcutta, Government Printing Office, 1905–06, 36–49. The inscription is dated 72 (Indian calendar) or ca.150 ACE.

2 Ramashankar Tripathi, *History of Ancient India, op. cit.,* 277–279; and D.N. Jha, *Ancient India in Historical Outline,* Delhi: Manohar, revised ed. (1998; first ed., 1977), 115–124.

3 Fleet, *Corpus Inscriptionum Indicarum: Inscriptions of the Early Gupta Kings and Their Successors,* Vol. 3 (1888), *op. cit.* #A, 17, 130–136, #B, 1–17; Bhandarkar, Chhabra, and Gai, eds., *Corpus Inscriptionum Indicarum: Inscriptions of the Early Gupta Kings* (1981) *op. cit.,* 215–220.

4 For the nationalist perspective, see R. Tripathi's chapter, "The Imperial Guptas", in *History of Ancient India, op. cit.,* 237–267.

5 D.N. Jha's chapter, "The Myth of the Golden Age", in D.N. Jha, ed., *Ancient India in Historical Outline, op. cit.,* 149–173.

6 R. Thapar's chapter, "Threshold Times", in R. Thapar, ed., *Early India: From the Origins to AD 1300, op. cit.,* 280–325, *vide.,* 280–302.

7 G. Buhler, trans., "Aśoka's Twelfth Rock Edict", in J. Burgess, E. Hultzsch, and A. Fuhrer., eds., *Epigraphica Indica, op. cit.,* 16–20. Aśoka stated that *dharma* was righteousness, the 'essential' doctrine underlying gifts and sectarian differences: (Line #2: '*Devanam priyo mañyati yatha kiti/salavadhi siya sarvapraśandanam/ salavadhi tu bahuvidha/tasa tu iyo mulayam vachagati*'). His last two line declare that he had sent his officials, some being women, to promote righteous 'essentials' as *dhamma:*(#9: '*Vapata dhrama mahāmatra yaccha mahabamatra vach bhumikañye cha nikaya/imamcha yetisa phalam yam atapraşadha vadhi; #10: dhrama sacha*

dipanā'). See also R. Thapar, *Aśoka and the Decline of the Mauryas, op. cit.*, 228–270, 254–255.

8 D.N. Jha, *Ancient India in Historical Outline, op. cit.,* 116–124; Ramashankar Tripathi, *History of Ancient India, op. cit.,* 211–234; R. Thapar, *Early India: From the Origins to AD 1300, op. cit.,* 226–244.

9 E. Hultzsch, ed., *Epigraphica Indica, op. cit.,* Vol. 8, "Junagadh Rock Inscription of Rudradāman 1905–06, 36–40, *ibid.*; Fleet, *Corpus Inscriptionum Indicarum, op. cit.,* 1–17, *ibid.*; Bhandarkar, Chhabra, and Gai, *Corpus Inscriptionum Indicarum: Inscriptions of the Early Gupta Kings* (1981) *op. cit.,* 215–220.

10

YĀJŇYAVALKYA AND *NĀRADA SMṚITIS*

I. *Yājňavalkya* and *Nārada Smṛitis*

The classical *Dharma Śāstras* reflect dynamic changes to the royal state and society on the subcontinent. As the first three *Dharma Śāstras* are separated by centuries, our search for the historical truth requires us to place each code in its sociopolitical context. This method sheds light on the authors' motivations and views and helps us to recognize them as simply human and not ideal divinities. By the later classical centuries, kingdoms were more dynastically stable, although these states did rise and fall due to numerous factors. Some states had complex economies based on agriculture, industry, and trade, while others had economies that were more uniform or simpler, sometimes with nomadic populations. The monarchs were also diverse, some being of local ethnic origin and others descended from immigrants; some had orthodox Vedic beliefs, others were more pragmatic and/or liberal, while others were heterodox. Their subjects were rarely from a single community but a varying mix of diverse ethnic, caste, sub-caste *jāti*, and tribal groups, with a growing tendency for patriarchal power structures, although many also retained forms of matriarchy. While classical Indian philosophies and literary and artistic creativity continue to inspire us today, early Sanskritic social hierarchies based on gender and caste may be increasingly irrelevant for a modern nation with a more equitable constitution.

Differences and similarities in the *Dharma Śāstras* reflect the original era of composition and the author's emphases and style, as well as those of his eponym/s. The early classical *Manu Smṛiti* has verses from a later Vedic *Dharma Sūtra*; the *Yājňavalkya Smṛiti* also has verses that resemble a *Dharma Sūtra*, but its cohesiveness suggests a single author in the pre-Guptan centuries (ca. 250 ACE); the lengthy *Nārada Smṛiti* from the Guptan Empire (ca. 400 ACE) has been embellished by at least one major posthumous author. While the *brāhman* authors defined *dvījā dharmas*, the *Dharma Śāstras* were primarily temporal laws (*vivāda*) for a patriarchal kingdom with *varna* social ranks, ruled by a monarch who was either *kşatṛiya* by birth or lived like a *kşatṛiya rājā*. Literary traditions include honoring the gods and *Vedas*, defining *vivāda* and court *vyavahāra*, and citing ancient sages with whom they agreed, but not maligning other sages.

In style, length, and attitudes, there is a substantial difference between the *Manu Smṛiti* and the *Yājñavalkya Smṛiti*. While Manu devoted six out of his twelve chapters to *varna* and *dvījā dharmas*, the *Yājñavalkya Smṛiti* is remarkably succinct, possibly because these duties were commonly known in the later classical era. While the author was conversant with Manu's rulings, especially on women and caste, other sections of the *Yājñavalkya Smṛiti* resemble Vasiṣtha's *Dharma Sūtra*. This suggests that it was perhaps derived from a Vedic *Yājñavalkya Sūtra* from the school of the *Yajur Veda*.[1]

The *Yājñavalkya Smṛiti*'s three chapters are of nearly equal length, and they emphasize temporal *vivāda* and the king's *rāja dharma*, indicating that king's chief function was to mete out court justice in this era. Its Chapter 1 ('Āchārādhyāyah', *YS* 1.1–398) praises the gods and *Vedas* (*YS* 1.1–9), then defines the *varnas*; lists male *dvījā dharmas* in just the first two life phases (*āśramas*), that is, of the celibate student and householder; describes marriage within a caste (*savarna*) and outside (*asavarna*); gives rules on eating, washing, and pollution; and describes ancestral rites invoking god Ganapati (*YS* 1.11–52–308). The final third of this chapter describes the king's *dharma* to protect all subjects, probably to guide *kṣatṛiya* kings and immigrant/local non-*dvījās* who lived like *kṣaṭriyas* (*YS* 1.309–398). Its Chapter 2 ('Vyavahārādhyāyah', *YS* 1–310) resumes the central theme of royal juridical *vivāda* and *vyavahāra*. This indicates that in later classical kingdoms like the Guptan, the monarch's chief function was to serve justice in court relying on a specific *Dharma Śāstra*. Although decentralized governance sanctioned local communal laws, the king was clearly the final court of appeal in crimes as well as in disputes. Chapter 3 ('Prāyaśchittādhyāya', *YS* 1–334) is the final section, and it describes crimes, penalties, atonements, women, and the economic functions of the *varnas*.[2]

The *Nārada Smṛiti* reveals that juridical functions constituted the king's main responsibility. The author bypassed the literary tradition of invoking gods and *Vedas* and of describing *dvījā dharmas* and life stages, as these were now well known.[3] Instead, Nārada plunged into legal arguments, during the course of which he described the economic roles of each *varna*, caste guilds for skilled artisans, and a guild solely for women (*NS* 1.135); rules on menial laborers, apprentices, and slaves (*NS* 5.1–42); and rules on birth castes (*varna-jāti*), and royal duties (*NS* 18.1.4–6, 16–52). These arguments indicate that caste stratification and even slavery were features of Guptan society. The *Nārada Smṛiti* has two sections, the main body of twenty chapters entitled 'Vyavahārapādini', indicating that the author's primary purpose was to define temporal *vivāda*, *vyavahāra*, crimes, and penalties, and an eponymous prologue, 'Mātrika', with three sub-sections, that is, 'Vyavahāra', 'Dialogue' (Bhāṣā), and 'Court' (Sabhā). 'Mātrika' is an eponymous work attributed to the later legalist Kalyāṇabhatta, who may also have modified sections of 'Vyavahārapādini', according to scholar Lariviere.[4] Unlike the main *Nārada Smṛiti*, 'Mātrika' contains a fleeting but distinct *namaskār* to the gods. Like Yājñavalkya, Nārada and his eponym emphasized that the paramount duty of the king and his magistrates was to discover the truth as *dharma* in each legal case, as this constituted unbiased justice, since people of all *varnas* committed crimes. This confirms what scholars conclude about the *Yājñavalkya Smṛiti,* that the king's chief function was often more juridical than military in stable dynastic states. Two manuscripts attributed to Nārada have been discovered in the south and Nepal, while eponymous recensions occur across the subcontinent. These discoveries, and the code's emphasis on unbiased justice, explain why the *Nārada Smṛiti* influenced the legal practices in later kingdoms.

This chapter has three sections, each with sub-sections: Section II is on kings, justice, and *varna* in classical India, with a comparative analysis of the *Yājñavalkya Smṛiti* and the *Nārada Smṛiti.* Section III is a separate analysis of women and *varna* in the *Yājñavalkya Smṛiti.* Section IV is a separate analysis of women and *varna* in the *Nārada Smṛiti.*

II. Kings, justice, and *varna*: *Yājñavalkya* and *Nārada Smṛitis*

A. Royal justice

Political and social events in the Vedic-classical millennium expanded the meaning of '*dharma*'. Once connoting the sacred duties of individuals in a society based on patriarchy and *varna* ranks, '*dharma*' in the first law codes also signified the temporal laws of states. The question then emerges as to how, in a society based on hierarchies of patriarchy and *varna*, *brāhman* authors defined the king's *rāja dharma* to mete out justice in an unprejudiced manner. In the later *Dharma Sūtra*, author Vasiṣṭha recognized the importance of more precise rules on court procedures (*vyavahārā*). This became even more important in the vast Mauryan Empire, as the ruler's juridical duties increased significantly. Kauṭilya thus expanded the term *dharma* in his *Arthaśāstra* to include both temporal laws (*vivāda*) and *vyavahārā* procedures. The early classical *Manu Smṛiti* reveals some authorial conflict, as the author ordered *kṣatṛiya* kings to exploit *śudra* labor and wealth yet to mete out justice precisely by using credible witnesses and *vyavahārā* (*MS* 8.16–26). After a period of political upheavals, amid more stable later classical dynastic kingdoms, Yājñavalkya and Nārada reiterated that the king's primary *dharma* was to mete out equitable justice (*nyāya*) by unveiling the truth hidden by superficial evidence, so that all guilty persons were punished, irrespective of caste or gender.

Yājñyavalkya was influenced by Kauṭilya's description of kingship in the *Arthaśāstra* but with a greater emphasis on *nyāya* in court. Yājñyavalkya thus declared that the righteous king's primary responsibility was to protect all subjects by meting out *nyāya* using precise rules on *vyavahāra*. Yājñavalkya's lucid verses on *rāja dharma* (*YS* 1.309–398) advised the king to rise early, focus on governance, and employ spies to weed out corrupt officials. The righteous king forgave the *brāhman* (*'brāhmaṇeṣu kṣmī'*), was brotherly to colleagues (*'syārāja bhṛtyavargeṣu'*), and was paternal to all subjects (*'prajāsu cha yathā pitā*), yet showed anger to enemies (*'krodhanoariṣu'*). In the Guptan Empire, Nārada reaffirmed these views on kingship, and while he did cite Manu's legal views, he avoided his virulent biases. These early verses equated *nyāya* with moral governance, with social and religious implications. If the king failed to protect subjects, he bore the weight of that sin, but by protecting those whom he taxed, he reaped a final reward for his virtuous acts (*YS* 1.335–337). A king without *nyāya* levied unfair taxes, but in the process, he would destroy his people and land, so that the eternal fire of grieving subjects would consume him, his family, and his wealth (*YS 1.341: 'prajāpīdan santhāpāt sabhudbhuto hutāśanah; rajah kulaṃ priyaṃ prāṇāṃśchādagadhvā na nivarte'*). Yājñavalkya advised the king to appoint 'loyal, able, honest officials, energetic men to collect and distribute wealth' (*YS* 1.322); and that:

> (*YS* 1.323): The king must give wealth from war to *vipras* (*brāhman s* who perform domestic rites), as this act, and protecting subjects from fear were his highest *dharmas*.[5]

Yājñyavalkya was also influenced by Kauṭilya in another way. He too was a *brāhman* who looked beyond rituals and advised kings how to govern. The *Arthaśāstra* thus informed the king that his 'religious vow is readiness to action' (*'rājō hi vṛitaṃ utthānaṃ yajnyah kāryānuśāsanaṃ'*; *AŚ* I.19.33ab) and that 'in the happiness of his subjects lies his happiness' (*'prajāsukhe sukhaṃ rajah, prajānāṃ cha hite hitaṃ'*; *AŚ* I.19.34ab).[6] Yājñyavalkya now advised the king to act firmly, but not recklessly, to promote subjects' welfare, as that ensured his own, and to make friends with his enemy's enemy (*YS* 1.334). He also borrowed Manu's analogy (*MS* 9.294–297) to describe the seven limbs (*saptanga*) of the state as king, officials, subjects, fort, treasury, weapons, and allies (*YS* 1.353). Yājñyavalkya's second chapter on *vyavahāra* directed the king and his *brāhman* magistrates to use *vyavahāra* with circumspection so that the truth emerged. He advised them to rely 'on the *Dharma Śāstras*, after having conquered anger and greed' (*YS.2.1: 'Dharmaśāstranusāraṇai krodha lobha vivarjitah'*). If the king could not attend court, Yājñavalkya forbade the judge to be vindictive, lest he be punished like a criminal (*YS* 2.3–4).

B. Varna

Living in a society based on *varna*, Yājñavalkya and Nārada realistically accepted its hierarchical order of castes and sub-castes, while Nārada even described slavery. Yet both authors refrained from disparaging women, *śudras*, and *chāṇḍālas*, and they also recognized that these groups were habitually exploited. Their answer to such injustice was for the king to protect his subjects by meting out *nyāya* in court, irrespective of the litigant's caste (*jātī*), guild (*śrenī*), or group (*gaṇa*), since *dvījas* and *śudras* committed crimes. Yājñavalkya advised the king to punish even his 'family, *jātī, śrenī, gaṇa*' and to set them on the right path (*YS* 1.391).[7] Nārada warned that 'if the king did not punish all castes when deviating from their paths, the kingdom and the subjects would be destroyed' (*NS* 18.14).[8] The *Yājñavalkya* and *Nārada Smṛitis* ordered the king and his magistrates to unmask the truth beneath false evidence, to rely on precise *vyavahāra*, as *nyāya* was *dharma*, which was the essence of truth. For a society that believed in Truth as divine, this was a significant ideal of court justice. While Yājñyavalkya and Nārada and his eponym cited Manu, they were more humane in their rulings. Yājñyavalkya advised the king that his chief duty was to protect subjects. This meant that the king had to weigh evidence impartially and to 'rely on the *Dharma Śāstras*, after conquering anger and greed' (*YS*.2.1).[9] The eponymous section 'Mātrika' in the *Nārada Smṛiti* stipulated that: 'One fourth of the guilt goes to the perpetrator; one fourth to the witnesses, one fourth jointly to the members of the court; and one fourth to the king' (*NS* 'Mātrika' 3.11).[10]

C. Women in classical India

India's social fabric was woven with intricate new designs in this normative millennium, due to marriage and interaction among *varnas*, local groups, and immigrants. Cultural assimilation was common among Sanskritic patriarchal clans, local matriarchal/matrilineal groups, and those who spoke Dravidian, Mongoloid, and Austro-Asiatic languages. With the establishment of the Sanskritic royal state, whose kings were *kṣatriyas* or lived like *kṣatriyas*, their learned *brāhman* advisors emphasized patriarchy and the *varna-jāti* order. The *Dharma Sūtras* legalized both hierarchies, the *Artha Śāstra* validated patriarchy, and the *Dharma Śāstras* ensured these as legal fixtures whenever the king or his magistrates meted out justice in court. Meanwhile, Sanskritic patriarchal norms subtly pervaded local matrilineal communities, who now attached greater value to premarital virginity and early marriage for women. While these norms probably deterred some molesters, they also empowered male relatives to wreak retribution on those who broke these iron-clad norms.

As in the *Dharma Sūtras*, the *Dharma Śāstras* validated women's subordination. Vasiṣṭha's decree that the son of a *dvīja* and his *śudra* wife was a *śudra* was echoed by Manu, who also reiterated the old adage that women must be dependent on the father, then on the husband, and finally on the son (*MS* 9.71–73). Yet it is conceivable that women often resisted great oppression or simply ran away and that many *śudras* left menial jobs and moved by assuming a new *dvīja* identity. While inviting community censure, or possibly being taken to court, the outcome would have depended on the king's choice of a code. The Guptans relied on the less censorious *Yājñavalkya* and *Nārada Smṛitis*, which rejected hearsay and false testimony as *adharma* and referred to the women as *svairīnis*, who may have become courtesans.

Female education

When the Sanskritic royal state grew more powerful in the later Vedic era, *dvīja* women were increasingly restricted to domestic pursuits. Fewer *brāhman* and *kṣatṛiya* women participated in public assemblies, but an expanding economy afforded *vaiśya* and *śudra* women opportunities to farm, sell goods, and work as artisans. The *brāhman* authors of all Vedic-classical *dharma* codes viewed women solely through the prism of family life. As they defined the first life phase (*āśrama*) of the celibate student (*brahmachārin*) as pertaining only to *dvīja* males, *dvīja* girls and *śudras* were largely excluded from Vedic schools. Yet other sources such as historical inscriptions and literature depict powerful educated women.[11] Such women include queens Kunti and Draupadi in the epic *Mahābhārata*; Maitreyi and Gārgi, who studied the *Vedas* from *ṛṣi* Yājñavalkya in the *Brihad Āranyaka Upaniṣad* (ca. 700 BCE; *BAU* 2.4.2–4. 3.6.1, 4.5.3–5); Guptan queens Prabhāvati and Kuberanāgā described in inscriptions (4th c. ACE); Buddhist canon (70 BCE) depictions of Mahāpajāpati, who founded the order of nuns; Jaina saints Nemi and Ajja Chanda described in heterodox canon (1st c. ACE);[12] the *Yājñavalkya Smṛiti*'s reference to wives who managed household budgets (*YS* 1.83); the *Nārada Smṛiti*'s dicta on the 'sonless widow' who repaid her husband's debts (*NS* 1.13–14); and wives of launderers, hunters, cowherds, and liquor sellers who supported their families (*NS* 1.16). Few *dvīja* girls sat openly with boys in Vedic schools, but they were probably taught at home to read secondary texts (*smṛitis*) like the epics and *Purāṇās* and basic math to manage their *strīdhana* and household accounts.

There are more references in the classical Tamil Sangam literature to women in the public arena. The anthology *Puranānūrū* describes female minstrels (*pāṭiṇi*) and dancers (*viṛali; ātumakaḷ*) who celebrated a king's victory and the advent of rains by lighting lamps and washing and offering flowers to icon pillars (*skanda*) and hero stones in temple halls (*potiyil*). Notable poets were the respected woman sage Auvaiyār (3rd c. ACE) and male sage Kapilar (*Pur.*,103, 109; 128).[13] The famous epic *Śilappadikāram* by Iḷango Adigal (3rd–4th c. ACE) revolves around three powerful women, nun Kavundi, courtesan Mādhavi, and heroine Kaňnaki.[14] An intriguing question for scholars is whether and when the *viṛali* and *pāṭiṇi* developed into the temple courtesan (*devadāsis*) of south India. Kersenboom-Story proposes that they were 'antecedents of the devadasi', as their job was not just to entertain but to add luster to the king. She argues that Mādhavi in *Śilappatikāram* 'exemplifies the change of the *viṛali-pāṭiṇi* into the courtesan called '*gaṇikā*' known in Sanskrit literature'.[15] Mādhavi composed poetry, sang, and retold legends. In real life, such courtesans were born to a courtesan mother or became one to escape an unhappy marriage. The *Yājňavalkya Smṛiti* uses the term '*svairiṇī*' for a woman who left her husband and was now unchaste (*YS* 1.67). The *Nārada Smṛiti* elaborates on four kinds of *svairiṇī* and the legal implications (*NS* 12.49–52, 77–78), indicating that in the Guptan urban scene, the *svairiṇī* occupied a familiar niche. It is possible that the large temples built by post-classical dynasties like the Chālūkyas, Pāndyas, and Pallavas sites attracted pilgrims and also became refuges for courtesans, who danced before sacred icons. The courtesan's role in purveying ancient legends indicates that they were taught secondary scriptures (*smṛitis*). Pre-modern sources from south India indicate that *dvīja* girls and courtesans were taught these *smṛitis* in inner school rooms, while boys sat on the open verandah (*pyal*) and chanted the *Vedas* (*śruti*). The girls often memorized the *śruti* verses, although they were forbidden to chant them aloud.[16]

D. Women and varna*: comparative assessment of three* Dharma Śāstras

In a society with waves of immigrant settlers, there were questions of how a person's *varna* was determined. Despite the disapproval of orthodox elite *dvījas* like Manu, the reality was a web of complex sub-castes due to ongoing sexual relations across communities. Yājňyavalkya's first chapter on *dvīja* identity and duties modified the Vedic *Dharma Sūtras*' rules on identity and progeny to suit later classical society. Baudhāyana's *Dharma Sūtra* and Kauṭilya's *Arthaśāstra* had decreed earlier that the progeny of a *dvīja* father and *śudra* mother were *dvījas*. Manu had disagreed with this view, claiming that a person was *dvījā* only if both parents were *dvījas* (*MS* 10.6). This seems to indicate that in the early classical era, *varna* was increasingly defined by birth (*jāti*). Some centuries later, Yājňyavalkya and Nārada agreed with Manu that a person's *varna* was based on his birth, that a *dvījā* had to have two *dvījā* parents, and that a marriage was most respected if the couple came from the same *varna* (*savarna*). While Yājňavalkya's discussion of mixed *varna* unions was brief, Nārada's was much longer and more detailed, perhaps due to increasing sex across castes, which produced more complex sub-castes in the Guptan era. Yājñavalkya stated that he 'disagreed with those who said that *dvījas* can take a *śudra* wife, since the *ātman* is born there (in her) as a *śudra*' ('*tistro varṇānu purvyeṇa dve tathaikā yathākramaṃ; brāhmaṇā kṣatṛiya viśāṃ bhāryā svā śudra janmanah*': *YS* 1.57).[17] Nārada declared that it was 'the king's duty to prevent the mixing of castes' (*NS* 12.117).[18]

Both authors frowned on inter-caste sex (*YS* 1.90–96, 1.90–96; *NS* 12.1–117), but as they realized that these strictures were being broken, they ranked various types of mixed marriages. Both writers ranked as higher marriages between a high-caste man and lower-caste woman (*anuloma*), whose progeny they recognized. They ranked as lower marriages between a low-caste man and higher-caste woman (*pratiloma*), and their children were of lesser rank. Yājñavalkya excluded the children of *pratiloma* from Vedic rites ('*śūdrājātastu chāṇdāla sarva dharma bahiṣkriti*': *YS* 1.93). He described *anuloma* unions as 'true/good' (*sat*), but *pratiloma* as 'untrue/bad' (*asat*), *vide.*, '*asat santastu vijñeyāh pratilomānulomajā*' (*YS*. 1.95),[19] and he philosophized that virtuous acts could result in a higher birth in a future life (*YS* 1.96).

In extreme cases, Nārada allowed a wife/widow to remarry if her husband died, disappeared after being outcaste, or became a hermit or eunuch (*NS* 12.97).[20] He allowed a *dvīja* man to form an *anuloma* union with a *śudra* woman but disapproved of a *pratiloma* union between a *brāhman* woman and *śudra* man, as this 'mixed the *varnas*' ('*pratilomyena yajjanam sa jñeyo varnasaṃkarah*': *NS* 12.103). As Nārada branded *pratiloma* offspring as '*chāṇḍālas/sūta/vaidehakā*', clearly these now became outcaste *jātis* (*NS* 12.106–109).[21]

Yājñyavalkya and Nārada advocated separate *varna* professions like Manu, but they were less harsh. Yājñavalkya and Nārada believed that separate professional skills learned in childhood brought benefits, as *dvījā* learning produced strong kings, *brāhman* advisors, and *vaiśya* merchants, and *śudra* artisanal training enriched the economy. Yājñvalkya cited the ancient 'highest sages' (*paramāmatā*; *YS* 3.38), who had decreed that people follow their *varna* occupations and atone with rites if necessity compelled them to take up another job (*YS* 1.113–129; 3.35–41). Yājñyavalkya's fourteen verses on *śudra* and *chandala* professions (*YS* 1.10, 1.21, 1.56–57, 1.90–96, 1.127, 1.166–168) reveal his conviction that exploiting *śudras* was unjust and '*adharma*'. In one magnanimous verse, he affirmed that everyone, including *śudras*, deserved respect for wisdom, worthy acts, age, friends, relatives, and wealth (*YS 1.116: 'vidhyā karmavayo bandhu vittairmānyā yathākramaṃ; aytaiha prahutaiha şūdroapi vārdhake mānmarhati*'). The metaphoric next line advised travelers to give way to those who carried a burden, kings, Vedic scholars, women, bridegrooms, and invalids (*YS*

1.117). Yājñyavalkya's verses reflect his social milieu but also some magnanimity. His second chapter on *vyavahāra* states that a slave (*dāsa*) must be freed by the owner if he was forced into slavery, if he was sold by a thief, if he saved his master, or if he had sold himself to get food (*YS* 2.185). Yājñyavalkya decreed that if a monk or nun forsook mendicant vows and returned to society, he/she became the king's slave, and that a person could be enslaved by a higher-caste person but not by a lower-caste person (*YS* 2. 1.86)

Yājñvalkya's code describes such heinous crimes as the murder of a *brāhman* or a woman of any caste, incest, rape of a maid, sex with an elder's wife, abortion, and consuming alcohol (*YS* 3.227–243). Women were outcaste for aborting fetuses, and a *dvīja* woman was outcaste for cohabiting with a *śudra* (*YS* 3.297–298). These rules on exclusion offend today, but in that society, some would have regarded it as better than the castration decreed earlier by Manu. It is also clear, that despite elite threats, some punishments may not have been rigidly enforced, as evident in Manu's lengthy chapter on *varna* and mixed groups (*MS* 10.1–130).

While Manu described *dvījā dharmas* in six chapters, Yājñavalkya devoted less than a hundred verses to them (*YS* 1.219–308). Yājñyavalkya emphasized the social aspects, probably as most *dvījās* were familiar with their *dharmas* and many immigrants had merged into local society. Yājñyavalkya described two rituals in detail, namely those for ancestors (*pitr*) invoking Ganapati and those atoning (*prayaśchita*) for serious crimes (*YS* 3.1–334). In his third chapter on penance, Yājñyavalkya gives us a glimpse of his personal devotional (*bhakti*) yearnings when he describes the Creator Iśvara as Ātman/ Brāhman:

> (*YS* 3.34): The ancient sages have declared that by doing our *varna* duties and respecting the learned, our intellect is cleansed, so that it knows that the Atman is Iśvara.[22]

Yājñyavalkya's philosophical leanings also appear in a rare and sensitive artisanal analogy when describing Brāhman as the Source of five gross elements (ether, air, fire, water, earth) and Ātman as the Perceiver/Soul (*YS* 3.145):

> (*YS* 3.146–148): Just as a potter puts a lump of earth on his wheel to make a pot, as the builder uses wood and mud to build a house, as the goldsmith uses gold to make many things, as the silkworm makes a web from his saliva, just so does the soul take the elements and senses to make the body act and it becomes fettered.[23]

Manu had claimed more leniency for *brāhmans* in this verse: 'if individuals of the three *varnas* give false testimony, a righteous king should first fine and then execute them; but that a *brāhman*, on the other hand, he should send into exile' (*MS* 8.123).[24] In contrast, Yājñavalkya described all the *varna* occupations as sacred *dharmas*, including those of *śudras*, and he emphasized that only if justice were equitable could such *dharma* be Truth.

While *Nārada Smṛiti* lacks a separate section on *dvīja dharmas* and *varna*, the author described their legal implications while making his arguments. The first chapter, 'Non-Payment of Debts' ('Hriṇādanaṃ'), stated that *śudras* could acquire wealth only if given by *dvījas* (*NS* 1.50). Nārada forbade the *brāhman* and *śudra* to perform each other's work, which would make them outcastes (*'na kathaṃchana kurvīta brāhmanāh karma vārṣalaṃ; vriṣalah karma brāhmanām patanīye hi te tayoh'*: *NS* 1.53). His next *śloka* ends by stating that the work of *kṣaṭriyas* and *vaiśyas* as 'the middle groups' was allowed to all (*NS 1.54: 'madhyeme karmāṇī hitvā sarva sādharane hite'*).[25] The two sections of the *Nārada Smṛtī* reveal the author's perfunctory interest in religion. The eponymous 'Introduction' ('Mātrikā') gives a valedictory *namaskār* to Vedic traditions, and to Manu as the first lawgiver, before plunging into issues such as the court, legal terms, procedures, judges. 'Legal Procedures' ('Vyavahārapadāni') has twenty-odd chapters on debts, deposits, partnership, marriage, property, disputes, and punishments.

The *varna* occupational order was based on the religious and political authority of *dvījas* rather than on affluence, although wealth increased power. Many *brāhmans* remained fairly poor, most *kṣaṭriyas* were soldiers rather than rich landowning kings, the majority of *vaiśyas* were smalltime shopkeepers, and just a handful of *śudra* artisans acquired property. In the thriving Guptan Empire, some *brāhmans* entered the 'middle professions' of *kṣaṭriyas* and *vaiśyas* as soldiers, officials, and merchants, and despite *dvīja* disapproval, some *śudras* ventured into non-traditional professions. People also defied *dvīja* strictures against sexual mingling, as the classical codes list a growing number of mixed *jātīs*. This astounding fact indicates that far from being static, the caste system evolved in politically stable, prosperous classical kingdoms and in those marked by poverty. What is interesting, however, is that when the Guptan state was at its peak, Nārada's code indicates that the religious-social *varna-jātī* order had started to stagnate into an economic class system. By the time of Huna invasions, there was greater poverty; *śudras*, *chāṇḍālas*, and mixed *jātīs* were being reduced to semi-serfs and slaves. When these invaders destroyed key urban industrial centers, the economy crumbled. The bright spot on the horizon was that when north India revived under capable rulers like Harṣa, the professional *jātīs* resiliently produced and sold products overseas to Asia and Arabia.

Nārada focused on *vivāda* and *vyavahāra*, and he cited Manu on *varna* occupations. His fifth chapter on breach of contract describes five types of service, four being 'pure work' by students, apprentices, hired laborers, overseers, and fifteen types of slaves (*NS* 5.1, 5.5. 23–42). Slaves were born into a household, bought, gifted, inherited, and acquired in battle or gambling, or they had sold themselves to escape a famine or other dire straits or had married a female slave. The author ordered the king to free slaves captured by robbers, but it also reveals that he lived in and accepted his unequal society. One section, possibly added by an eponym, decreed that persons of higher *varna* could not be enslaved by lower *varnas* and that slaves and wives could not be owned directly, nor could they own property (*NS* 5.39). This extraordinary parallel between women and slaves denied women's primary right to *strīdhana* given in the *Rig Veda* and repeated in all later codes. In contrast, the *Nārada Smṛiti*'s more liberal 'Matrika' eponym echoed Yājñyavalkya's view of *dharma* as Truth and faulty judgments as *adharma*. He stated that, as the king's first duty was to mete out justice, 'he must resort to fact alone since *dharma* is the root of prosperity' (*NS* 'Mātrika' 1. 25).[26] The next verse directs the king to serve only Truth in the manner of Yamā-Vaivasvata, god of Death:

> (*NS* 'Mātrika' 1. 26–27): Just as the fire has seven flames, the *dharmic* king who presides over *vyavahāra* with discipline has seven rewards, truth as *dharma*, wealth, fame, success, the subjects' support, esteem, and a definite place in heaven;[27]
>
> (*NS* 'Mātrika' 1. 28): Therefore, when the king takes the judgement seat, he should abandon selfishness, be neutral to all beings, and take on the vow of Vaivasvata.[28]

'Mātrika' ordered the king to select judges who were 'good bulls', capable of undertaking difficult cases (*NS* 'Mātrika' 3.3).[29] They had to 'know the *dharma smṛitis*, belong to a good family, adhere to truth, be unprejudiced, as the king was the center of *dharma*, even if appointed magistrates presided in court (*NS* 'Mātrika' 3.4–6); to be without deception and hatred', and to speak with *dharma* or go to hell (*narak*) (*NS* 3.14).[30] The final *śloka* declares:

> (*NS* 'Mātrika' 3.17): A court is not a court if there are not elders. Elders are not elders unless they pronounce dharma. Dharma is not dharma unless there is truth. Truth is not truth if it is mixed with sophistry.[31]

In the main code, Nārada ordered the magistrate to punish all guilty persons, irrespective of caste (*NS* 18.5–21); to know the *Vedas* (*śruti*) and sacred texts (*smṛiti*); and never to confiscate a person's tools of livelihood (*NS* 18.11–12). He declared that: 'The king is the only man who has neither beginning nor end, for he is illustrious and sacred, as long as he does not swerve from his path' (*NS* 18.13).[32] While Nārada tried to be fair, as a *dvīja*, he clearly feared *śudra* ascendancy:

> (*NS* 18.14–15): If the king did not wield his *danda* to punish all castes straying from allotted paths, his subjects would be ruined. The *brāhman* would neglect duties as a priest; the *kṣatṛiya* would be powerless; the *vaiśya* would cease to work; and the *śudra* would become the most superior of all.[33]

III. Women in the *Yājñyavalkya Smṛiti*

A. Marriage and remarriage

This section examines the *Yājñyavalkya Smṛiti*'s dicta on women's marriage, remarriage, *strīdhana*, and rights to paternal/spousal property. The *Yājñyavalkya Smṛiti* reified the tradition of writing for male *dvijas*, especially the two higher ranks of *brāhmans* and *kṣatṛiyas* who most frequently attended Vedic schools. Yājñavalkya first reified social distinctions between male *dvijas*, women, and *śudras* when describing some important rites. These included prayers for a pregnant woman to have a male fetus (*puṃsavanam*; *YS* 1.12); the sacred thread ceremony (*upanāyanam*) for only *dvijā* males but originally also undertaken by *dvija* women; and the purificatory *brāhma tīrtha* water rite for *dvīja* men, modified for women and *śudras* (*YS* 1.21). When describing marriage, the author reaffirmed gender ideals, such as virgin brides (*YS* 1.53–54, 59–64), chaste wives, and lifelong dependency (*YS* 1.70–90). A bride could be given away by the father, brother, grandfather, or uncle, but in their absence, it was preferable that she gave herself rather than an unqualified person (*YS* 1.63–64). Like earlier law givers, he listed the *brāhma, daiva, ārṣa, kāyah, aśura, gāndharva, rākśasa,* and *paiśāscha* forms of marriage. Yet Yājñavalkya also sanctioned the remarriage of a girl promised earlier but not claimed by another man, after which she could ritually purified as a 'reborn' *punarbhū* (*YS* 1.66–67). In the second case, if her husband died early or disappeared before giving her a son to maintain her and perform her funeral, rites of purification allowed her to remarry his younger brother (*niyoga*; *YS* 1.69). Yājñavalkya ordered the wife to live in her husband's home, obey his wishes as her 'highest duty', to manage household chores and budget, and to 'salute the feet' of his parents (*pāda vandanaṃ*; *YS* 1.83). If a wife eloped with a man of her caste, she was an unchaste '*svairiṇī*' ('*svairiṇī yā patim hitvā savarna kāmatah śrayet*': *YS* 1.67). If she committed adultery but returned, she was reprimanded, shorn of all rights, forced to subsist on meager rice balls (*piṇḍa*), and to sleep on bare earth. At the same time, Yājñavalkya warned that if the husband did not maintain his wife, he bore a weighty sin (*YS* 1.70, 74).

Yājñavalkya repeated Vasiṣṭha's ideas on menstruation as a gift from the Moon goddess. He forbade men to punish a chaste woman for adulterous thoughts, as long as she did not act on them, as the menstrual flow cleansed a chaste woman, who 'reaps great fame in this world, and sports with Uma in the next' (*YS* 1.71–75). Yājñavalkya forbade the husband to neglect, misuse, or discard a chaste wife who bore sons and was docile, but if she were barren, sick, had only daughters, or squabbled with him, he could remarry. Yet he had to give his chaste first wife up to a third of his property before he remarried (*YS* 1.76–78).

While Yājñavalkya agreed with Manu on some social norms, he was far less abrasive to women. Manu instructed *dvijas* that 'having children only from a *śudra* wife' was 'degrading' (*MS* 3.64) and 'a downward path' for the *brāhman*, who could become an outcaste (*MS* 3.14, 17).[34] Yājñavalkya gently restated that: 'It is said that *dvījas* can choose *śudra* wives; I do not agree, as the *ātman* goes from there to the son' ('*yaduchyate dvījatīnāṃ śudra dadāro pasamgrihah; naitanmama mataṃ yasmāt tatrāyaṃ jāyet svayaṃ*'; *YS* 1.55).[35] He lauded marriages within the *varna* (*savarna*), as such Brahma unions sanctified the *varna* for twenty-one generations (*YS* 1.58). He also said that:

> *YS* 1.90: *Savarna* sons are born from *savarna* unions, which ensure this male lineage till eternity (*savarnebhyah savarnāsu jāyante hi sajātayah; anindhyeṣu vivāheṣu putrāh santāna vardhanāh*).

Yājñavalkya's second chapter defined laws on property that affected women. Yājñyavalkya did not advocate primogeniture but authorized the father to distribute his property equally among sons or give a larger share to the eldest. If he gave equal shares to his sons, they had to pay off his debts and allot an equal share to his wives without *strīdhana* for her subsistence (*YS* 2.117). A widowed mother received an equal share of her husband's property, as did her son/s (*YS* 2.126). If the mother died, daughters paid off her debts, then divided her *strīdhana* equally among themselves, but in the absence of daughters, her sons shared her matrilineal wealth (*YS* 2.119). The next verses give superior rights to the wife who bore his son to a share of his property over that of kinsmen (*YS* 2.130). The next verses reveal women's rights to spousal property, with a range of related possibilities that reflect the sexual practices and mores of Yājñavalkya's society. His code thus stipulated that if a man died without a son, his heir could be an 'appointed daughter's son' who offered *pinda* at his funeral; the heir born to his wife in a *niyoga* rite with an appointed brother/paternal kinsman; his own son born at home secretly to a married woman servant; his *kānina* son born to an unmarried woman relation from his maternal line; his pregnant widow's unborn son; or an adopted son 'gifted by his parents or himself, or had been deserted' (*YS* 2.131–134). If a man lacked a son, his wife inherited his property, or, in her absence, the man's daughter, parents, brothers and their sons, or kinsmen (*YS* 2.135) received the property. Yājňyavalkya also recognized the rights of the man's son from a *śudra* maid (*dāsyā śūdraṇa*; *YS* 136–137).

B. Property and inheritance rights

The *Yājňavalkya Smṛiti* punished men who cheated women and raped non-*dvīja* servant women. It reaffirmed women's control of *strīdhana* and the rights of widows and daughters to inherit spousal/paternal property. Yājňavalkya allowed *dvīja* men to take a second or third wife of another *dvīja varna*, after which he could marry a *śudra* wife. He listed their progeny based on their ranks, and he gave specific names to sons of mixed *jātis* (*YS* 1.88, 91–96). Yet he also decreed that if a husband took a second wife, he must give his first wife monetary compensation, especially if she did not have *strīdhana*, and if she did, half the amount to maintain her (*YS* 2.151). As described earlier, Yājňyavalkya also sanctioned a young widow's *niyoga* remarriage to her deceased husband's younger brother (*YS* 1.69),[36] thus allowing her to resume marital life.

Although the code expected women to be chaste, it allowed polygamy for men, but it forbade men to ill-treat or cheat women, even those who were *śudra* servants. The fine for public sexual activity was heavier for men than for women (*YS* 2.288); a man who raped even a servant woman paid a hefty fine (*YS* 2.293–294), as did the husband who sexually degraded his wife or the man who had sex with a mendicant nun (*YS* 2.296–297). Yājňyavalkya made the adage on female dependency more humane by decreeing that fathers must provide for daughters until marriage and husbands must take care of even 'childless wives' (*YS* 2.144–145).

The *Yājňyavalkya Smṛiti* reaffirmed the ancient laws on *strīdhana* as gifts from a woman's 'father, the mother, the husband, or a brother, or received by her at the nuptial rite' and gifts from her husband's family or if he married a second wife (*YS* 2.146–147). If she died childless, gifts from her family were returned to her family; those from her husband were returned to him (*YS* 2.146–150). While the husband was not compelled to return money that he had borrowed from his wife during calamities like famine and sickness, he had to provide for his chaste wife, especially one without *strīdhana,* by giving her monetary compensation if he married a second wife while his first wife was still alive (*YS* 2.151).

Yājňyavalkya Smṛiti lists serious crimes such as abortion, murdering a woman who was menstruating (*YS* 3.251), murdering a *brāhman* (*YS* 3.227), and murdering one's husband (*YS* 3.297). Rape or sex with a friend's wife, a virgin, or a woman of low *jāti* were sins as serious as having relations with a teacher's wife or daughter, for which a man was castrated and killed (*YS* 3.321). Similarly, a man who committed incest with an aunt, daughter, or daughter-in-law was castrated and killed (*YS* 332–233). Sins that could be expatiated with penances included killing an 'unchaste' woman of any *varna* (*YS* 3.268–269) or having sex with a wife during her menses (*YS* 3.287).

Yājňavalkya's code is remarkably succinct on juridical details, condensing in its second chapter ('Vyavahārādhyāya') two lengthy chapters of the *Manu Smṛiti* (*MS* 7 & 9). To ensure equity in criminal cases, Yājñavalkya listed three types of evidence as 'documents, legal ownership, witnesses' (*YS* 2.22), and he prioritized documents above witnesses (*YS* 2.86–96), which Manu had emphasized. The *Yājňavalkya Smṛiti* improved trial procedures by requiring five ordeals (*divya prakāraṇaṃ*; *YS* 2.97–115). It also changed Manu's order of eighteen litigation titles, which facilitated trials involving commercial crimes, such as counterfeiting, selling cloth owned by another, acting as surety in father-son quarrels (*YS* 2.53–54), adulterating goods, false trade in local and foreign goods, bribing officials, and being a physician without proper training (*YS* 2.241–261).[37] While these were clearly improvements, two *ślokas* (*YS* 2.72–73) reveal that Yājňavalkya shared his era's social attitudes, as he forbade testimony from these persons, beginning with: 'Women, old men, boys, gamblers, drunkards, mad men, defamed persons' (*YS* 2.72). He also forbade performers, heretics, forgers, outcastes, the deformed, friends of the litigant, and those involved in the case.[38]

The *Yājňyavalkya Smṛiti*'s second chapter, 'Vyavahārapada', concerns civil and criminal court cases, and its precise rulings on commercial transactions probably improved juridical procedures in the Guptan Empire. One section of particular importance for women is entitled 'Dāyabhāgaprakarṇaṃ', as it defines the inheritance rights to paternal/spousal property, and it is more liberal to widows (*YS* 2.116–152). The *Yājňyavalkya Smṛiti* and *Nārada Smṛiti* were later cited in two medieval commentaries (*prabandhas*), which became the laws in many regions of the subcontinent.

The first commentary was Vijňāneśvara's *Mitākşarā* (ca. 11th c. ACE), composed for the Chālukyā kingdom in the Deccan. Vijňāneśvara cited the *Yājňavalkya Smṛiti* to give wives and widows rights to spousal property, by innovatively interpreted a key funeral rite in which male heirs offer a rice ball (*piṇda*) representing a transcended ancestor's soul (*atman*). The *Mitākşarā* decreed that a pregnant widow and the child she bore had a closer physical relationship to her deceased husband than his distant male relatives, and thus she had a greater right to inherit spousal property. This practical, rather than metaphysical, interpretation of *pinda* enabled the *Mitākşarā* to spread from the Deccan to the south Maharashtra, Benares (U.P.), and Mithila (Bihar). *Mitākşara* operated as local customary law, even after the British framed their colonial Hindu Law based on the *Manu Smṛiti*.

After Indian independence, as jurists cited *Mitākṣarā* as the more 'secular' code, it helped to shape the Hindu Succession Act, section #6 (1956).[39] The *Yājñavalkya Smṛiti* gave widows and daughters first rights to the property of their husband/father without a son, followed by rights given to his brothers, their sons, male relations, and fellow students of the same caste (*'patnī duhitaraśchaiva pitarao bhrātarastathā; tatsu gotrajā bandhu śiṣyasa brahmachāriṇah'*; *YS* 2.138).[40] This ruling shaped medieval property laws across several regions of the subcontinent. Although *Mitākṣarā* specified that a father shared his rights with his sons while alive, this ruling specified that a father could share his property with sons while alive and allowed a share to the widow and daughters.[41]

The second commentary to be shaped by the *Yājñavalkya Smṛiti* was Jimuthavāhanā's *Dāyabhāga* (12th–13th c. ACE). Jimuthavāhanā cited several *Dharma Śāstras* to make his points, but he specifically cited the *Yājñavalkya Smṛiti* to allow widows' rights to spousal property. He declared that upon the father's death, sons could not partition his estate while the mother still lived. The widowed mother thus assumed greater importance to her sons, as her consent was necessary for any dealings over her husband's property.[42] This ruling enabled *Dāyabhāga* laws on women to prevail in Bengal and Assam.[43]

IV. Women in the *Nārada Smṛiti*

A. *Marriage and property*

This section is on the *Nārada Smṛiti*'s rulings on women's marriage, remarriage, *strīdhana*, and rights to spousal/paternal property. The prologue, 'Mātrika', was probably composed later by Kalyānabhatta, who may also have added verses to the main code, 'Vyavahārapradhāni'. The first eleven chapters of 'Vyavahārapradhāni' define civil laws on debts, deposits, partnership, gifts, breach of contract, wages, sales, guilds, and land disputes, including those with widows who inherited spousal property. Chapter 12 describes laws on gender relations, including marriage ('Strīpumsayogah'); Chapter 13 is on inheritance rights ('Dāyabhāgah').

In 'Strīpumsayogah', Nārada declared that a marriage was legal only when the couple joined hands while sacred *mantras* were chanted, not earlier when bride and groom were chosen. This rule allowed women who were first promised, but not claimed, to legally wed another man. Nārada praised *savarna* marriage as the ideal, but he legally validated inter-*varna* marriages among *brāhmans, kṣatṛiyas, vaiśyas,* and *śudras*. He considered an *anuloma* union between *dvīja* men and women of a lower *varna* as preferable to a *pratiloma* union in which the woman was of a higher *varna* than the man (*NS* 12.2–5).

As male virility was highly prized, since that gave a couple a son to perform their funeral rites and to inherit paternal property, Nārada carefully described some sexual scenarios (*NS* 12.8–18). If the husband was sterile or had been castrated, or if he were impotent with his wife but not other women, Nārada advised the wife to wait for a year before she left him. If he was sexually shy, fearful, sick, or had homosexual urges, he advised her to stay and help him. Nārada pungently rephrased the old analogy of woman as simply the field, while the man was the seed and the owner of both field and offspring:

> *NS* 12.19: Women were created for offspring. The woman is the field, the offspring belong to the possessor of the seed. A field should be given to one who has seed; one without seed is not entitled to a field.[44]

Nārada ordered the father or male guardians of a girl to conduct her marriage before she attained puberty, and he instructed the girl to inform her close family when she had her first period. If the guardian failed to arrange her marriage soon after her first menstruation, his sin was equivalent to 'killing an embryo' (*syurbhūṇabih samāh*; *NS* 12.25.2). If the prospective groom disappeared before the wedding, the girl had to wait for three menstrual periods before marrying another man. The chaste wife was loyal to her husband, and she dutifully bore him sons.

Nārada categorized four types of marriages, that is, the *brāhma, prajāpatya, ārṣa,* and *daiva*, as righteous (*dharmasya*), and he tolerated the *gāndharva* elopement. He described three unions as unrighteous (*adharmasya*), that is, the *aśura* in which a groom paid a bride-price, the *rākṣasa* abduction of a woman, and the *paiśāscha* rape of an unconscious woman (*NS* 12.38–44). As girl and groom could both have flaws, Nārada forbade guardians to slander the other party, as they would then pay a fine (*NS* 12. 34–37). As a *dvīja*, Nārada believed that *savarna* marriages perpetuated Sanskritic male bloodlines, and he gave specific names to children from mixed caste unions as separate birth *jātis* (*NS* 12.103–112).

Nārada recognized seven types of women who could remarry, three being women 'reborn' as *punarbhūs* after purificatory rites (*NS* 12.45–52). Nārada's tone was censorious when describing two types of *svairīnīs* as unchaste women, but he was more compassionate for two others in dire circumstances. He allowed these three types of *punarbhūs* to remarry, namely those whose marriage was not consummated; those married in childhood, who ran away but returned; and in the absence of a brother-in-law, a widow was allowed to remarry another man of her caste in a levirate marriage (*niyoga*) in order to have a son. Nārada frowned upon these two *svairīnīs,* that is, the woman who left husband and children due to lust for another man and the widow who rejected *niyoga* with her brother-in-law to have relations with another man. Nārada was more sympathetic toward these *svairīnīs*, namely a foreign woman bought as child slave, now in such poverty that she offered herself to a protector, and a raped woman given by her family to another man as his mistress (*NS* 12.49–54).

Nārada used the analogy of the seed and field a second time when he described three types of struggles over custody of a child. If a man cast his seed in someone else's field, he had no right to the crop. If he cast his seed in another man's field with his consent, both men had a partial right to the crop. However, in ordinary marital squabbles, as field and seed were both needed for a crop, both mother and father had equal rights to a child (*NS* 12.55–59).

Roughly ten verses of the *Nāradasmṛiti* (*NS* 12.79–80, 96–102) describe widow remarriage, preferably through *niyoga* in order to get a son (*putrakāmyayā*). If a young widow was childless, family elders were instructed to arrange a '*niyukta*' relationship between the widow and her husband's brother, but after the birth of the *putra*, sexual relations had to be discontinued immediately, as the long-term practice was morally wrong:[45]

> (*NS* 12.79–80): If a woman's husband departs from
> this world without children; elders should conduct her
> *niyukta* remarriage to her brother-in-law to get a son.
> He can be her husband until a son is born; after the birth
> they must immediately stop, as that would be sinful.

Nārada advised the husband to be kind to a virtuous wife who had given him sons. At the same time, he told the husband that a wise man did not take pleasure in a dissolute or quarrelsome wife with only daughters (*NS* 12.93–95). The code decreed that if a woman with no known faults left her husband, but she did not elope with another man, the family had to arrange for her remarriage, but if she had no relatives, the woman was told to arrange her own remarriage. Nārada endorsed Yājñavalkya's views on a young widow's *niyoga* (*NS* 12.79–80) and a woman's remarriage in five cases, that is, if the husband disappeared or died or became a hermit, homosexual, or debauchee (*NS* 12.97; '*naṣtai mṛitai pravajitai lalībai cha patitai patau*').[46] He also decreed that if a husband disappeared, a *brāhman* woman with children waited for eight years to remarry, but if she were childless, she waited only for four years; a *kṣaṭṛiya* woman with children waited for six years to remarry, but only for three if there were no children; a *vaiśya* woman with children waited for four years to remarry, but only for two if she had no children; a *śudra* woman waited for a year. The author argued that Prajāpati created living beings to reproduce: 'if a woman goes to another man under these circumstances no sin is entailed' (*NS* 12.102; '*ato anyagamanai strīṇāṃeva doṣō na vidhyatai*').[47]

The author of *Nāradasmṛiti* described both light flirtation and sexual intercourse as adultery, but he forbade men to falsely accuse an innocent woman of adultery. The punishment for such sexual crimes varied, as a man who committed adultery with a higher-caste woman was killed. However, if he committed adultery with a woman of his caste, he paid the highest fine, but adultery with a lower caste women resulted in a lower fine. The punishment for deflowering a virgin was the loss of two fingers for a man but castration if he committed incest with his mother, aunt, sister, friend, student, teacher's wife, or a nun (*NS*.12.69–70, 72–75). A recension of the *Nārada Smṛiti* borrows Manu's penalty for incest, namely branding on the forehead with an image of a vagina and then being paraded on a donkey (*NS* 14.9).[48] Nārada sanctioned sex outside marriage with women who were *svairīnīs*, non-*brāhmans*, low caste, prostitutes (*veśya*), or slaves (*dāsi*) without a master (*niṣkāsinī*) (*NS* 12.77). Yet, Chapter 14 on violent crimes ('Sāhasaṃ') decreed that the assault and murder of another man's wife were the most serious crimes (*NS* 14.2–5).

Like Yājñavalkya, Nārada ordered the husband to punish an unfaithful wife by shaving her head and forcing her to sleep on bare earth, wear old rags, eat sparsely, and clean household waste. If she was dissolute, aborted a fetus, or plotted to kill her husband, she was thrown out (*NS* 12.91–93). Yet Nārada also directed the king to punish men who were cruel to or abandoned a faithful wife who had given them sons (*NS* 12.95). In the last verses of this chapter, Nārada returned to the subject of *anuloma* and *pratiloma* marriages, reiterating Yājñavalkya's dicta on the ranks of these mixed *jātis* but with more specifics. The *anuloma* offspring of a *śudra* mother and *brāhman* father were called *ugra*, of a *śudra* mother and *kṣatṛiya* father were *pārasva*, and of a *śudra* mother and *vaiśya* father were *niṣāda*. The *pratiloma* offspring of a *brāhman* mother and *kṣatṛiya* father were known as *sūta*, of a *brāhman* mother and a *vaiśya* father were *vaidehaka*, and of a *brāhman* mother and *śudra* father were *cāṇḍāla*. Despite orthodox disapproval, the long lists suggest that mixed unions were common, and their offspring were seen as legitimate mixed *jātis* in the Guptan era. Moreover, as the magistrates also came from this society based on these ranks and having such sexual mores, they would have regarded the *Nārada Smṛiti* as more equitable than the *Manu Smṛiti* and more detailed on *vyavahāra* than the *Yājñavalkya Smṛiti*.

B. Property rights

Several sections of the *Nārada Smṛiti* describe women's rights on property. The most significant are: Chapter 1 on debt relief ('Hṛiṇadānaṃ', *NS* 1.4–5, 10, 13–24, 73–76, 135,183, 205), Chapter 5 on breach of contract for services ('Abhyupetyāśuśrūśā', *NS* 5.37, 39), Chapter 6 on not paying wages ('Vetansyānapākarma', *NS* 6.20–21), and Chapter 13 on inheritance ('Dāyabhāga').

The first chapter freed widows from the burden of repaying debts incurred by the husband, accorded the widow some rights to inherit spousal property, and acknowledged women workers' contribution to their families. Nārada began by declaring that a deceased man's debts had to be repaid by the son/heir or the man who married his widow and raised his son/s (*NS* 1.4–5). The wife was not held responsible for debts incurred by the husband or son unless she had jointly undertaken these. If she went into debt in order to sustain her family, her son or heir had to repay these sums. A man without a son or male heir could appoint his widow as his rightful heir, and she would then repay his debts (*NS* 1.13–15), a ruling that clearly gave the widow a right to inherit spousal property.

Nārada also declared that if a 'mother abandons her son' to live with another man, her son was the sole heir to his father's property, and the wife received nothing. If, however, she took her children and her *strīdhana* to live with another man, that man repaid her deceased husband's debts (*NS* 1.17–18). She was a *punarbhu* if she undertook purification rites allowing her to remarry, but if she simply lived with a lover, she was a *svairini*. Those exempt from repaying a husband's debts were the wives of 'washer men, hunters, cowherds, and liquor merchants', as these working women's incomes often supported their families (*NS* 1.16).[49] In another verse (*NS* 1.35), Nārada stipulated that the truth would emerge only if the witness was a woman like the plaintiff or belonged to the witness's caste or guild. He rejected evidence given by the plaintiff's enemies or by dissolute criminals, gamblers, and murderers (*NS* 1.135–136,141).[50] Nārada warned that false testimony was dangerous *adharma* that caused misery, want, loneliness, and perennial neglect like that endured by 'a superseded wife' (*NS* 1.183–185).[51]

While these verses accorded women some respect, some others in the *Nārada Smṛiti* are so pungently patriarchal that they suggest an eponym's hand. Lariviere argues that while early scholars believed that the authors of the *Manu Smṛiti* and *Nārada Smṛiti* were single individuals, it is now clear that the codes were both expanded and condensed by later eponyms.[52] This is seen in the next two verses from the *Nārada Smṛiti*. In the first verse, the author emphasized that the male seed was always superior to the female field (*NS* 1.33), thus rejecting even Manu's conciliation that occasionally both seed and field were each superior to the other (*MS* 9.33):

> (*NS* 1.33): The father is the more important parent as his seed is clearly dominant. In the absence of the owner of the seed, the mother is dominant, or in her absence, the first son.[53]

In another example, a *Nārada Smṛiti* verse (*NS* 1.73) depicts women as male property, although some erroneously interpret the word 'women' as referring only to women servants:

> (*NS* 1.73): A pledge, a boundary, the property of children,
> unsealed and sealed deposits, women, the king's property, and
> a learned *brāhman*'s property are not lost through possession.[54]

This chapter has a more enlightened ending, as it declares that Truth was the eternal Atman (*Satyamātmā*). The author issued a dire warning that those who lied were plunged into a deep 'darkness' that neither friends nor wealth could remove and that falsehood was as vile a crime as killing a *brahman*, woman, or child (*NS* 1. 202–205).[55]

Chapter 5 on breach of contract for services ('Abhyupetyāśuśrūṣā') describes fifteen types of slaves who performed menial jobs (*NS* 5.23–41). They included men and women born into slavery, bought, or acquired in a famine; those who offered themselves due to indebtedness or those offered by others as surety for debt; renunciants who left their noble calling; those sold by robbers; war captives; and men declared slaves for having sex with a woman slave. A verse chillingly declares that: 'A wife, a slave, a son are similar as neither owns property; what they get belongs to the owner' (*NS 5.39: 'adhanāstraya evokttā bhāryā dāsasthā sutah; yattai sammadhi gacchanti yasya te tasya taddhānaṃ*'). As in Chapter 1, Chapter 5 ends graciously by declaring a master could free his slave at any time (*NS* 5.40–42).[56]

Chapter 13 on inheritance ('Dāyabhāga') was especially important, as it helped to shape medieval laws on women's rights in many regions. If the first line speaks of paternal property, the second interjects the rights of daughters and widows:

> *NS* 13.2: Upon a father's death, sons share his property;
> daughters share the mother's property; if there are no
> daughters, their children do.[57]

The next verses indicate that paternal or maternal property was generally divided among heirs after the parent's death or when neither mother or father could have another child. If the father divided up his estate when he was still alive, he was instructed to keep two shares for his own maintenance, another for his wife, and the rest for his sons (*NS* 13.12). Occasionally, a father entrusted his eldest son to complete the task of dividing the property after he had died. While the *Nārada Smṛiti* did not advocate primogeniture in which one son took everything, it did sanction a larger or even two shares to the eldest, who acted as a surrogate father to siblings (*NS* 13.4–5). On the whole, sons took equal shares, including those legitimately born from a levirate union or to a lower-caste mother (*NS* 13.14). While sons who committed a serious sin, were outcaste, or impotent did not get a share of the father's property, sick, crippled, blind, or insane sons had a right to maintenance, but their shares went to their sons (*NS* 13.20–21). This ensured that weaker family members, widows, and unmarried daughters were either maintained or received sums for their maintenance:

> (*NS* 13.12): When dividing his estate, the father must keep two shares. Upon his death, the mother gets a share like the sons.

> (*NS* 13.13): The eldest son must get two shares, as this is righteous (*dharma*). The other sons and unmarried daughters must get equal shares.[58]

At the end of this important chapter, the author made a dramatic statement free of any gender biases, as he declared that both sons and daughters were progeny who carried the family line forever (*santāna*). Lariviere translates this line thus:

> (*NS* 13.47): If a man has no sons, his daughters inherit since they are as much a part of his lineage; both son and daughter continue the lineage of the father.[59]

A recension of *Nārada Smṛiti* calls the father the 'master' of his property with the right to divide it at his will, but another version questions this ruling if he were senile or 'raging'. Some property was not inherited, namely the father's rewards for courage, gifts from a wife, and his scholarship awards (*NS* 13.6–7). As with paternal property, the mother controlled her *strīdhana*, which she could dispense as gifts in her lifetime. In almost the same words as in the *Manu Smṛiti*, the *Nārada Smṛiti* lists six forms of *strīdhana* as 'what she receives in front of the wedding fire, what she gets on being taken away, gifts of love from her husband, brother, mother, father'. It also stipulates that her children inherited her *strīdhana*, but if she had no offspring, her husband received it, but only if theirs was a *brāhma, prajāpatya, ārṣa,* or *daiva* marriage. If theirs was one of the other unions, that is, the *gāndharva, asura, rākṣasa,* or *paiścha*, her *strīdhana* was given to her parents (*NS* 13.8–9). The verses suggest that the author disliked these forms of marriage, which often involved male sexual compulsion, including raping women.[60]

The *Nārada Smṛiti* describes various complex social scenarios of illegitimate offspring, their rights to property, and their need to perform funeral rights for their parents. Sons of an unwed mother and a known father, of a woman pregnant during her marriage, or of an unfaithful wife were regarded as the sons of the man married to the mother, hence receiving a share of his wealth and being allowed to perform his funerary rites. If the son's father was unknown, the son could perform funerary rites for his maternal grandfather and take a share of his grandparent's property, but not that of the man she later married (*NS* 13.16–19).

Conclusion

The *Nārada Smṛiti*'s verses reveal that Guptan society was less stringent on sexual and patriarchal mores, as it gave women more inheritance rights. At the same time, the code reveals that caste stratification was now deeply embedded as *varnāśramadharma*, clearly encroaching upon distinctions based on economic class, so that serfdom was an established feature of this society. The author apparently felt that if royal justice was predicated on the principle of *dharma* as truth and justice, the potential for violent upheavals would be reduced. Moreover, he emphasized that in such a vast and diverse empire ruled through decentralized administration, the king could be the central pillar of strength by ensuring equitable justice in the royal court. Justice, then, was the monarch's key function. One of the last chapters is devoted entirely to asserting the superior authority of the monarch, echoing Kauṭilya a millennium later (*NS* 18.2, 5–13–16, 22–50). The author praised the king as one who upheld *dharma* as described by the scriptures (*śāstras*; *NS* 18.5–7) as the earthly lord, 'the only man without beginning nor end as long as he does not stray from his path' ('*anādiśchāpyanantaścha dvīpadāṃ prithvī pati*'; *NS* 18.13); a monarch venerated by subjects just as a wife venerated her husband (*NS* 18.22); a ruler who forbade the castes to intermingle sexually, as this was sinful (*varna saṃkara doṣa*; *NS* 18.3); and who instructed each *jāti* to perform its function without assuming 'undue superiority' (*NS* 18.6–9, 14–16), but who gave the highest honor to *brāhmans* for upholding *dharma* (*NS* 18.32–37, 40).

Although Guptan emperors sanctioned communal laws on marriage and property in their vast and diverse empire, it is clear that more cases on family law appeared before royal magistrates, as they had acquired a reputation for serving justice more equitably. This may have moved the author to tighten the laws on paternal and maternal property inheritance rights. Similarly, the *Nārada Smṛiti*'s large section on commercial crimes, as distinct from violent crimes, strongly indicates that legal industrial issues were more common in a complex economy. Some verses offer a rare glimpse of equity in an otherwise unequal world based on caste and gender hierarchies. The first verse decreed that when two angry people assaulted each other, the one who forgave (*kṣama*) was admirable, but the one who still seethed deserved punishment (*NS* 15–16.8). The second verse declared that the individual who maligned another was as guilty of a crime as the one he accused, and he was doubly so if he maligned falsely (*NS* 15–16.22). The *Nārada Smṛiti*'s verses offered subjects a glimmer of hope that whatever their caste, royal justice would be closer to the high ideal of *dharma* as truth. Clearly, the primary aim was to ensure legal justice, not the equal rights we aspire to today. This makes it imperative for those who read the code to view it as a mirror of that early society and mores rather than ours in the modern world.

Notes

1 A fine discussion on *Yājñyavalkya Smṛiti* is by Robert Lingat, *The Classical Law of India,* translated from the French by J.D.M. Derrett, Berkeley: University of California Press, 1978, 97–100.

2 I am grateful for two excellent critical translations: M.N. Dutt, trans., ed., *Yājñavalkyasmṛiti,* K.L. Joshi (rev. ed.), New Delhi: Parimal Publications, 2005; Richard W. Lariviere, trans., ed., *The Nāradasmṛiti,* Delhi: Motilal Banarsidass Publishers, 2003.

3 On *Nārada Smṛiti,* see Robert Lingat, ed., *The Classical Law of India, op. cit.,* 100–103; Richard W. Lariviere, trans., ed., *The Nāradasmṛiti, op. cit.*

4 Richard W. Lariviere, trans., ed., *The Nāradasmṛiti, op. cit.,* 15–19. Lariviere makes a strong case for an 'Eponymous Nārada', whom he believes to have been Kalyānabhatta.

5 My translations of *Yājñyavalkya Smṛiti*: *YS* 1.322: '*tatra tatra cha niṣṇātāna dhyakṣāṇa kuśalāñaśuchāna; prakuryādā yankarmāntavya karmasu chodhyatān*'; and *YS* 1.323: *nātah parataro dharmo nrpāṇām yadraṇārjitama; viprebhyo dīyate dravyam prajābhyaśchābhayam sadā.*' Also see M.N. Dutt, *Yājñavalkyasmṛiti, op. cit.,* 77.

6 The *Arthaśāstra* in Sanskrit is found at: www.patheos.com/blogs/hindu2/2014/09/chanakya-niti-pdf-downloads/. For the English edition, see R. Shamasastry, trans., ed., *Arthaśāstra, op. cit.,* 38–39.

7 My translation of Yājñyavalkya's Sanskrit verse: *YS* 1.391: '*Kulāni jātīh śreṇīścha gaṇāñjān padānapi; svadharmācchalitānājā vinīya sthāpayet pathi*'. See M.N. Dutt, ed., *Yājñavalkyasmṛiti, op. cit.,* 85.

8 My translation of Nārada's Sanskrit verse: *NS* 18.14: '*Yadi rājā na sarveṣāṃ daṇdadhāranāṃ; kuryātpatho vyapetānān vinayśyeyurimāh prajāh*'. Richard W. Lariviere, trans., ed., *The Nāradasmṛiti, op. cit.,* 222.

9 The second line of Yājñyavalkya's verse reads: *YS* 2.1: '*Dharmaśāstranusāraṇai krodha lobha vivarjitah*'). M.N. Dutt, trans., ed., *Yājñavalkyasmṛiti, op. cit.,* 87.

10 Nārada's Sanskrit verse reads: *NS*, 'Matrika' 3.11: '*pādō dharmasya pādah sākśiṇa mṛchchati; pādah sabhāsadah sarvānpādō rājānamṛhchchati*', *vide,* Richard W. Lariviere's trans., ed., *The Nāradasmṛiti, op. cit.,* 88, 270.

11 Sita Anantha Raman, *Women in India: A Social and Cultural History, op. cit.,* 30–37, 75–101.

12 Susie Tharu and K. Lalitha, eds., *Women Writing in India, 600 BCE to the Present, op. cit.* Also see Padmanabha S. Jaini, *Gender and Salvation, op. cit.,* 14–35, 58–59, 82–91, 105–106; Padmanabha S. Jaini, ed., *Collected Papers on Jaina Studies, op. cit.*

13 Auvaiyar's poem to the dancer (*Puranāñūru* 103) and Kapilar's poem to the singer (*Puranāñūru* 109). See A.K. Ramanujan, trans., *Poems of Love and War, op. cit.,* 129–130, 142–144, 152.

14 Alain Danielou, trans., ed., *Shilappadikaram* (The Ankle Bracelet) by Prince Ilango Adigal, New York: New Directions, Paperback, 1965.
15 Saskia C. Kersenboom-Story, *Nityasumaṅgalī: Devadasi Tradition in South India,* Delhi: Motilal Banarsidass, 1987, 10–11, 16.
16 Sita Anantha Raman, *Getting Girls to School, op. cit.*, ix.
17 My translation of *Yāĵñyavalkya Smṛiti* (*YS* 1.57). Also see M.N. Dutt, ed., *Yājñavalkyasmṛiti, op. cit.,* 15.
18 Lariviere's translation: (*NS* 12.117): *'rājā parīkśyaṃ na yathā jāyathe varnasaṃkarah; tasmādāĵā viśeṣeṇa triyī rakṣyā tu saṃkarāt'*. See Richard W. Lariviere, trans., ed., *The Nāradasmṛiti, op. cit.,* 203, 400.
19 My translation of *Yāĵñyavalkya Smṛiti* verses 1.94–95. *YS* 1.94:'A son of a *kśatṛiya* (mother) and *vaiśya* (father) is a *māgadha,* of a *kśatṛiya* (mother) and a *śudra* (father) is *kṣattā*; of a *vaiśya* (mother) and *śudra* (father) is an *ayogava*'; *YS* 1.95: 'The son of a *mahiṣyā* (N.B. whose father is a *kśatṛiya* and mother is a *vaiśya* or *śudra*) and a *karaṇa* woman *(N.B.* with a *vaiśya* father and a *śudra* mother) is a *rathakāra*. The offspring of *pratiloma* are not good (*asat),* the offspring of *anuloma* are good (*sat*)'. See M.N. Dutt, trans., ed., *Yājñavalkyasmṛiti, op. cit.,* 23–25.
20 The Sanskrit verse reads thus: *NS* 12.96: *'naṣte mṛite pravrajite kklībe cha patitepato; paṇchasvāpatsu nārīṇāṃ patiranyo vidhiyate'*. Richard W. Lariviere, trans., ed., *The Nāradasmṛiti, op. cit.,* 201, 397.
21 My translation of the Sanskrit verse *NS* 12.103. Also see Richard W. Lariviere, trans., ed., *Nāradasmṛiti, op. cit.,* 202, and his translation on 398.
22 My translations of *Yāĵñyavalkya*'s Sanskrit verse (*YS* 3.34); *'bhūtātmanstapo vidhye buddherĵnānaṃ; kṣtraĵnyasy eśvara ĵnānādvi śuddhih paramāmata'*.
23 M.N. Dutt, trans., ed., *Yājñavalkyasmṛiti, op. cit.,* 1.98.
24 The Sanskrit *ślōka* reads: *MS* 8.123: *'kauṭasākṣyam tu kurvāṇāms trin varṇān dhārmiko nṛpah; pravāsayed daṇdayitvā brāhmaṇām tu vivāsayet'*.

Websites for *Manu Smṛiti* are: http://hinduonline.com/Scriptures/Smriti/ManuSmriti.html and www.esnip.com/doc/1333237a9-b9bd-4823-b37e9555 e3d0f70. Also see P. Olivelle, *The Law Code of Manu: A New Translation Based on the Critical Edition, op. cit.,* 2009 (pbk), 132.
25 My translation of *Nārada Smṛiti's* Sanskrit verse *NS* 1.54. Also see Lariviere's ed. with complete Sanskrit text and translation, *Nāradasmṛiti, op. cit.,* 110, 292.
26 I have retained Lariviere's translation, *Nāradasmṛiti, op. cit.,* 60, 259. The Sanskrit verse is *NS* 'Matrika' 1.25: *'Tatra śiṣṭhaṃ chalam rājamarṣe dharmasādhanah; bhūtameva prapadhyeta dharmūlā yatah śriyah.'*
27 My translation of *Nārada Smṛiti* 'Matrika' 1. 26–27, *'Dharmaśchārthaścha kīrthi ścha lokapakti rūpagṛhah; prajābhyo bahumānaścha svarge sthānaṃ cha śāśvataṃ'*. *vide.,* Lariviere, *Nāradasmṛiti, ibid,* 61.
28 Lariviere, *Nāradasmṛiti, ibid.,* 61. *NS* 'Matrika' 1.28 reads: *'Tasmād dharmāsanaṃ prāpya rājā vigatamatsarah; samah syātsarva bhūteṣu bibhrad vaisvataṃ vratam'*.
29 Lariviere, *Nāradasmṛiti, ibid.,* 86, 269.
30 My synopsis of these three verses, *vide.,* Richard W. Lariviere's trans., ed., *Nāradasmṛiti, ibid.,* 86–87.
31 Lariviere, *Nāradasmṛiti, ibid.,* 90, 271. *NS* 'Matrika' 3.17 reads: *'na sā sabhā yatra na santi vṛiddha, vṛiddha na te ye vadanti dharmas; nāsau dharmo yatra na satyamasti, na tat satyam yacchalenānuviddham'*.
32 My translation of this Sanskrit verse given by Lariviere, trans., ed., *Nāradasmṛiti, ibid.,* 222.

33 Lariviere's translation, *Nāradasmṛiti, ibid. NS* 18.14 reads: '*yadi rājā na sarveśāṃ varnāṃ daṇda dhāraṇaṃ; kuryātpatho vyapetānāṃ vinhaśyeyurimah ḳṣātramṛithyusrijet*'; *NS* 18.15: '*brāmaṇyaṃ brāmaṇo jahyāt ḳṣatriyah ḳṣātram-utsrijyetl; sarva karma jahyādvayśyastu śūdrah sarvā nivaśeṣayet*'.

34 http://hinduonline.com/Scriptures/Smriti/ManuSmriti.html. Also see P. Olivelle, *The Law Code of Manu: A New Translation Based on the Critical Edition, op. cit.*, 44, 48.

35 My translation of the Sanskrit verse (*YS* 1.56) in M.N. Dutt, ed., *Yājñavalkyasmṛiti, op. cit.*, 14.

36 M.N. Dutt, trans., *Yājñavalkyasmṛiti, op. cit.*, 18.

37 Robert Lingat, ed., *The Classical Law of India, op. cit.*, 97–100.

38 *Yājñyavalkya Smṛiti* verses are: *YS* 2.72: '*strībālavriddhakitavamattonmattābhiśasta kāh:raṇgāvatāripākhaṇiṇakūtakriddhikale indriye*'); (*YS* 2.73: '*patitāptārsambandhi sahāyariputaskārāh; sāhasī driṣtadoṣaścha nirdhūtādhyāsatvsākśiṇāh*'). See M.N. Dutt, trans., *Yājñavalkyasmṛiti, op. cit.*, 107–108.

39 See this insightful analysis by Markandey Katju, Chief Justice, Madras High Court, "The Importance of Mitakshara in the 21st Century", Speech at Gulbarga University, December 12, 2004, at this website: ebc-india.com/lawyer/articles/2005_7_3.htm. Also see S. Chattopadhyaya, *Social Life in Ancient India in the Background of the Yājñyavalkya Smṛiti*, Calcutta: Academic Publishers, 1965, 106–139; and N.N. Bhattacharya, "Property Rights of Women in Ancient India", in L.K. Tripathi, ed., *Position and Status of Women in Ancient India*, Vol. I, Varanasi: Benares Hindu University, 1988, 62–71.

40 M.N. Dutt, trans., *Yājñavalkyasmṛiti, op. cit.*, 123.

41 Ashutosh Dayal Mathur, *Medieval Hindu Law: Historical Evolution and Enlightened Rebellion*, Delhi: Oxford University Press, 2012, 71.

42 Ludo Rocher also describes *Jīmutavāhanā's Dāyabhāga: The Hindu Law of Inheritance in Bengal*, Oxford & New York: Oxford University Press, 2002.

43 Also see Ludo Rocher, trans., ed., *Jīmutavāhanā's Dāyabhāga: The Hindu Law of Inheritance in Bengal, op. cit.*, 1–32, 177–186.

44 Richard W. Lariviere, trans., ed., *Nāradasmṛiti, op. cit., vide.*, 194, 382. The Sanskrit verse *NS* 12.19 states: '*Apatyārthaṃ strīyah sṛiṣtāh strī kśetraṃ bījinah prajāh; kśetraṃ bījavate deyaṃ nā bījī kśetra marhati*'.

45 Richard W. Lariviere, trans., ed., *Nāradasmṛiti (NS* 12.79–80), 199 (Skt.), 393 (English). I have chosen to translate these Sanskrit verses: *NS* 12.79–80: '*anutpanna prajāyāstu patih preyādyadi strīyāh, niyuktā gurubhir gaccheddevaran putrakāmyayā; sa cha tāṃ patipadhyeta tathaivā putra janmatah, putre jāte nivarteta viplavah sayādato anyathā*'.

46 My translation of *Nāradasmṛiti, (NS* 12.96). Lariviere translates this line thus: 'If the husband disappears, dies, becomes a world-renouncer, becomes a eunuch, or an outcaste'. Richard W. Lariviere, trans., ed., *Nāradasmṛiti, op. cit.*, 201, 397.

47 Lariviere, *ibid.*

48 Lariviere, *ibid.*, 414.

49 Lariviere, *ibid.* (*NS* 1.13–33), 99–105 (Skt.), 281–286 (Eng.)

50 Lariviere, *ibid.* (*NS* 1.135–141), 138–139 (Skt.), 316–317 (Eng.)

51 Lariviere, *ibid.* (*NS* 1.183–185), 149 (Skt.), 325 (Eng.).

52 Lariviere's "General Introduction", in Richard W. Lariviere, trans., ed., *Nāradasmṛiti, op. cit.*, 2–5.

53 I have translated this verse from the Sanskrit, *Nāradasmṛiti, (NS* 1.33): '*tayorapi pitā śreyānbīja pradhānya darśanāt; abhāve bījino mātā tad bhāve tu pūrvajah*', *vide.*, Richard W. Lariviere, trans., ed., *Nāradasmṛiti, op. cit.*, 105 (Skt.).

54 Lariviere, *ibid.*, 1.73, 115 (Skt.), 298 (Eng.).
55 Lariviere, *ibid.*, 1.202–205, 151 (Skt.), 328 (Eng.).
56 My translation of *NS* 5.39, *vide*, Richard W. Lariviere, trans., ed., *Nāradasmṛiti, op. cit.*, 175 (Skt.)
57 My translation of these *Nārada Smṛiti* Sanskrit verses: *NS* 13.2: '*pitaryūdharven mṛitai putrā vibhajaiyur dhanaṃ pituh; māturduhitaro abhāve duhiṭriṇāṃ tadanvayah*'. Richard W. Lariviere, trans., ed., *Nāradasmṛiti, op. cit.*, 205 (Skt.).
58 My translation of these *Nārada Smṛiti* Sanskrit verses: *NS* 13.12: '*dvāvāṃśo pratipadhyet vibhajannālmanah pitā; samāṃśā bhāginī mātā putrāṇāṃ syānmṛitai patau*'. *NS* 13.13: '*jyeṣthāyāṃ śoadhiko deyah jyeṣthāya tu varah smṛitih; samāṃśabhājah śeṣoh syuraprattā bhāginī tathā*'. See Richard W. Lariviere, trans., ed., *Nāradasmṛiti, op. cit.*, 205 (Skt.)
59 *NS* 13.47 reads: '*putrābhāve tu duhitā tulyasantāna darśanāt; putraścha duhitā choktau pituh santāna kārakau*'.
See Richard W. Lariviere, trans., ed., *Nāradasmṛiti, op. cit.*, 209 (Skt.), 411 (Eng.).
60 My translation of the Sanskrit verses: *NS* 13.8: '*adhyagnya dhyāvahinikaṃ bhartri dāyasthaiva cha; bhrātṛi mātri pitri bhyaścha ṣaṇvidhaṃ strīdhanaṃ smritaṃ*'; *NS* 13.9: '*strīdhanaṃ tadpatyānāṃ bhartṛigāmya prajāsu cha; brāhmanā diṣu chatuhaṣvāhuha pitṛigāmītareṣu tu*'. See Richard W. Lariviere, trans., ed., *Nāradasmṛiti, op. cit.*, 205 (Skt.).

Bibliography

Primary

A. Sanskrit Texts & Critical Translations

Artha Śāstra

Olivelle, Patrick, trans./ed., *King, Governance and Law in Ancient India: Kautilya's Arthaśāstra, A New Annotated Translation*, New York: Oxford University Press, 2013.

Sabhlok, Sanjeev, ed., *Chanakya (Kautalya)'s Arthashastra in Sanskrit*, and R. Shamasastry, trans. (1915), Melbourne, Australia, 2012, at this site: https://www.sabhlokcity.com/2012/09/chanakya-kautilya-arthashastra-chanakya-niti-chanakya-sutras-full-text-sanskrit-and-translations/.

Shamasastry, R., trans./ed., *Kautilya's Arthaśāstra* (1915), Mysore: Mysore Printing and Publishing Works, 1967 (8th ed.).

Dharma Sutras

Dharma Sutras (Sanskrit), at http://www.hinduonline.co/DigitalLibrary.html, Scriptures/Sutra, apastamba_dharma_sutra.pdf.; baudhayana_dharma_sutra.pdf.; gautama_dharma_sutra.pdf.; vasishta_dharma_sutra.pdf.

Olivelle, Patrick, trans./ed., *Dharmasūtras: The Law Codes of Ancient India*, New York: Oxford University Press, 1999.

Dharma Śāstras

Olivelle, Patrick, trans./ed., *Manu's Code of Law: A Critical Edition and Translation of the Mānava-Dharmaśāstra*, co-edited by Suman Olivelle, Oxford and New York: Oxford University Press, 2005.

Doniger, Wendy, and Brian Smith, trans./ed., *The Laws of Manu*, London: Penguin Classics, 1991.

Dutt, Manmatha Nath (trans.), and K.L. Joshi (ed.), *Yājñavalkya Smṛti* (Sanskrit Text, English Translation, Notes), New Delhi: Parimal Publications, 2005.

Jolly, Julius, trans., *The Minor Law-Books: Nārada, Bṛihaspati*, Volume XXXIII of *Sacred Books of the East*. Ed. by F. Max Muller (1889), New Delhi: Motilal Banarsidass, 1965 (reprint).

Lariviere, Richard, trans./ed., *Nāradāsmṛti* (Sanskrit text, English Translation, Notes), New Delhi: Motilal Banarsidass Publishers, 2000.

Olivelle, Patrick, ed., *The Law Code of Manu: A New Translation Based on the Critical Edition*, Oxford: Oxford University Press (Oxford Classics), 2004.

Manu Smṛti (Sanskrit), at http://www.hinduonline.co/DigitalLibrary.html, Scriptures/Smriti, 14Manu_Smriti.pdf.

Vedas

Griffith, Ralph T.H., trans., *The Rig Veda*, (1892), reprint, New Delhi: Motilal Banarsidas, 1973, www.sacred-texts.com/hin/rigveda.

Haug, Martin, ed./trans., *Aitareya Brāhmanam of the Rigveda: Rites of the Vedic Religion*, Bombay: Govt. Central Book Depot, 1863, reprint by Sudhindra Nath Vasu, Bahadurganj, Allahabad, 1922, University of Toronto, 2008, at this website: https://archive.org/stream/aitareyabrahmana04hauguoft/aitareyabrahmana04hauguoft_djvu.txt.

Keith, Arthur Berriedale, trans., *The Taittirīya Saṃhita*, Cambridge, MA (1914); New Delhi: Motilal Banarsidass, 1967 (reprint).

Mādhavānanda, Swami, trans., *Bṛhadāraṇyka Upaniṣad*, Chennai: Sri Ramakrishna Math, 2000.

Max-Műller, Friedrich, and Julius Eggling, trans., *Śatapatha Brāhmana According to the Text of the Madhyandina School (Sacred Books of the East)*, Vol. 12 (1882), New Delhi: Motilal Banarsidass, 1988.

Sarvānanda, Swami, trans., *Aitareyopaniṣad,* Chennai: Sri Ramakrishna Math, 2001.

Sastri, R. Anantakrisna, ed., *Aitareya Brāhmana*, Vol. I, Travancore: University of Travancore Sanskrit Series CXLIX, 1942 at: https://archive.org/streaming/aitareyabrahmana014460mbp.

Subramania, Sarma, ed., *Taittirīya Brāhmana,* 2005, from Hari Narayana Apte, ed., *Taittirīya Brāhmana*, 3 Volumes (1898; 1998 reprint) at: www.sanskritweb.net/yajurveda/tb-1-05.pdf.

Swāhananda, Swami, trans., *Chāndōgya Upaniṣad*, Chennai: Ramakrishna Math, 1980 (5th ed).

Swami Sarvananda, trans., *Isavasyopanisad*, Chennai: Ramakrishna Math, 2015 (20 ed; 1st ed., 1998).

Swami Sarvananda, trans., *Aitareyopanisad*, Chennai: Sri Ramakrishna Math, 2001.

Swarupananda, Swami, *Shrimad Bhagavad Gita*, with Sanskrit Text, English translation, Calcuttta: Advaita Ashrama, Mayawati, 1976 (1st ed., 1909).

B. Buddhist Texts

de Bary, William Theodore, ed., *The Buddhist Tradition in India, China and Japan*, New York: Vintage Books, 1972 (Random House, ed., 1969).

Embree, T. Ainslie, *Sources of Indian Tradition: From the Beginning to 1800*, Volume I, New York, Columbia University Press, 1991 (2nd ed.).

Rhys Davids, T.W., transl., *The Questions of Milinda*, from *The Sacred Books of the East*, Vol. 35 (1890) and Vol. 36 (1894), Oxford: Clarendon Pres; website: www.sacred-texts.com/bud/milinda.htm.

Rhys Davids, T.W., and J.E. Carpenter, eds., *Dīghā Nikāya*, 3 vols. 1899–1911, London: P.T.S.

Warren, Henry Clark, *Buddhism in Translations: Passages Selected from the Buddhist Sacred Books and Translated from the Original Pali into English 1896*, New York: Atheneum Press, 1982 (11th reprint).

C. Epigraphica Indica & Government

Bűhler, Georg, trans., "Asoka's Twelfth Rock Edict: Shāhbāzgarhi Version", in James Burgess, Eugene Hultzsch, and Anton Fűhrer, eds., *Epigraphica Indica: A Supplementary to the Corpus Inscriptionum Indicarum*, Vol. I (1892), Calcutta: Archaeological Survey of India 1983 (rev. ed.).

Bűhler, Georg, trans., "The Siddhapura Edicts of Asoka", Vol. III (1893–95), in Eugene Hultzsch, ed., *Epigraphica India and Record of the Archaeological Survey of India,* Calcutta: Archaeological Survey of India 1979 (rev. ed.).

Chhabra, B. Chandra, and G.S. Gai, *Corpus Inscriptionum Indicarum: Inscriptions of the Early Gupta Kings*, Calcutta: Archaeological Survey of India, 1981.

Fleet, John F., *Corpus Inscriptionum Indicarum*, Vol. III (1888), 'Inscriptions of the Early Gupta Kings and Their Successors' (rev. ed. by Devadatta R. Bhandarkar).

Forrest, G.W., ed., *Selections from the State Papers of the Governors-General of India*, Vol. I: Introduction & Vol. II: Warren Hastings Documents, 295–296, Oxford: B.R. Blackwell, 1910.

Kielhorn, L. Franz, trans., "Junagadh Rock Inscription of Rudradaman", in Eugene Hultzsch, ed., *Epigraphica India and Record of the Archaeological Survey of India*, Vol. VIII (1905–06), Calcutta: Govt. Printing Press, 1905–06.

D. Tamil Texts

Drew, W.H., and John Lazarus, *Thirukkural* (Tamil with English translation; 1886), Madras: Asian Educational Services, 1988.

Hart, George III, *The Poems of the Ancient Tamil: Their Milieu and their Sanskrit Counterparts*, Berkeley: University of California Press, 1995.

Ramanujan, A.K., trans., *Poems of Love and War from the Eight Anthologies and the Ten Long Poems of Classical Tamil*, New York: Columbia University Press, 1985.

Sastri, K.A. Nilakanta, *Foreign Notices of South India: From Megasthenes to Mahuan,* Chennai: University of Madras, 2001.
Somasundaram, P.V., ed. *Ilango Adigal Iyarrunaruliya Cilappatikaram* (Tamil), Chennai: Saiva Siddhanta Sociey, 1969.
Somasundaram, P.V., ed., *Akanānūru* (2 vols., Tamil), Chennai: Saiva Siddhanta Society, 1970.
Sundaram, P.V., trans., *Tiruvalluvar: The Kural,* Madras: Vijyalakshmi Graphics, 1987.

Secondary

Agarwal, Bina, *A Field of Ones Own: Gender and Land Rights in South Asia,* Cambridge: Cambridge University Press, 1994.
Agnes, Flavia, "Women, Marriage, and the Subordination of Rights", in Partha Chatterjeee and Pradeep Jeganathan, eds., *Subaltern Studies XI. Community, Gender and Violence,* 106–37, New York: Columbia University Press, 1995.
Agnes Flavia, Sudhir Chandra, Monmayee Basu, Eds. *Women and Law in India,* New Delhi: Oxford University Press, 2004. An Omnibus in three parts: Flavia Agnes, "Law and Gender Inequality", "The Politics of Women's Rights in India", "Pre-Colonial Legal Structures"; Sudhir Chandra, "Enslaved Daughters: Colonialism, Law and Women's Rights"; Monmayee Basu, "Hindu Women and Marriage Law: From Sacrament to Contract".
Balbir, Nalini, "Women in Jainism", in *Women in Indian Religions,* edited by Arvind Sharma, New Delhi: Oxford University Press, 2002, 70–107.
Barnes, Nancy, "Women and Buddhism in India", in *Women in Indian Religions,* edited by Arvind Sharma, New Delhi: Oxford University Press, 2002, 38–69.
Basham, A.L., *The Wonder that Was India,* New York: Macmillan, 1954.
Behl, Benoy H., "Harmony in Stone", in *Frontline Magazine,* 24, 18 (September 8–21, 2007), at www.fronline.in/static/html/fl2418stories/20070921505066OO.htm.
Behl, Benoy H., "Sacred Stupas", in *Frontline Magazine,* 25, 23 (September 8–21), at www.frontline.in/static/html/flstories/20081121252306600.htm.
Bhargava, Purushottam Lal, *Chandragupta Maurya,* Lucknow: The Upper India Publishing House, Ltd., 1935, 28.
Bhattacharya, N.N. "Property Rights of Women in Ancient India", in L.K. Tripathi, ed., *Position and Status of Women in Ancient India,* Vol. 1, 62–71. Varanasi: Benares Hindu University, 1988.
Buehler, Georg, *The Laws of Manu,* SBE 25, Oxford: Oxford University Press, 1886.
Chakrabarti, Dilip K., *India: An Archaeological History: Paleolithic Beginnings to Early Historic Foundations,* New Delhi: Oxford University Press, 2003 (2nd ed.).
Champakalakshmi, R., *Trade, Ideology and Urbanization: South India 300 BC to AD 1300,* Delhi: Oxford University Press, 1996.
Chattopadhyaya, Sudhakar, *Social Life in Ancient India (in the Background of the Yājñavalkya Smṛti),* Calcutta: Academic Publishers, 1965.
Chawla, Monika. "Rights of Female", *Central India Law Quarterly* (Online). Vol. 18 (2007), 443–511. http://www.indiankanoon.org.
Craven, Roy C., *Indian Art: A Concise History,* London: Thames and Hudson, 1997 (2nd ed.).
Danielou, Alain, trans., *Shilappadikaram (The Ankle Bracelet) by Prince Ilango Adigal,* New York: New Directions, 1965.

Dehejia, Vidya, *Indian Art,* London: Phaidon, 2000 (3rd ed.).

Deshpande, Indu, "Position and Status of Women in the Sūtra Literature", in L.K. Tripathi, ed., *Position and Status of Women in Ancient India*, Vol. 1, 55–61. Varanasi: Benares Hindu University, 1988.

Doniger, Wendy (O'Flaherty), *Tales of Sex and Violence: Folklore, Sacrifice, and Danger in the Jaiminīya Brāhmana*, Chicago: University of Chicago Press, 1985.

Falk, Harry, "The Yuga of Spuddhivaja and the Era of the Kusanas", in *Silk Road Art and Archaeology*, Vol. VII (2001), Kamakura, Japan: Institute of Silk Road Studies, 121–136.

Falk, Harry, "The Kaniska Era in Gupta Records", in *Silk Road Art and Archaeology*, Vol. X (2004), Kamakura, Japan: Institute of Silk Road Studies, 167–176.

Falk, Nancy Auer, "The Case of the Vanishing Nuns: The Fruits of Ambivalence in Ancient Indian Buddhism", in Nancy Auer Falk, and Rita M. Gross, eds., *Unspoken Worlds: Women's Religious Lives*, Belmont, CA: Wadsworth Publishing Company, 1989.

Gimbutas, Maria, "Primary and Secondary Homeland of the Indo-Europeans", *Journal of Indo-European Studies*, Vol. 13 (1985), 185–202.

Gimbutas, Maria, *The Goddesses and Gods of Old Europe, 6500–3500: Myths and Cult Images*, Berkeley: University of California Press, 1982 (1st ed. 1974).

Gurukkal, Rajan, "The Beginnings of the Historic Period: The Tamil South (Up to the end of the fifth century AD)", in Romila Thapar, ed., *Recent Perspectives of Early Indian History*, 237–265, Bombay: Popular Prakashan, 1995.

Harle, *The Art and Architecture of the Indian Subcontinent*, New Haven: Yale University Press, 1994 (2nd ed.).

Hart, George III, *The Poems of the Ancient Tamil: Their Milieu and their Sanskrit Counterparts*, Berkeley: University of California Press, 1995.

Jaini, Padmanabha S., *Gender and Salvation: Jaina Debates on the Spiritual Liberation of Women*, Berkeley and Los Angeles: University of California Press, 1991.

Jaini, Padmanabha S., ed., *Collected Papers on Jaina Studies,* New Delhi: Motilal Banarsidass, 2000.

Jaising, Indira, ed., *Men's Laws, Women's Lives: A Constitutional Perspective on Religion, Common Law and Culture in South Asia,* New Delhi: Women Unlimited & Kali for Women, 2005.

Jamison, Stephanie. *Sacrificed Wife/Sacrificer's Wife: Women, Ritual, and Hospitality in Ancient India*, New York: Oxford University Press, 1996.

Jamison, Stephanie. "Women 'Between the Empires' and 'Between the Lines' ", in Patrick Olivelle, ed., *Between the Empires: Society in India 300 BCE to 400 ACE*, 191–214, Oxford and New York: Oxford University Press, 2006.

Jha, D.N., *Ancient India in Historical Outline,* New Delhi: Manohar Publishers, 1998 (1st ed., 1977).

Joseph, Tony, *Early Indians: The Story of Our Ancestors and Where We Came From*, Juggernaut Publications, 2018.

Kane, P.V., *History of Dharmaśāstra*, Pune: Bhandarkar Oriental Research Institute (1920).

Katju, Justice Markandeya, "The Importance of Mitakshara in the 21st Century", 7SCC (J) 3, 2005, Lucknow: Eastern Book Company of India, site: http://www.ebc-india.com/lawyer/articles/2005_7_3.htm.

Keay, John, *India: A History,* New York: Grove Press, 2000.

Kenoyer, J.M., et al., "An Upper Paleolithic Shrine in India?" *Antiquity*, Vol. 57 (1983), 88–94.

Kenoyer, J.M., *Ancient Cities of the Indus Valley Civilization*, Oxford University Press and American Institute of Pakistan Studies, Karachi, 1998.

Kenoyer, J.M., "Socio-Ritual Artifacts of Upper Paleolithic Hunter-Gatherers in South Asia," in Gregory Possehl, ed., *South Asian Archaeological Studies*, 233–251, New Delhi: Oxford IBH, 1992.

Kenoyer, J.M., et al., "Preliminary Report on Excavation at the Late Paleolithic Occupation Site at Baghor", in G.R. Sharma, and J.D. Clark, eds., *Palaeoenvironment and Prehistory in the Middle Son Valley (Madhya Pradesh, North India)*, 117–142, Allahabad, 1983.

Koller, John M., *The Indian Way: An Introduction to the Philosophies and Religions of India*, 154–160, NJ: Prentice-Hall/Pearson, 2006 (1st ed. 1982).

Konow, Sten, *Kautalya Studies*, Oslow: Kommisjon Hos Jacob Dybwad, 1945.

Kulke, Hermann, and Deitmar Rothermund, *A History of India,* London and New York: Routledge, 1999 (3rd ed.).

Lingat, Robert, and J. Duncan M. Derrett, trans/ed., *The Classical Law of India.* Berkeley and Los Angeles: University of California Press, 1973.

Mahadevan, Iravatham, *Early Tamil Epigraphy from the Earliest Times to the Sixth Century,* Harvard Oriental Series, Harvard University Press (rev. ed., 2014).

Mahadevan, Iravatham, "The Earliest Inscription in Malayalam", *The Hindu*, June 7, 2012.

Mahadevan, Iravatham, "An Epigraphic Perspective on the Antiquity of Tamil", *The Hindu*, January 24, 2010.

Mahadevan, Iravatham, *Indus Script – Texts, Concordance and Tables*, New Delhi: Archaeological Survey of India, 1977.

Mahadevan, Iravatham, "Parpola and the Indus Script", *The Hindu*, June 17, 2010.

Mahadevan, Iravatham, M.V. Bhaskar and Iravatham Mahadevan, "Unearthing Stories from Stone", *The Hindu*, January 5, 2013.

Majumdar, R.C., H.C. Raychaudhuri, and Kalikinkar Datta, *Ancient India: An Advanced History of India*, London: Macmillan, 1958 (2nd ed.).

Majumder, Partha C., "The Human Genetic History of South Asia", *Current Biology*, Vol. 20 (February 23, 2010), Elsevier Ltd., 184–187.

Mallory, J.P., *In Search of the Indo-Europeans: Language, Archaeology and Myth*, London: Thames and Hudson, 2001, 2nd ed. (1st ed., 1989).

Mathur, Ashutosh Dayal, *Medieval Hindu Law: Historical Evolution and Enlightened Rebellion*, New Delhi: Oxford University Press, 2007.

McCrindle, J.W., trans., *Ancient India as Described by Megasthenes and Arrian*, London: Trubner, 1877.

McGee, Mary, "Ritual Rights: The Gender Implications of Adhikāra", in Laurie Patton, ed., *Jewels of Authority: Women and Textual Tradition in Hindu Texts*, 32–50, New Delhi: Oxford University Press, 2002.

Mehta, Pratap Bhanu Mehta, "Authority, Religion, and the Indian State", in Indira Jaising, ed., *Men's Laws, Women's Lives: A Constitutional Perspective on Religion, Common Law and Culture in South Asia*, 56–86, New Delhi: Women Unlimited & Kali for Women, 2005.

Menski, Werner. *Hindu Law: Beyond Tradition and Modernity*, New Delhi: Oxford University Press, 2003.

Metspalu, Mait, Mayukh Mondal, and Gyaneshwer Chaubey, "The Genetic Makings of South Asia", in *Science Direct*, Vol. 53 (December 2018), 125–133, Elsevier Ltd.

Mukherjee, Bharati, *Kautilya's Concept of Diplomacy: A New Interpretation.* Calcutta: South Asia books, 1976.

Nair, Janaki, *Women and Law in Colonial India*, New Delhi and Bangalore: Kali for Women and National Law School of India University, 1996.

Narain, Harsh, "The Near-Incorruptibility of Women", in L.K. Tripathi, ed., *Position and Status of Women in Ancient India*, Vol. 1, 109–116. Varanasi: Benares Hindu University, 1988.

Olivelle, Patrick, ed., *Between the Empires: Society in India 300 BCE to 400 CE*, Oxford and New York: Oxford University Press, 2006.

Olivelle, Patrick, ed., *Dharma: Studies in its DHARMA – Studies in Its Semantic, Cultural and Religious History*, New Delhi: Motilal Banarsidass Publishers, 2010.

Olivelle, Patrick, *Language, Texts, and Society: Explorations in Ancient Indian Culture and Religion*, New Delhi: Firenze University Press and Munshiram Manoharlal, 2005.

Olivelle, Patrick, "Manu and the 'Arthaśāstra: A Study in Sastric Intertexuality", *Journal of Indian Philosophy*, Vol. 34, No.2/3 (June 2004), 281–191.

Pande, Susmita, "The Rights of Women in the Arthasāstra", in L.K. Tripathi, ed., *Position and Status of Women in Ancient India*, Vol. 1, 130–135, Varanasi: Benares Hindu University, 1988.

Parashar, Archana, "Just Family Law: Basic to all Indian Women", in Indira Jaising, *Men's Laws, Women's Lives: A Constitutional Perspective on Religion, Common Law and Culture in South Asia*, 286–322, New Delhi: Women Unlimited & Kali for Women, 2005.

Parpola, Asko, *Deciphering the Indus Script*, Cambridge: Cambridge University Press, 1994.

Parpola, Asko, "The Coming of the Aryans to Iran and the Cultural and Ethnic Identity of the Dāsas", *Studia Orientalia*, Vol. 64 (1988), 195–302, The Finnish Oriental Society.

Patton, Laurie, ed., *Jewels of Authority*, Oxford and New York: Oxford University Press, 2002.

Possehl, Gregory, ed., *South Asian Archaeological Studies*, New Delhi: Oxford IBH, 1992, 233–251.

Possehl, Gregory, *The Indus Civilization: A Contemporary Perspective*, Walnut Creek: Altamira, 1998.

Poznik, G. David, Yali Xue, Fernando L. Mendez, Peter Underhill, et al., "Punctuated Bursts in Human Male Demography Inferred from 1,244 Worldwide Y-chromosome Sequences", *Nature Genetics*, Vol. 48, 593–599 (2016 Macmillan).

Raman, Sita Anantha, *Getting Girls to School: Social Reform in the Tamil Districts, 1870–1930,* Kolkatta: Stree, 1996.

Raman, Sita Anantha, "Popular Pujas in Public Places: Lay Rituals in South Indian Temples", in *International Journal of Hindu Studies*, Vol. 5, No.2 (August 2001), 165–198.

Raman, Sita Anantha, *Women in India: A Social and Cultural History*, Santa Barbara, CA: Praegar, an imprint of ABC-CLIO, 2009.

Raychaudhuri, "Chandragupta and Bindusāra", in K.A. Nilkanta Sastri, ed., *Age of the Nandas and Mauryas*, New Delhi: Motilal Banarsidass, 1996 (1st ed., 1967).
Richards, Martin, M. Silva, M. Oliveira, D. Vieira, et al, " A Genetic Chronology for the Indian Subcontinent Points to Heavily Sex-biased Dispersals", *BMC Evolutionary Biology*, Vol. 17, No. 1 (2017). ISSN 1471-2148.
Rocher, Ludo, trans., *Jīmūtavāhana's Dāyabhāga: The Hindu Law of Inheritance in Bengal*, Oxford and New York: Oxford University Press, 2002.
Romila Thapar, ed., *Recent Perspectives of Early Indian History*, Bombay: Popular Prakashan, 1995.
Rowland, Benjamin, *The Art and Architecture of India: Buddhist. Hindu, Jain*, Baltimore: Penguin, 1953.
Roy, Kumkum, *The Emergence of Monarchy in North India: Eighth-Fourth Centuries BC as Reflected in the Brahmanical Tradition*, New Delhi: Oxford University Press, 1994.
Roy, Kumkum, "Women and Men Donors at Sanchi", in L.K. Tripathi, ed., *Position and Status of Women in Ancient India*, Vol. I, 209–223. Varanasi: Benares University Press, 1988.
Sastri, K.A. Nilakanta, ed., *Age of the Nandas and Mauryas*, New Delhi: Motilal Banarsidass, 1996 (1st ed., 1967).
Sharma, G.R., and J.D.Clark, eds., *Palaeoenvironment and Prehistory in the Middle Son Valley (Madhya Pradesh, North India)*, Allahabad: Abinash Prakasan, 1983.
Sharma, Ram Sharan, *Aspects of Political Ideas and Institutions in Ancient India*, New Delhi: Motilal Banarsidass, 1991 (3rd rev. ed.).
Shulman, David Dean, *Tamil Temple Myths: Sacrifice and Divine Marriage in the South Indian Saiva Tradition*, Princeton: Princeton University Press, 1980.
Sharma, Shubhra, "Position and Status of Women in the Sūtra Period", in L.K. Tripathi, ed., *Position and Status of Women in Ancient India,* Vol. 1, 47–54. Varanasi: Benares Hindu University, 1988.
Thapar, Romila, *Asoka and the Decline of the Mauryas*, New Delhi: Oxford University Press, 1997 (2nd ed.).
Thapar, Romila, *Early India: From the Origins to AD1300*, Berkeley: University of California Press, 2002.
Tharu, Susie, and K. Lalitha, eds., *Women Writing in India, 600 BC to the Present*, Vol. 1, New York: Feminist Press, 1991.
Trautmann, Thomas R., *Kautilya and The Arthasastra: a statistical investigation of the authorship and the evolution of the text*, Leiden: Brill, 1971.
Tripathi, L.K., ed., *Position and Status of Women in Ancient India,* Vol. 1. Varanasi: Benares Hindu University, 1988.
Tripathi, Rama Shankar, *History of Ancient India*, New Delhi: Motilal Banarsidass, 1942 (9th ed., 1999).
Thapar, Romila, *Ancient Indian Social History: Some Interpretations*, New Delhi: Orient Longman, 1998 (5th ed.).
Wolpert, Stanley, *A New History of India*, New York: Oxford University Press, 2000 (7th ed.; 1st ed., 1977), 92–94.

INDEX

For Product Safety Concerns and Information please contact our EU representative GPSR@taylorandfrancis.com
Taylor & Francis Verlag GmbH, Kaufingerstraße 24, 80331 München, Germany

www.ingramcontent.com/pod-product-compliance
Lightning Source LLC
LaVergne TN
LVHW021128300926
849160LV00010B/912
9780367496920